START & RUN A
CATERING BUSINESS

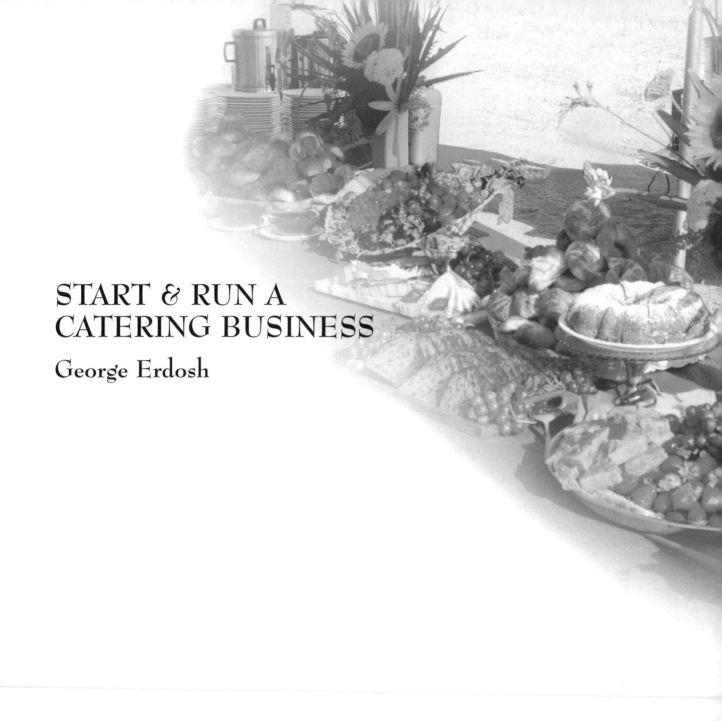

START & RUN A
CATERING BUSINESS

George Erdosh

Self-Counsel Press
(a division of)
International Self-Counsel Press Ltd.
USA   Canada

Self-Counsel Press acknowledges the financial support of the Government of Canada through the Book Publishing Industry Development Program (BPIDP) for our publishing activities.

Printed and bound in China by C&C Offset Printing Co., Ltd.

First edition: 1994; Reprinted: 1996
Second edition: 2001; Reprinted: 2003; 2005
Third edition: 2007

Library and Archives Canada Cataloguing in Publication

Erdosh, George, 1935–
    Start & run a catering business / George Erdosh. -- 3rd ed.

(Self-counsel business series)
First ed. has title: Start and run a profitable catering business from thyme to timing.
ISBN-13: 978-1-55180-736-2
ISBN-10: 1-55180-736-X

    1. Caterers and catering—Management. 2. New business enterprises.
I. Title. II. Title: Start and run a catering business. III. Series.
TX911.3.M27E73 2006   642'.4   C2006-904349-3

Self-Counsel Press
(a division of)
International Self-Counsel Press Ltd.

1704 North State Street
Bellingham, WA 98225
USA

1481 Charlotte Road
North Vancouver, BC V7J 1H1
Canada

CONTENTS

NOTICE TO READERS

The author, publisher, and the vendor of this book make no representations or warranties regarding the outcome or the use to which the information in this book is put and are not assuming any liability for any claims, losses, or damages arising out of the use of this book. The reader should not rely on the author or publisher of this book for any professional advice. Please be sure that you have the most recent edition.

Prices, commissions, fees, and other costs mentioned in the text or shown in samples in this book probably do not reflect real costs where you live. Inflation and other factors, including geography, can cause the costs you might encounter to be much higher or even much lower than those we show. The dollar amounts shown are simply intended as representative examples.

ACKNOWLEDGMENTS

"Too many cooks spoil the broth" goes the proverb; this is true for commercial and domestic kitchens. By choice, I am the cook both in my catering kitchen and in our home kitchen, and I like it that way. One cook is enough in a family.

One writer is enough in a family too, and that was true for some time in ours. My wife is a professional writer. Because of this, I was surrounded by writers, as several of our friends are writers, too. Writers' groups meet at our house and writing and editing successes and failures are frequent topics of conversations.

I thought I was immune to the writing bug and was quite happy to be the king of my kitchen. But eventually I caught the infection and once I got into it, I could see what keeps writers going. I could feel all the excitement of transmitting information to others who may benefit from reading it.

That's how this book was born. From the beginning, my wife, Marj Stuart, kept me going through the frustrating and doubting phases. By default she became the editor, and she even gave me a family rate. The book was my idea, but it would have succumbed to infant mortality without her help and constant encouragement. I would like to thank her for that and apologize for intruding into her territory as the only writer in the family.

I would also like to thank Nicky Major of Major, The Gourmet, a catering company in Vancouver, British Columbia, for helping me with the legal aspects of catering on the Canadian scene. Finally, I would like to acknowledge Mike Roman of CaterSource in Chicago, a selling/marketing and catering guru, for the information I obtained from his seminars.

INTRODUCTION: THE APPETIZER

Catering: the business of preparing, presenting, and serving great food (and tasting it along the way), then graciously but modestly accepting the compliments at the end of an event. Every guest wants to know who the caterer is and they all take a business card. The reputation of the caterer spreads at once (since word-of-mouth is the best advertisement of all) and the telephone rings all the time. People beg the caterer to reserve dates for them. Sounds like a truly lucrative business.

Is it really that easy? To an outsider who has had no inside contact with the catering business before, this scenario sounds ideal, a perfect way of making a good living while having fun. This is the main reason so many people turn to catering as a possible new business venture, part time or full time.

Many caterers jump into their new profession from completely different fields. My own experience is a good example; I was a mineral exploration geologist for some 25 years prior to establishing myself as a caterer. You don't need to be afraid of a complete career change; it really is not that uncommon.

Opening a restaurant seems to have an equally high appeal, though restaurants and their workings are a little more visible to the public. The failure rate in both businesses is extremely high, showing that the lucrative appeal is illusionary. No matter where you live, restaurants are opening and closing constantly. Some of them cannot stay in business even for a year. This is equally true for catering, except that business is much less visible. Most caterers don't want walk-in clients, so the public is often unaware of their presence.

However, the business of food catering is not quite as gloomy if you know what you are getting into from the very beginning. It can be fun and pleasurable to run a profitable catering business.

This book is written for people who either have already started catering on a very small scale and are struggling to establish themselves and their businesses, or who think they might enjoy opening a catering business but have little or no concept of what to expect. This book is also for those who already have the knowledge, experience, and financial backing to start a business right away. For those of you who think of catering as a possible future career, perhaps in retirement or once the children are raised, this book shows you how to get yourself ready.

It tells you what to expect, what you are risking, what skills are essential to have before you even consider getting into catering, and what skills are desirable though you can succeed without them.

Other books on catering are written from the point of view of large catering establishments, hotels, and banquet halls. But very few, if any, caterers ever started large. Most start tiny and grow as they succeed. This book is written by a small caterer for entrepreneurs who want to start small and become successful as small caterers.

This book is also for those who want to start with minimal financial backing and equipment, and minimum staff. It is targeted for those wanting to know what to learn, how to gain experience, and when to apply for a business license.

The dream of being a professional caterer is appealing to many: the lure may be the pleasures of cookery; creating or altering recipes and dishes; presenting them with an artistic touch that instantly stops conversation around the table; serving and pleasing guests; or simply the mistaken belief that catering is an easy way of earning a living.

Many people have considered catering as a profession; few have acted on that wish seriously. First of all, once you stop and think about all the logistics of starting a complex business like catering, you may quickly lose your belief that it is easy. But if you follow the advice and steps given in this book, you may realize your dream and enjoy the varied life of a successful caterer.

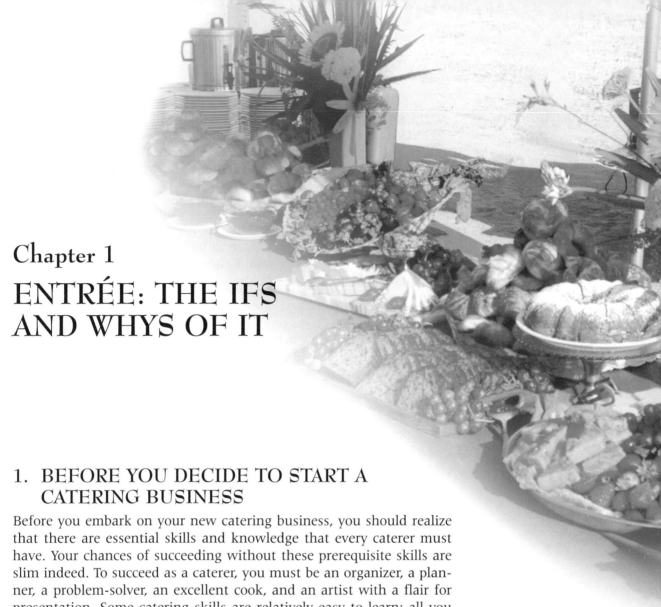

Chapter 1
ENTRÉE: THE IFS AND WHYS OF IT

1. BEFORE YOU DECIDE TO START A CATERING BUSINESS

Before you embark on your new catering business, you should realize that there are essential skills and knowledge that every caterer must have. Your chances of succeeding without these prerequisite skills are slim indeed. To succeed as a caterer, you must be an organizer, a planner, a problem-solver, an excellent cook, and an artist with a flair for presentation. Some catering skills are relatively easy to learn; all you need is practice. Others you have to be born with.

The knowledge and skill considered essential for catering is discussed in more detail in Chapter 3. You must decide for yourself how many of those skills you already have, where your weaknesses lie, and how you can overcome any problem areas.

When you operate a reasonably large catering business, you won't need to know how to do everything; someone else on the team may have the skills you lack. But if you want to start a small operation, often doing all the work by yourself, be sure there is no weak spot in your business: you need to have all the required skills and knowledge.

1

By the time you are ready to spread the word about your new catering service, you should be fully confident about your abilities. Of course, you'll learn through trial and error and through the day-to-day experience of running your business, but it will take years before you can call yourself an expert.

Even if you have employees or partners who complement your weak areas, you should not neglect those skills. After all, when your part-time food preparer with an artistic touch in food presentation cannot make it into the kitchen for a last-minute lunch order, you will have to take his or her place and attempt an almost equally glamorous presentation.

Even if your business is large enough to employ workers who can take over the various tasks required to successfully execute an elaborate wedding, your expertise in the different fields will make you a better manager, a better judge of your employees' work, and a better person to coordinate the event.

If you look at the list of essentials and find you're lacking several that won't be easy to acquire, perhaps it is time to reconsider. Maybe this avocation is not meant to be your next career. Can you learn to be extremely organized and efficient, or have these always been alien concepts to you?

Since you're now considering catering as a profession, chances are good that you already have a number of skills you'll need.

For now, let's assume that you consider yourself an excellent potential caterer and proceed to the next step.

2. TYPES OF CATERING

There are at least a dozen different types of catering niches or styles. Some are not exactly catering (e.g., preparing and serving food to clients) but they are closely related. All of them deal with food and food preparation. Decide which type of catering best fits your personality, skill level, interest, and expectations, and focus on that. As you learn more, you can expand into other areas without much effort, either slowly, gradually, or all at once.

First of all, catering services have two broad areas: corporate and social catering. Corporate catering is fairly routine, concentrating on breakfasts, luncheons, and occasional dinners. Corporate receptions, however, are not routine at all — they are often very lavish — and they let you express your full artistic creativity with food presentation.

Social catering (i.e., catering for private clients) calls for every type of food service imaginable. Most of these events are receptions, breakfasts, luncheons, and dinners. There are relatively few guests for full meals, and social receptions are not as large as corporate receptions. The difference is in the budget. Most corporations can be more lavish with their budgets. However, large private parties, such as weddings and bar mitzvahs, may also have substantial budgets and a large number of guests.

There is another catering niche that is less easy to classify: institutional catering. It includes off-premise catering for any institution or government agency, including schools, hospitals, various other public institutions, and government offices. Many of these catering jobs are routinely done in-house, but if the requirement is for better quality catering or if the in-house staff cannot accommodate catering needs, an outside contractor is called in.

The main difference between institutional and corporate catering is the budget. The budget for institutional catering is usually lower, sometimes far lower, than for corporate catering. It is a catering niche in the low-end or medium-quality sector.

Nearly all caterers do both corporate and social catering, but how much of each varies widely from business to business. On average, surveys indicate that caterers do about 60 percent corporate to 40 percent social catering.

Even if a caterer attempts to work in corporate catering entirely, never marketing to social clients, he or she will find that guests attending corporate events may call to request catering for social events. This kind of solicitation is hard to refuse. The same applies if you try to restrict your business to private parties. However, the two types of groups make a pleasant blend. Each requires a different approach and different types of service, and each poses different problems. They complement each other on your calendar, too. Corporate events are generally scheduled on weekdays, social events on weekends.

What separates caterers most from each other, however, is what class of catering they choose to do. The field varies from low-end to high-end (or low-budget to high-budget) with a complete spectrum in between. Decide where you want to be, but never attempt to span the complete spectrum. That is simply not good business philosophy. Large caterers may have a low-budget division along with their medium-budget business. Small caterers, however, should specialize in a narrow band of the spectrum.

IF YOU PREFER TO
HAVE WEEKENDS TO
YOURSELF, DIRECT
YOUR MARKETING
EFFORTS TOWARD
CORPORATE CATERING.

In low-budget catering, expect much higher volume, more competition, more production-line food preparation, and little leeway for creativity. Your business will be more in demand (though this also depends on the state of the economy), and you can expect lower profit margins, higher volume, better overall profits, and longer working hours.

In high-budget catering, you will have more fun, less competition, possibly less work, more exacting demands, and more tension. Your clients will be much more particular and expect more from you, but they will pay to have those demands met. Your business will be vulnerable to economic downturns because high-end catering is slashed quickly from both corporate and social budgets. Events are less frequent, but if you price them right and watch your costs, they can still be very profitable.

In addition to the broad catering areas outlined above, here are niches that are possible for a small caterer:

- Picnics
- Barbecues
- Vegetarian catering
- Cooking with organic foods
- Kosher catering
- Subcontracting to large caterers
- Selling to retail outlets
- Subcontracting to hotels, banquet halls
- Corporate gifts
- Coffee breaks, meeting breaks
- Breakfasts and brunches
- Food styling
- Fundraising
- Catering for small groups only
- Last-minute catering
- Producing private-label food items

The last item, producing private-label food, is not strictly catering, but if you find the right food item, it can be very profitable. Thousands of new food items hit the market every year, but only a small number make it to long-term profits. The other niches are fairly obvious and can be profitable. Food styling is not exactly catering but is an artistic niche you may consider. Some caterers hire food stylists on a consulting basis to present their food displays for particularly fancy events.

Two areas are in great demand: catering for small groups and last-minute catering. Few caterers want to do either. Small groups are simply not profitable unless this is your niche and you are set up specifically to do such events. Caterers get many calls for small events, such as lunch or dinner for five to ten guests, but are reluctant to take them unless they are for good, steady clients.

Similarly, there are many last-minute calls, mainly from corporations, when unexpected events call for a meal in the boardroom. Many caterers take such contracts reluctantly or refuse them. If you decide to market yourself as a last-minute caterer, you may find another niche here. Advertising in the Yellow Pages and letting other caterers know your niche will help in getting small and last-minute events.

3. WHAT TO EXPECT IN CATERING

Today, more than ever before, buyers expect excellent service. Diverse industry surveys consistently have found that buyers prefer businesses that offer good service even over those that offer good quality and low price. Catering is a pure service industry; with excellence in service, a catering business has a good chance of success.

What's more, catering is one of the rare businesses in today's world of superstores and mega-warehouses where small means personal and yet can be competitive. While small drugstores, grocery stores, and hardware stores are absorbed by impersonal big-box stores with no staff in sight to ask questions of, catering businesses can still remain small and yet be competitive by focusing on service.

The industry is characterized by small- and medium-sized businesses, with very few large ones. Large caterers mainly offer mass-produced, airline-type food; the quality suffers due to the huge volume produced. There are exceptions, but in general, large caterers are unable to provide high-quality food. Have you ever had high-quality catered food from hotel and banquet establishments?

Your small operation can successfully compete with any large caterer in your area. You can offer competitive prices and far better quality than they can.

What can you expect in catering? Briefly, long hours and little profit, at least in the beginning. As you establish your business, the profits will slowly creep up and the number of working hours hopefully will slide down. Yet a survey by the Department of Food and Beverage Management at Cornell University School of Hotel Administration, responded to by 340 US caterers, showed the following frightening answer: average work week for caterers is 58.7 hours but ranging up to 100 hours.

Don't expect catering to be a get-rich-fast business. However, if you find just the right niche for yourself and you are good at what you do, there is no reason not to expect a very handsome profit.

Be warned that the burnout rate in the food business is very high, in both restaurants and catering. If you put all your energy into the business for several years, you are likely to feel the symptoms. In the beginning the business will demand all your energy and enthusiasm, but eventually you have to channel your life in other directions as well or burnout will come even sooner. Mike Roman, president of Catersource, a respectable Chicago-based catering education institution, states in one of his 10 catering rules: "Caterers have the right to a personal life away from business … make time for yourself, burnout is worse than bankruptcy."

In spite of these gloomy warnings, there are bright aspects to catering. If there weren't, the business would not have any interested followers. It can be a glamorous, show business-type world if you are in medium- to high-end catering. It is varied, rarely monotonous, and whenever there is a lot of routine work to do, it means you have a large party that will bring in a good profit if you priced your event right. That prospect surely brightens the hours of messing with unruly phyllo dough.

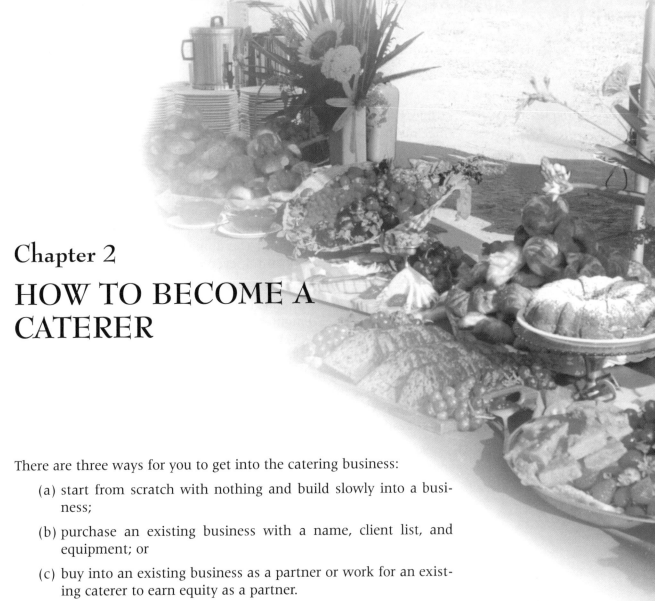

Chapter 2
HOW TO BECOME A CATERER

There are three ways for you to get into the catering business:

    (a) start from scratch with nothing and build slowly into a business;

    (b) purchase an existing business with a name, client list, and equipment; or

    (c) buy into an existing business as a partner or work for an existing caterer to earn equity as a partner.

The first method is by far the least expensive way to start, but without a client base, it is a slow rise to the top.

Purchasing an existing business can be quite costly, but you are running a business from day one with a cash flow, presumably a positive one. Often the purchase agreement stipulates that the former owner will assist for several months with the smooth running of the business and perhaps even deal with the clients you inherit. You have all the equipment and staff in place.

Buying into an existing business as a partner may also be costly, but you don't take on all the responsibility and the tremendous tension of running a business all by yourself all at once. Here you can ease into the business and partnership over several months or even years. These three methods are discussed in detail in this chapter.

1. STARTING OUT ON YOUR OWN

Most catering businesses start with one individual simply starting from scratch. Perhaps you are known as a good cook and organizer, have been in charge of several church dinners for 100 to 150 guests, and have pulled each one off beautifully. The dinners were great: the food was served on time and was plentiful; everyone was served promptly; and you were showered with praise.

Then someone who attended one of the dinners calls you and asks if you could cater her daughter's wedding reception for 50 guests. You are stunned with the request and you give a noncommittal answer. You want to think about this for a day. But once you have a chance to consider the idea, it begins to take shape in your mind. What a challenge it would be! An exciting possibility to earn money while having fun at the same time. A career change is on your mind and by pure coincidence, an interesting possibility suggests itself: catering.

So you agree to do the wedding, but before that event happens, someone else asks you to cater a classy dinner party for eight guests, which turns out to be a fabulous affair. You are gaining confidence, and by the time you're getting ready for the wedding reception, you've not only earned a little unplanned income, you've also earned a great deal more self-confidence. You managed to cater two completely different events all by yourself. You may have made a few errors at the wedding reception, but neither the hostess nor the guests noticed anything thanks to your quick thinking in resolving the problems.

This example illustrates how a large number of catering businesses start. When it is not by chance, it takes deliberate planning to begin a catering service. You may have worked for a caterer and come to the conclusion that you could do it even better. So you decide to go out on your own and perhaps even give yourself a tentative date to start your business.

Virtually all caterers start out part time from their own kitchens on a very small scale and generally grow the business by word-of-mouth. This kind of catering is illegal in most, if not all, communities. Serving the public from a home kitchen is against health department standards; nonetheless, it is done all the time. As long as your business remains small, chances are you will not be investigated by the local health inspectors.

Many caterers work out of their kitchens for years without a problem. But as the volume of business increases, you will attract more and more attention. If the local health department finds out about your catering business, an inspector will be ringing your doorbell and asking questions. Under very strict codes, you are legally allowed a limited number of meals served out of a home kitchen, perhaps eight meals a day, but this number varies in different municipalities.

The next problem is your competitors. Once you challenge a significant part of their market share and undercut their prices (your overhead is almost nil when working from a home kitchen), they will report you to the health inspector. Zoning laws probably do not allow a commercial operation in your residential neighborhood, so an unfriendly neighbor may report you, too.

Finally, chances are you are operating without insurance to cover your catering activities. Unless you are in commercial, approved facilities, you cannot be underwritten for a policy. It is unwise and dangerous to operate a food service business without substantial liability insurance. In our litigation-prone society, it would not take much provocation for a disgruntled client to sue you. Spoiled food that a guest became sick from, an olive pit inadvertently left in that broke a tooth, or a fish bone someone choked on when you served boneless fish fillets — all of these situations can result in a lawsuit that ruins your business. With no permit, no health inspection, no business license, and no sales tax registration, you don't have a leg to stand on. That would be the permanent end to your catering career.

Look into the laws in your area and decide for yourself if you want to start from your home to see if this field is for you. You may realize that the catering business is not just the pleasure of cooking, presenting, serving, and then waiting for the praise and the client's check. Since you have invested very little money so far, you can easily change your mind. If you make arrangements for a commercial facility, you cannot change your mind without a great loss of investment, not to mention the blow to your ego.

I know a caterer who worked eight years out of her home kitchen before trouble started from her competitors. She managed to avoid detection from the authorities for that long because her business started from a niche that didn't bother the competition: she made the most sumptuous holiday fruitcakes.

The business was seasonal at first. Her small operation was perfectly legal (though I doubt that her income tax form ever showed profits from

LOOK INTO THE LAWS IN YOUR AREA AND DECIDE FOR YOURSELF IF YOU WANT TO START FROM YOUR HOME TO SEE IF THIS FIELD IS FOR YOU.

the fruitcakes), and her reputation spread in the local community. In a few years the demand was so great that she baked fruitcakes for five to six months a year and froze them for the Christmas season.

Pretty soon calls started coming in to cater dinner parties, and in no time she was running a full-fledged catering business. The holiday fruitcakes remained a part-time operation. The competition started to notice and called the health inspector. She was told to go legal or close the business.

She found a commercial, approved kitchen, and in a few weeks her operation continued as if it had never been interrupted, although it now had higher prices, more staff and equipment, substantially expanded space, and a great deal more overhead expenses and headaches.

Her business soon grew big enough to hire an office manager/receptionist and a kitchen manager/chef. She spent all her time coordinating events, dealing with clients, and marketing her business. She rarely went to functions unless they were exceptionally classy. Instead she played tennis in the morning, dropped by the kitchen mid-morning to have her coffee and taste a little bit of everything that was on the prep tables, and proceeded to deal with clients for a few hours. By mid-afternoon she left the facility in the capable hands of her staff. This is one of the few successful catering stories I know. It illustrates how catering can start from a small niche — in this case, a great fruitcake.

You may find a similar niche for yourself. This is indeed an excellent and legally acceptable way of starting a food service from your home. The right product is very difficult to come up with, however. The market is flooded with every conceivable food product, and hundreds of new products come out every month. Only an extremely small percentage survive. If one of them is yours, you are in business.

Once you have made your decision to be a caterer, work toward your goal with a deliberate plan that includes distinct steps, each of which will give you the required knowledge, skills, and information.

Many would-be caterers want to slip into the business slowly on a part-time basis while holding down another job. This concept sounds feasible, but rarely works in practice. A full-time commitment is necessary. Catering requires your full attention. Potential clients who call to ask questions (usually about prices) get discouraged by an unanswered telephone, a telephone answering machine, or even an answering service. Very few will leave a message on your answering machine unless they know you personally.

If you have another occupation that allows you to answer catering calls on your cell phone as they come in, then part-time catering may be feasible. Call forwarding to a cell phone is an excellent solution, provided that you can answer the telephone with your catering business name. Otherwise you lose precious business every time you are unable to answer the phone.

The widespread use of the Internet and e-mail is also making part-time catering more feasible. If you have your e-mail address and cell phone number on your business cards and brochures, and perhaps even your own website, potential clients will be more likely to approach you with a click of the button and a quick message. Provided that you check your messages regularly and answer promptly, clients will consider you easily accessible. Taking advantage of communication technology may allow you to hold a part-time job to generate the necessary income while you are starting your catering business.

Another solution that I discuss below is a partnership. If your partner is a friend or a mate, then telephone answering may be divided between the two of you, freeing you up to earn the money you need to support your catering business.

2. PURCHASING AN EXISTING BUSINESS

In order to get into catering by purchasing an existing business, you need the following prerequisites:

- You must have funds to purchase the business outright or at least secure it with a down payment. You must also have a significant financial cushion left to purchase additional equipment and run the business for many months with a possible negative cash flow.

- You must be an accomplished caterer with significant skill and knowledge related to every aspect of the business. You must be able to take over, manage, and run the business by yourself, even if the former owner promises to help you during the first three months.

- You must be able to devote up to 16 hours a day to the running of your business for the first five to six months until you know your clients well and your business intimately. After that initial period, you should be able to slowly relax, reduce your working hours, and resume your social activities.

2.1 Buying a business directly

Restaurants and catering services are often available for purchase, which makes it a buyer's market. In the restaurant business, the hours are very long; in catering, the pressure is extreme. In both industries, the profit margins are low and the rate of burnout is high.

If you live in a large town or city, chances are you can find a catering business for sale. Along with responding to advertised businesses for sale, write a letter or send an e-mail to every genuine catering establishment in town. Even delis with sideline catering or small restaurants may be possibilities. Unless they are located in high-volume downtown areas where rents are prohibitive, their health department-approved kitchen facilities may be reason enough to consider the purchase. You can always scrap the deli or restaurant part if the purchase price is right. (If you are interested in the restaurant business, have a look at *Start & Run a Restaurant Business*, another title in the Self-Counsel Business Series.) However, if catering is a restaurant's sideline business, their client base may be too small to be of much value to you as a caterer.

A fair purchase price is tricky to determine. Larger businesses with good record keeping are easier to assess, but smaller ones are notoriously poor when it comes to bookkeeping. You must know the true annual gross and net of the business for several years back to determine the fair price. The higher the annual gross, the better the business looks in the eye of the buyer, and the more the net profit is, the more the business is going to be worth. Good record keeping by the current owner is a must, although it is as rare as a new client who pays in full, in advance, for an event three months from now.

Get a lawyer to help you with the purchase and an accountant to decipher just how true the records are. Income tax returns are not reliable and the seller isn't likely to show them to a buyer since the reported gross earnings on these returns are often not as high as the true gross earnings.

There are different formulas to help determine the fair price of a business: one calculates the percentage of the last full year's gross profits; another is based on the average of the last three years' net profits. You should discuss this topic with experts, which is why you need a lawyer who can protect your interests and an accountant who will thoroughly check all records, verify their authenticity, and tell you his or her opinion of how realistic those records are. Naturally, you should study the records very carefully yourself. Working with the present owner for a while will likely give you a clue to how good the bookkeeping records are.

If the books and records have been maintained by professionals, you'll know they are reasonably accurate. But a bookkeeper can only do as good a job as the records given to him or her allow. You never know if receipts are missing due to neglect or if unrelated receipts have been added. For example, when the owner bought a food processor for her home use, did she include the receipt as a business expense in order to reduce her business's net income? Always be suspicious.

Check the client list carefully and see how often each one uses catering services. Discuss with the owner the style of catering service, the prices charged, the average size of events, minimum and maximum number of guests, suppliers, credit lines, the labor force he or she uses, pay scale, and so on. Other questions to ask yourself: Is this the style of catering I want to do? Can I run the business without the former owner's help?

Before you utter even one word expressing serious interest in purchasing the business, ask if you can work in the kitchen for a week or two with the crew and go with them to several events — at no charge, of course. Even better, don't ask, insist on doing so. You will learn a lot about the business and whether it is for you. Remember, you are likely to be in a buyer's market and the owner will try to bend over backwards to please you. You can do this frontline work while your lawyer and accountant are doing their work.

Remember, total immersion in every aspect of the business is essential. Do nothing else. Drop your social life to a minimum. Live with the business you are interested in buying. Do your research, either in a library or on the Internet, on legal and financial aspects. Perhaps even check out the suppliers, but for now only a cursory check is needed.

Whenever you have free time, work on your recipe collection and food preparation techniques. Work on your efficiency as well.

Once you have worked in the business for two to three weeks, attempt to figure out the costs of labor, insurance, rent, utilities, taxes, vehicles, and so on. Compare your figures with those reported by the owner. Then estimate food costs, or even better, ask for a current monthly food and supplies total and calculate roughly what the current month's gross and net profits (or losses) are. This exercise will certainly give you some indication of the authenticity of the owner's records. Discuss your findings with your accountant. Keep in mind that catering

WORK FOR A CATERER AND CAREFULLY OBSERVE EVERY ASPECT OF THE BUSINESS.

income is seasonal and can vary from month to month. The two and a half weeks of Christmas holiday season could bring you 50 percent to 70 percent of your annual gross income!

Then it is time to develop the purchase agreement and negotiate the price. The owner will likely come up with an asking price, and you will, in consultation with your lawyer, give a much lower figure based on what you feel the business is worth. No matter how far apart you start, eventually you usually can come to a mutually satisfactory agreement.

How you are going to come up with the dollars is not the subject of this book; it could be cash up front, or payments over a year or two, or there could be conditions attached to your payments regarding the seller's true representation of the business. It will depend on your situation.

Before a purchase agreement is prepared, you and the owner should do a thorough inventory of all equipment and vehicles that are a part of the business. Prepare a complete list of everything, including vehicles, office furniture and equipment, even an approximate amount of china, glassware, silverware, napkins, and tablecloths. Make a separate list of items that will be excluded from the sale, if any. The owner is likely to have personal items, perhaps a collection of cookbooks, files, pictures, and so on. The list of items included with the business should show anything having an approximate value of $50 or more.

The purchase agreement is now the lawyer's territory. It should include the purchase price, the full list of all equipment and vehicles that are part of the purchase price, and any contracts or events in progress. For example, if much work has already been done on an upcoming event, the owner could be entitled to some of the net proceeds. That, too, should be outlined and included in the agreement.

If the seller is willing to train you or assist you during the takeover period, contract with him or her for a specified number of hours over a period of weeks or months in the purchase agreement. Be specific about what the contracted work will include. For example, the seller might be contracted to attend all catered events for the first month.

The agreement should also include a list of clients with addresses, telephone numbers, e-mail addresses, and contact names; a copy of the rental lease; and many other clauses for mutual protection, like goodwill. Goodwill encompasses the client list, the name of the business, the value attributed to years of marketing, word-of-mouth recommendations, client satisfaction that generates future revenue, and everything else that is part of a successful business.

The third major piece of the agreement is a covenant not to compete. Insist on this. Without this covenant, the seller could set up in another location and keep his or her faithful clients, leaving you sitting by a quiet telephone. The covenant should be for a minimum two-year period, preferably more, and it should specify a geographic area of a 30- to 40-mile radius around your kitchen.

Chances are, once you take the business over, you will lose some clients, perhaps many. You cannot exactly duplicate your predecessor's style, charm, food, and service. But why would you want to? You have your own style, cuisine, service, and presentation to develop. If you suddenly lose many clients, start worrying and ask clients about what changes they would like to see in your service or menu.

2.2 Buying through a business broker

Another common way to buy a business is through a business broker. Business brokers are like realtors; the best way to find them is through recommendations. Your local chamber of commerce is also a good source. The broker finds buyers on behalf of a seller and takes care of the paperwork. According to contract law, a business broker represents the seller, because the seller pays the broker's commission. A few brokers are willing to represent the buyer. The broker can also assist in selecting an escrow officer. He or she can help in reassigning the seller's lease to you if there is one on the premises. Brokers' fees are high since most of them don't like to deal with small businesses. Their commission is about 12 percent and a minimum of about $8,000.

If you are considering purchasing or expanding an existing business and you don't have ready cash, your challenge is to borrow money or equity, either by selling shares or stocks or by bringing in partners with ready cash or equity. Both options have advantages and disadvantages, but it is beyond the scope of this book to delve into a discussion on this subject. I mention it here so you are aware of the possibilities.

3. BUYING INTO AN EXISTING BUSINESS AS A PARTNER

If you buy into an existing business as a partner, make sure you know that business well: the owner, the staff, and the style of catering. There is only one way to know a business really well, and that is to work in it for some time. This usually means forming a partnership with someone who has common goals and interests, and complementary expertise.

THE BROKER FINDS BUYERS ON BEHALF OF A SELLER AND TAKES CARE OF THE PAPERWORK.

THERE IS AN
UNWRITTEN LAW
THAT SAYS THAT THE
WEEK YOU TAKE OFF
FOR YOUR OWN
PLEASURE WILL BE THE
WEEK EVERY CLIENT
YOU HAVE CALLS
ABOUT AN
IMPORTANT EVENT.

The business must be able to run profitably without serious friction between the two of you.

Business partnerships are unpredictable. You may get along well with a partner today but you may grow in different directions later. Like marriages, some partnerships succeed, some fail, and some float along without much satisfaction for either partner. If you find a good business partner, you have many advantages, including shared workload, responsibility, expenses, and decision making. In a partnership you don't have to be an expert in all aspects of catering. In the best circumstances, your weakness is complemented by your partner's strength. It is also pleasant to take some time away from the business without worrying about leaving it in dubious hands. Taking a week or two off for a well-deserved vacation is especially hard when you are the only key person. There is an unwritten law that says that the week you take off for your own pleasure will be the week every client you have calls about an important event.

You have two choices when buying into a business. You either buy or earn part of the business up to a predetermined share and become a partner, or you work toward becoming a full owner over a period of several years. For instance, you may have worked in a catering business for a while and the owner is approaching the age when he or she wants to retire. This is an ideal situation since you have the time to pay for the partnership slowly over time or add the so-called "sweat equity" of your own labor toward ownership instead of cash. You work for little or no compensation and the value of your time applies to your equity in the business at a predetermined rate. This is not easy unless you also have an income-producing job and the effort you put into the catering business is part time. It is also hard to work for something that gives no immediate return. What if you have worked 1,000 hours over a year (averaging 20 hours a week), which earned $10,000 equity in the business (at a rate of $10 per hour) and all of a sudden business drops off significantly because of an unexpected economic downturn? Since you have not earned enough equity yet, you have no control. You may see your equity slowly lose its value as the business suffers from neglect. At this point your best option is to borrow the money to buy the business outright in order to save the equity you have already built up.

Look out for diminishing personal interest in the business by the current owner. Once the end is in sight, enthusiasm weakens, and you may find yourself taking the brunt of the responsibility, worries, and workload while the owner takes much of the profit.

However you approach buying into an existing business, you must be sure that there is a crystal clear understanding between you and the owner. Everything must be on paper and legally binding. The help of a lawyer familiar with partnerships is essential.

Resolve critical issues before a partnership deal is finalized. For instance, define contributions to the partnership (cash, expertise, property) and the percentage of ownership granted to each partner at the inception of the deal. Arrange for a method of obtaining additional funds in the event of operating cash deficits. Define the responsibilities and remuneration for each partner. Also define when and in what order of priority cash will be distributed. Finally, make sure there are adequate provisions for buying out or removing a partner in the event of unexpected problems, if a partner wishes to terminate the venture, or if a partner dies.

Before making the decision to get involved in a business, here are some sobering statistics to consider:

- According to the National Federation of Independent Business (NFIB), owners who have worked with the same products or services in prior jobs have a 10 percent better chance of surviving over owners who have not.

- Another study conducted by the NFIB and American Express states that 80 percent of small-business people who worked between 60 and 69 hours a week remained in business after three years.

- The same study found that companies emphasizing good service had a higher survival rate than those offering low prices to promote business.

- Of the firms surveyed, 84 percent that started with $50,000 or more investment had a 10 percent better chance of making it than those that started with less than $20,000.

- A survey by the US Small Business Administration found that 65 percent of all new businesses fail within the first five years.

No doubt, the first year or two are going to be critical. There are many government websites, both in the US and Canada, and small-business oriented websites that feature information on starting a business. Here is a list of good places to start your research:

- The United States Small Business Administration, Business Start-up Guide, www.sba.gov/starting_business/startup/guide.html

MAKE SURE THERE ARE ADEQUATE PROVISIONS FOR BUYING OUT OR REMOVING A PARTNER IN THE EVENT OF UNEXPECTED PROBLEMS, IF A PARTNER WISHES TO TERMINATE THE VENTURE, OR IF A PARTNER DIES.

- Welcome Business USA, www.welcomebusiness.com
- Canada Business, Business Start-up Assistant, http://bsa.cbsc.org
- Business Development Bank of Canada, www.bdc.ca
- Small Business Information, http://sbinformation.about.com

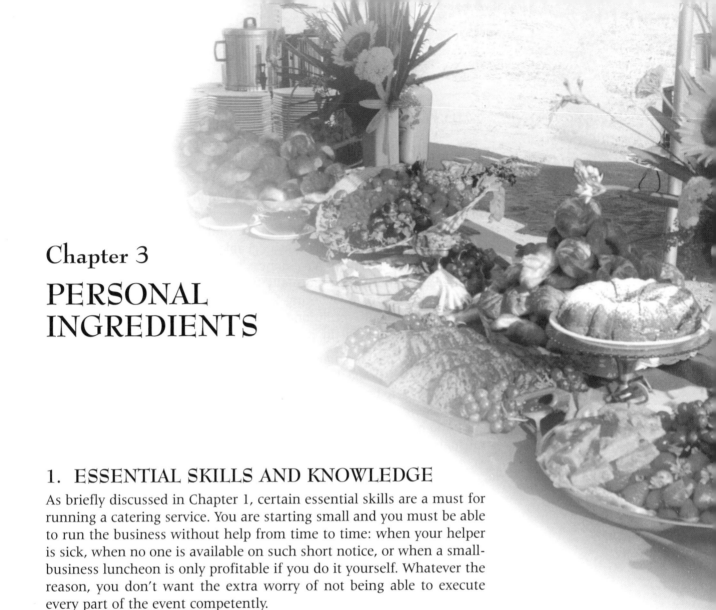

Chapter 3
PERSONAL INGREDIENTS

1. ESSENTIAL SKILLS AND KNOWLEDGE

As briefly discussed in Chapter 1, certain essential skills are a must for running a catering service. You are starting small and you must be able to run the business without help from time to time: when your helper is sick, when no one is available on such short notice, or when a small-business luncheon is only profitable if you do it yourself. Whatever the reason, you don't want the extra worry of not being able to execute every part of the event competently.

Here are the essential skills and knowledge you must have:

- Competency in cooking and food preparation
- The highest degree of planning and organizational skill
- A high degree of efficiency
- Ability to work well under pressure
- Skill in problem solving and crisis management
- An artistic touch in food presentation
- Ability to deal with clients confidently and successfully

Let's discuss each of these essentials individually.

1.1 Cooking and food preparation

A high degree of skill in cooking, as well as ease, efficiency, and speed in food preparation are by far the most important prerequisites for a successful small caterer. Many would-be caterers start as good home cooks with a moderate-sized repertoire and better-than-average food preparation skills. Some are knowledgeable about cookery, its chemistry and physics, while others have done a lot of food research and experimentation. Still others are formally trained food professionals, such as chefs who are tired of working for someone else with low pay, long hours, and difficult conditions in tiny, poorly equipped, inefficient, overcrowded, and hellishly hot kitchens.

Your cooking skill should be far better than that of a good gourmet cook, and you should have a sizable repertoire of well-tried recipes. Also, you need to be well versed in preparing all kinds of dishes, including hors d'oeuvres, entrées, side dishes, salads, desserts, breads, and beverages. You not only have to know how to prepare all these items, but you must also be able to present them in an appetizing, appealing way.

How are you going to acquire all that cooking skill and knowledge? Practice, more practice, courses, and plenty of reading, research, and Internet surfing. The information is available, but you must find it. The place to practice is your own kitchen with readily available and eager testers — your family and friends — sitting at your table daily.

If you haven't had any formal culinary training, get some. It can be done, and you can have a great deal of pleasure and fun doing it. You don't need the entire curriculum of a cooking school, or even the majority of it. A small fraction will be quite sufficient for your catering business; which fraction will depend on what type of catering you choose. It is hardly necessary to learn dozens of French sauces when you have no intention of using any more than a few basic ones (many are out of date anyway). If a demanding client insists on having boulettes of beef with sauce financière, don't worry. Just look it up in your extensive reference collection and prepare it. If it is a complicated sauce, you may not get it right on the first try. Do it again — well before the event, of course. With a basic cooking background and some experimenting, you will come up with the perfect dish in no time at all. And you will also have a satisfied, amazed, and impressed client.

1.1a Classes, seminars, and cookbooks

Cooking classes may or may not be a good idea for you. Nearly all of them are geared to home cooks, and although they may be fun, professionals will learn little. Try a few classes offered in your local area. If the instructor is good, observe his or her techniques — that's where the lessons may pay off. Videotapes and television cooking programs can help in the same way. Most cooking programs on the Food Network are geared to entertaining home cooks, but you can learn kitchen techniques from the hosts. Don't pay much attention to the recipes themselves; rather, watch how chefs work.

There are seminars and cooking camps for experienced chefs, too, on both cooking and presentation. They don't come cheap: expect to pay several hundred dollars for a two- or three-day cooking seminar, plus accommodation and related expenses. Catersource has regular one- and two-day seminars in various major cities in the US (see www.catersource.com). Their seminars are excellent, geared to caterers, expensive, and usually worth the fees. During the breaks you can network with other caterers and make valuable contacts. You go home enthusiastic and totally jazzed up.

There are a truly awesome number of food- and cooking-related websites on the Internet, but only a very small fraction of these are useful to a professional. The CD-ROM enclosed with this book includes a list of links to websites that I have found worth a visit.

No matter how you choose to do it, total immersion in cooking and cooking techniques for an extended period is what you want. Keep on reading books on food and cooking, even simple cookbooks. No matter how poor a cookbook is, it will likely contain some useful information.

Learn to cook an entire cross section of dishes, but emphasize the ones you want to prepare in your catering business. Sounds like a formidable task, but it really isn't. Once you get into the rhythm of preparing new and unusual food with unaccustomed kitchen techniques, trying other new items becomes easier and easier.

Mark each of your recipes with significant information you've discovered in preparation — anything you might need to know for future preparation of the dish. Ingredients should be slightly adjusted to your own taste as well as to current trends. Older recipes use less spices and herbs than today's more sophisticated palates demand. Sugar used to be used more generously, too, producing the over-sweetened desserts that are not much in favor today. Oils and cooking fats were used more

THE CD-ROM ENCLOSED WITH THIS BOOK INCLUDES A LIST OF LINKS TO WEBSITES THAT I HAVE FOUND WORTH A VISIT.

generously than our present awareness about good nutrition tolerates. So adjust the recipe accordingly and make sure to note the adaptation and results.

You will need a substantial collection of recipe books for yourself as well as reference books on cooking and food. Your choices will be dictated somewhat by the kind of catering you want to do. Of the enormous selection of cookbooks available, most will be useless to you. There are very few books with original recipes, but those are the ones you need, both for their ideas of new things to try and for your own reference.

You will also need several good reference books on cookery, basic food chemistry and physics, and nutritional information. These books should be read and reread, studied and re-studied. It is very important to understand the basics of food and cooking and to know where to look up the information when you need it. As Samuel Johnson famously said, "Knowledge is of two kinds. We know a subject ourselves, or we know where we can find information upon it." When it comes to cooking, there is no single source as comprehensive as *Joy of Cooking*.

A classic since its original publication in 1931, *Joy of Cooking* is the best and most comprehensive cookbook ever written in English. In its revised form, it is still America's most loved cooking companion and it should definitely be on your bookshelf. The amount of information and research that went into *Joy of Cooking* is simply incredible, and the information is useful and up to date on most subjects.

1.1b Cooking and catering software

There are many cooking software programs available, designed for both the professional and the home cook. These programs not only offer new recipes, but also allow you to organize and manage your own recipes. They scale ingredients up and down for smaller or larger yields, create shopping lists, provide dietary information, and more. Personally, I have never found cooking software useful for my professional needs. You can download and test most software to see if it fits your catering style.

Professional catering and event management software programs are several steps above cooking software. There is a large selection to choose from; the Internet is the best source for research. To briefly summarize, most programs are designed for large banquet and catering companies, hotels, and restaurants, but some are designed with small businesses in mind. Many of these complex programs are designed for people who work full time managing a large staff, inventory, food orders, and many events and reservations. These are not user-friendly programs. Besides, they are expensive, starting at around $1,500 for the basic version. You can request a CD-ROM or download a demonstration version from the manufacturers' website. Testing the software will give you a feel whether it will help your business or is an unnecessary business expense.

Software suitable for a small catering business tends to be simpler and more user-friendly, and starts at about $700. There are not many programs available. One program I tested that appears to be user friendly and suitable for a small-business caterer is CaterPro (www.caterprosoftware.com). My suggestion is to start your business manually. Eventually, request trial software to test it and decide for yourself.

1.1c Achieving consistency

There are two basic ways for cooks and chefs, whether professional or amateur, to work: either following a recipe or free-form cooking (i.e., sampling the dish while cooking it until it tastes just right.) In catering, free-form cooking is not advisable, particularly in preparing large quantities of food. Food should be consistently prepared from one event to the next, and therefore be very predictable. If you have an excellent memory, you may be able to do it without using a recipe as a checklist, but it is certainly much safer to use one. This way you never need to taste or adjust ingredient amounts. Most chefs who use recipes produce the food and serve it without even tasting it. They check and double-check recipe ingredients, making sure that nothing was left out and the right quantities were used. When the dish is finished, it is ready to be served. The chef knows exactly what it tastes like without sampling it.

Most food preparation techniques involve chopping, dicing, cutting, cleaning, peeling, and preparing at least half a dozen different types of doughs and batters. Even though machines are now used for most of these jobs, you must learn to do all the basic techniques by hand. In a small catering business, the use of a machine, even if it is available, may not be justified for a small job. Knowing how to do jobs by hand is also valuable when machines are suddenly unavailable.

The same applies to the many yeast and baking-soda breads, muffins, scones, biscuits, crêpes, pies, and puff and choux pastries you will be preparing: you must know the right technique for each by both hand and machine.

MOST CHEFS WHO USE RECIPES PRODUCE THE FOOD AND SERVE IT WITHOUT EVEN TASTING IT.

One more hint: Use your hands often. Your hands are perfect tools for the job. They accomplish the tasks quickly and are easy to clean. But don't abuse them. Use rubber gloves if you don't want to have your hands in water constantly. Kitchen work is not easy on your skin, so save your hands as much as you can. A restaurant kitchen cook can get by with rough, red hands, deadened nerve endings (also called asbestos fingers), split skin, and cracked fingernails. But in catering you need well-cared-for hands — they are exposed to the full view of the guests, particularly at full-service meals. In fact, they are the only part of you most guests will ever look at.

1.2 Planning and organization

Few fields of work require such a high degree of skill in planning and organization as off-premise catering. Industrial catering with a mobile kitchen, bulk-prepared food for retailers, large-event catering, or even barbecues are relatively simple to organize, but off-premise catering compels you to plan and organize for each event.

In off-premise catering, all food and equipment must be brought to the place of the event. Nothing should be missing, and the food must be in prime condition at the time of serving, even though several hours may have passed between the crew's departure from the kitchen and the serving of the first guests. The hot food must be hot and the cold food must be icy cold. The facilities at which you are serving may have no kitchen whatsoever or only a tiny office kitchen, so you must bring all your equipment. Imagine if someone miscounted the silverware and you are short one fork. What can you do? How can you produce a single fork during the next 20 minutes when the crew's every minute is planned for the next three hours? The answer is to avert such disasters by careful planning. If an unforeseen mishap does occur, then you quickly switch to your next prerequisite skill as a caterer, resolving crises and emergencies.

If you think that you are a reasonably good planner and organizer, you can improve those skills by diligent effort and careful checklists. Review your first few events. Did you remember to take everything? Was planning adequate? Did what you anticipated happening happen? If so, you are capable of organizing and planning progressively larger parties.

Planning for an event must be done well in advance of its occurrence. Even the smallest event demands some thinking four to five days ahead of the date to schedule the various phases of preparation, such as defrosting food and ordering supplies. Large events need even more advance planning because you must reserve staff time, rental items, and maybe additional subcontracted services.

Advance planning and organization has five major parts:

- Securing supplies and rental items
- Scheduling food preparation
- Reserving staff time
- Preparing equipment and invoices
- Planning the event

The chapters that follow will deal with all these aspects of planning in greater detail.

1.3 Efficiency

Efficiency is important in most professions, but in some fields, it is an essential skill to ensure success; food service is one of those fields. The food the guests are waiting for must arrive at their table as quickly as possible. Preparation time must be kept to a minimum; only a high degree of efficiency can achieve this.

You quickly discover what you can prepare far in advance of the event and what must be done at the last minute so that staff time is used efficiently. With careful planning, organization, and good efficiency, you'll pull it off with the minimum staff possible to protect your profit margin. Fine-tuning allows a small safety factor of time for unexpected problems that notoriously crop up at the last minute. If you're not a very efficient person, or are unwilling or incapable of learning how to be one, hire a good catering or kitchen manager who is. Then you can concentrate on other aspects of the business, such as selling and marketing, food styling and presentation, or financial management.

Efficiency is necessary for several reasons. First, you must be able to shape masses of raw material into gorgeous food in the shortest possible time or you'll never get to the culminating step: feeding people. Second, many items can be prepared only at the last minute. Some foods hold well hot but every extra half hour of standing will lower the peak serving quality. Many foods don't keep well if they are chilled too long either. Salads and fruits lose their crispness. An extra hour does make a noticeable difference. One more hour, and even the host or hostess will notice. Such foods must be prepared at the last minute, so the end of preparation signals the beginning of serving with no time lag. That requires meticulous preplanning so nothing goes wrong. Some catering tricks you'll learn along the way will help alleviate the last-minute rush and tension. Maybe what you'll learn is how to deal with the pressure.

1.4 Tension: If you can't stand the heat

To be a caterer, you must be able to live with and work under pressure and not show it. Outwardly you must be cool, smiling, apparently doing your work with ease, without rushing. Inwardly you may have five different things to worry about (e.g., the guest who is back at the buffet table to pile another ten shrimps on his plate when you allowed two-and-a-half per person; whether the Sterno under the chafing dishes is going to hold out; and countless other potential minor disasters). Nothing is predictable during an event. The guests at each one are completely different: they prefer different food, eat different portions, and interact with you and your staff completely differently.

When it is obvious that the guests like your food and ooh and ah at the elegant presentation, then you can relax and quit worrying. Once the guests and host or hostess are pleased, they will overlook slight problems, such as a missing punch ladle. If they are not pleased from the beginning, however, even small errors will grow into gross negligence and there will be no forgiveness.

1.5 Crisis management and problem solving

Off-premise catering, no matter how well planned and organized, is bound to have unexpected problems. Occasionally, problems reach crisis proportions. When so much equipment, food, drinks, staff, and peripheral items must be transported and set up for a complex event, problems will crop up from time to time. In the best scenario, your event is flawless as far as the client is concerned, though you and your staff know of the little bumps that you successfully overcame.

Just think of the numerous little things that must be on hand for you to prepare an elegant meal for 35 guests at home. Then think of the further complications when a similar meal must be served for 135 at an unfamiliar location. Then add the complication of another crew in your kitchen preparing a reception for 50 at the same time. Everything that goes into the refrigerator is carefully labeled according to which event it belongs to. When loading, you must be really careful that you don't accidentally take the other crew's ingredients or equipment. No matter how much care is taken, there is a possibility that some things could end up in the wrong vehicle.

Other problems occur at the event site. No matter how carefully you discuss every detail with the client, expect surprises. One of the things you must learn is not to despair or panic, but quickly find a way out of it, preferably before your client notices and, if at all possible, before the guests notice. Some problems can be solved with the help of the host or hostess. If an important piece of equipment or tool or ingredient was left behind, he or she may have something you can use. But usually you are better off solving it yourself without consulting the client, even if it means a quick trip to the store.

To successfully solve problems, you must expect them to happen. Remain cool and rational. Talk with your staff. Someone might come up with a good idea. For some problems there is no easy solution. If you left your ice in the freezer back in your kitchen, check the hostess's freezer to see if she has enough to last while you send someone for more ice. If all else fails and you must delay the bar setup, explain the situation to the hostess with apologies and make the delay as short as possible.

Crises are more difficult to solve, but they should be expected occasionally, too. On your way to the event, someone pulls in front of you and you have no choice but to hit the brakes hard (something you should never do in a catering truck!) and four lemon cloud pies scoot at high speed against the lip of the shelf. They are now misshapen and can only be served to your staff, their families, and yours. There is no time to get a comparable pie from the local French patisserie; your only option is to stop at a nearby supermarket and buy their flavorless, over-sweetened pies with artificial topping. It is that or serve no dessert.

Should you mention it to the client and give her a discount on the invoice? The decision is yours. I would be tempted to not say a word about it to anyone and serve the second-rate pies, feeling red-faced and guilty. Chances are, no one will mention the pies, provided the rest of the dinner is excellent. Should the hostess tell you later that she was a little disappointed in your lemon cloud pie, admit your guilt and apologize. Deduct enough from the invoice to console her and promise to send her two genuine lemon cloud pies.

It is a little scary to be in a profession where you are in the limelight, where everything must go smoothly and there is so much chance for errors to happen. Accept it, learn to live with it, even learn to love it.

NEVER PANIC IF SOMETHING GOES WRONG AT AN EVENT. A QUICK BRAINSTORMING SESSION WITH YOUR STAFF OFTEN BRINGS SOME SOLUTION.

Eventually, solving the problems and crises will come naturally, and you'll have plenty of anecdotes to share with trusted friends and family.

1.6 The artistic touch

Food presentation is extremely important in many catering businesses, especially for high-end, upscale catering. For fundraising projects with minimum budgets, there is less emphasis on presentation. High-class presentation takes time and money, and you can only afford to do it if someone is willing to pay for it. That doesn't mean that the low-end caterer can get away with dumping food on disposable aluminum platters. Food can be presented nicely with minimal effort and cost, small additional garnishes, and a touch of artistic presentation. (See photographs of food presentation on the enclosed CD-ROM.)

Demand for high-quality food presentation is higher in affluent, sophisticated areas of the country. In some places, and especially for some clients, presentation is so important that they neglect the food quality. As long as it is beautiful, elegant, and artistic, you can serve sawdust on arugula leaves with squash blossoms, drizzled with motor oil.

In some circles artistic presentation of food has gone too far, especially in the trendiest areas of California. The kitchen and chef put more emphasis on presentation than flavor. Mercifully, the trend appears to be fading. Presentation and flavor should be balanced, but flavor shouldn't suffer because of presentation. I would rather see a few simple but carefully placed garnishes on a plate to complement a delicious entrée than the time-consuming creation of a food stylist.

1.6a Keep it simple

Even if you are not artistically inclined, you can learn the art of simple and tasteful garnishing. There are many books on garnishes, and you should have at least a couple on your shelf. Read them, pick out a few ideas that appeal to you, and practice using them. Depending on your dexterity, you can try more elaborate garnishes.

A prepared garnish, such as a simple radish rose or scallion flower, takes time. You have to weigh this time spent against the importance of the event and the budget. If you feel the time spent is justified, then do it. But keep it as simple as possible. When the food arrives at the table, it is the entrée that guests' eyes should be focused on and only then should they wander to the side dish and the garnish. If the garnish is too elaborate, that is what guests see first. You don't want the guests to be so dazzled by small details that they miss the main attraction.

1.6b Getting ideas

Glance through recent food magazines and cookbooks and look at food ads and beautiful full-page photos. Check out food websites that have photos that are obviously the work of food stylists. These are all sources of good ideas produced by professional cooks and food stylists (see recommended websites on the enclosed CD-ROM). Adapt these ideas to your catering business. Copy them and after a while you'll be devising your own. Have meals at restaurants in which food presentation is emphasized and learn from what the chef created on the plates. (Keep the receipts; these expenses are legitimate business costs.)

Look around when you go to the supermarket and see what is interesting in the produce department. Use contrasting textures and colors to complement the food you are serving. For example, if it is a Tex-Mex dinner, a thin slice of round jicama could be the base on top of which you carefully place tiny slices of red and green chilis and a sprig of cilantro. All these garnishes can be prepared ahead of time and carried to the job site, ready to be placed on plates. It takes only ten extra seconds per plate once the food is on it.

1.6c Decorations and garnishes

Plate garnish can only be done when the meal is full-service. For self-service, the decoration is on the table and on the serving platters. Magazine pictures will give you ideas, but most decoration in such photos looks artificial, commercial, and cold.

If you prefer something a little more casual, which looks as though a real person created it, then add your own personal touch. I like to use a variety of fruits and vegetables in different shapes, colors, and sizes scattered around the table, encircling the serving platters.

A few unusual, eye-catching items are fine, but don't overdo it. A good supermarket produce department or your local farmer's market will have all kinds of interesting items, but you need keen eyes to find them. Look for things such as an elephant garlic with its long stem topped with a flower. Or use more common items such as a fresh, shiny Japanese eggplant, or bright red and green chilis.

Another simple decoration is fresh carrots with the green tops left on. Place them on the table in a loose, wreathlike fashion or create a bouquet in a vase. A bouquet of combined vegetables is simple and effective, not overpowering, and reusable. The next event's guests will see the vegetables in a different form — on their plates.

A cream pitcher filled with cherry tomatoes, wine goblets with oil-cured olives, a glass vase with a bouquet of two-foot long vermicelli — all are good examples of attractive focal points on the serving table.

1.6d Use attractive serving dishes and utensils

Creativity is required for serving pieces, too. There are only a few points to keep in mind. First, the serving piece must not chemically react with or discolor the food. Take special care when presenting acidic foods such as salads, pickles, or marinated vegetables.

Second, the serving piece must look appealing. No matter how pretty a porcelain bidet is, or a brass spittoon, they are not suitable containers for a reception table.

Third, the material must suit the event. Highly polished silver is not commonly used anymore except for very formal, strictly traditional affairs. Anything rustic and exotic is in style: terra-cotta flowerpots and saucers, rough wood, and antique baskets. Clay, bricks, and stones all add a certain air to your table for informal catering.

1.6e Collect special props for theme parties

For theme parties, look for table decorations in secondhand shops, thrift stores, and at flea markets. You may want to start a collection of special props for catering to corporate clients. If you have several law firms, for instance, use a few old leather-bound law books; for health-related organizations, use a small collection of old medicine bottles or antique health books. To decorate the reception table for a construction company, buy small eye-catching toy tractors and bulldozers or some rusty old tools. Your guests will remember that your table didn't have the same dull, standard look as dozens of other catered parties. It is a good marketing technique and is worth the extra expenditure and personal time.

1.7 Dealing with clients

Being a small caterer, you will be dealing with your clients personally most of the time. (If you have a sales and marketing person, he or she may be the first contact with a potential new client.) From that first contact the deal will be determined mainly by your relationship with that client. It will be your personal interaction that determines whether there will be any future business from that client. This is where your skill in working with people enters the scene. (See Chapter 8 for further discussion on dealing with clients.)

Contact with strangers is intimidating to many people, while others feel immediately comfortable with anyone. But even the most timid person can learn to be perfectly at ease when meeting potential new clients, introducing the business to them, and letting them know what you have to offer and at what price. Evening courses on public speaking are popular, and there are helpful books and audio guides that offer techniques on good communication and presentation skills.

Based on an initial introduction, the client will decide if you are the right caterer. If you are, start selling yourself and your business. A great deal of your success depends on how well you can do that. Catering, particularly small catering, is a very personal business. It is you and not your company that the client will hire. Your reputation and recommendations from satisfied clients will help a great deal, but if you personally don't impress your client (and the first impression is always the most important), you may not have a deal. He or she may want to talk to someone else before deciding. If you give the right impression, the client may decide right away with a deposit check.

For a small catered affair, that first contact may be the only face-to-face meeting you and the client have until you arrive on the agreed-upon date with the agreed-upon food. If the event is a large wedding, chances are that you will be dealing with the client several times. Some clients will call you daily, even several times a day, for the entire week preceding the wedding. You have to know how to reassure this type of client so that he or she will relax.

With the convenience of e-mail and fax, you may not meet your client in person until the day of the event. If you were recommended, the client may not insist on a face-to-face meeting, and the event may be arranged through the magic of instant electronic transmission, saving time and money for both parties.

2. DESIRABLE SKILLS AND KNOWLEDGE

No one can be so perfectly well rounded that he or she has all the necessary and desirable skills and knowledge for running such a complex business. You are a fortunate person if you have all seven of the essential skills just discussed; if you do, you have a good chance of becoming a successful caterer. However, there are another six skills that are very desirable, although not essential, to have. The following are definitely ingredients for success, too:

(a) Well-developed marketing and selling skills, and ability to network

GOOD SALES AND
MARKETING PEOPLE
ARE RARE. IT IS OFTEN
EASIER AND CHEAPER
TO FIND A GOOD
CATERING AND
KITCHEN MANAGER.

(b) Good record keeping and bookkeeping skills

(c) Ability to manage staff

(d) Solid financial backing along with good budgeting skills

(e) Financial and emotional stability to deal with seasonal highs and lows

(f) Ability to deal with extreme pressure and stress, especially during the holiday season

Let's look at each of these desirable skills in detail.

2.1 Marketing and selling

It is a great advantage to have solid marketing and selling skills when you own virtually any business, particularly if you are a sole proprietor. Unless you have few competitors and what you provide is much in demand, you have to sell your service.

If you live in a small town with few competing caterers and many social and corporate clients who need catering services, you may not need to spend so much time and money on marketing. If, through word-of-mouth and repeat clients, your business is operating at the level of your expectations, marketing is again optional. But these are rare cases.

You may or may not have the time to do marketing and selling while running a catering business alone. It depends on your volume and the other time requirements the business imposes on you. To properly market your business and sell your services you will need to put in at least 10 to 20 hours a week, possibly 30 to 40 hours if you want to do aggressive marketing. Can you sacrifice that much time from the catering side?

Many caterers who have all the essential skills to run a good catering business, but who also can sell and market, prefer to do the latter and delegate the catering end either partly or entirely. The choice is yours as long as you can find competent, reliable help. Good sales and marketing people are rare. It is often easier and cheaper to find a good catering and kitchen manager.

Networking is an important part of marketing. To be good at networking, you need self-confidence and social skills. If you have decided to hire a person to do your marketing, you can either do your own networking or delegate it to your marketing person. Many marketing people love networking and are good at it. Networking will bring in business both directly and through referrals.

2.2 Record keeping and bookkeeping

Many, if not most, small-business owners detest the numerous chores that keep popping up at the record keeping end of their business. They consider record keeping and bookkeeping unnecessary headaches and procrastinate as long as possible, except when it comes to depositing the checks. The longer administrative chores are postponed, the more difficult they become to do, not only because of the sheer volume of the work but because you forget the useful little details you didn't record when they were still fresh in your memory.

The best way to approach office chores is to do them daily, keeping up to date on every record keeping system you use. There will be some extremely busy periods in your business when you simply cannot get into the office. Fine. Postpone the office stuff, but only until the next opportunity comes for a free hour or two. Don't let your mind tell you there is no free time. Much of the office work approached this way can be, if not exactly fun, at least tolerable. Adding up your books every month can definitely be fun, provided your cash flow is a healthy, positive one. Whether you prefer the traditional low-tech tools of bookkeeping or newer accounting software programs, you have to add your own numbers to know how your business is doing.

Without good records you face many potential problems. You don't know how much you owe your staff. You'll have to rely on their record keeping — a very poor practice. You don't know how much to charge clients. You forget a scheduled event because it wasn't written on your calendar! You don't know how your business is doing, what your actual expenses and your total receipts are, and what your gross and net profits (or losses) are. Your business is doomed under these conditions, no matter how good your food is.

Your other choice is to hire someone to do all the office chores. But remember, if someone else is doing your bookkeeping, you will still have to hand your records to him or her, and the bookkeeping won't be any better than your record keeping.

2.3 Staff management

In a survey of a large number of US catering companies in the late 1990s, an overwhelming majority of the respondents indicated labor issues are their largest concern, including hiring chefs and kitchen personnel, service staff (both full and part time), and sales staff. Over the years such concerns became more acute and caterers (like other business owners) constantly complain about finding competent and reliable

WITHOUT GOOD RECORD KEEPING, YOUR BUSINESS IS DOOMED, NO MATTER HOW GOOD YOUR FOOD IS.

help even if they are willing to pay good money. Should you be able to find good staff, appreciate them, nurture the relationships, and count your blessings.

If you are basically a one-person operation, with on-call staff only, your staff and production-control problems will be minimal. If your business is a little larger and you employ part-time or even full-time staff and perhaps a sales representative and marketing person as well, the ability to deal with your staff becomes important.

2.3a Good serving staff

One ingredient of a successfully executed event, besides your excellent food, good planning, and timing, is the gracious and superb service your staff provides. How your people present themselves, how they interact with the guests, how much they are interested in serving the food and not just receiving their weekly checks, is what the client perceives as service. Good food with mediocre service will not bring you repeat clients. Good food with poor service gives rise to complaints.

There are two common problems with serving staff. One is accepting that being a server puts them in a subservient position. This is often a problem with better-educated staff from middle-class backgrounds who take catering jobs to earn extra income. They resent being treated like servants. A second problem occurs with serving staff being overly friendly with the guests, talking with them and treating them as equals, even engaging them in lengthy discussions while the food is getting cool on the serving trays they are supposed to be passing around.

When hiring your staff, make it clear to them that you are in a service business and their role is to serve the invited guests, not just to dispense food as a host or hostess would. (See Chapter 7 for further discussion on staffing.)

Determine how to give good service. Choosing and motivating your staff are two essential parts of this. These two items also apply to your kitchen staff. In the kitchen you are dealing with a staff whose duties include work that is often monotonous and unpleasant, such as cleaning a small mountain of shrimp. Rotating your staff from monotonous to creative work is helpful. Doing the routine work in teams is also a good way of easing the burden.

Your relationship with your sales and marketing staff will probably also be reflected in their performance, unless you are lucky enough to find someone who works well without supervision.

2.3b Combating employee theft

Theft is a serious problem in virtually all food service facilities; the bigger the institution, the bigger the problem. The main problem is the staff stealing your raw ingredients. This is not easy to deal with. If the amounts taken are relatively small and the food value low, poorly paid staff may hardly consider it dishonest to take a package of butter or half a dozen chocolate chip cookies. The issue is more serious if half a dozen pieces of filet mignon disappear regularly. Even $20 worth of food taken from your kitchen by the staff can have an impact on your profit margin if it happens routinely.

To make matters worse, in a small business you don't purchase many extra supplies. If you need 23 steaks for a dinner, you may buy a few extra in case the guest count increases at the last minute or as insurance against one steak being ruined beyond repair, or being dropped in the dog dish in front of the client. Six steaks taken from the refrigerator can spell disaster.

Theft is usually not much of a problem in a small business with a small staff. You know each other well and your relationship is cordial. Once your business and your staff grow and you hire minimum-wage dishwashers and extra food prep staff, theft could become a real problem, particularly if you are frequently absent from the kitchen.

Larger restaurant, hotel, and institutional kitchens deal with the problem by daily and weekly inventory control. This does discourage theft since the staff know about the strict control. If they are taking the butter, it will be limited to one pound instead of four. The disappearance of a package of butter is hardly noticeable when a lot of food is being prepared; four packages missing will be noticed. Large kitchens put someone in charge of logging everything coming into the kitchen in raw form and keeping track of each item and quantity being used. (This serves as more than theft prevention; it is also the system for ordering and restocking.)

In your much smaller business, the idea of inventory control is still valid. You have to know what you have in your freezer and refrigerator, on your shelves, and in the bins. You don't need to itemize every last article, but at least keep track of the major items (e.g., how many chicken breasts, how many cans of caviar). Do your best to make your staff understand that you know every spoonful of vanilla in the vanilla bottle and every cup of flour in the flour bin.

EVEN $20 WORTH OF FOOD TAKEN FROM YOUR KITCHEN BY THE STAFF CAN HAVE AN IMPACT ON YOUR PROFIT MARGIN IF IT HAPPENS ROUTINELY.

Another way to make the staff less likely to take food behind your back is generously sharing the delicious extra food after a successful party.

2.4 Financing and budgeting

Records compiled by the Small Business Administration indicate that a significant number of small businesses fail because of undercapitalization. What a waste! Would-be entrepreneurs start their undertakings full of enthusiasm, hope, diligence, skill, and a willingness to put in 80-hour work weeks — but without enough money. All their resources are put into the business — the money from a second mortgage on the house, a spouse moonlighting for extra funds — just to end up losing it all.

No amount of work and enthusiasm compensates for undercapitalization. You must have sufficient financial backing to start a business, to pay monthly fixed expenses even in negative cash flow months, and to have a cushion for unexpected expenses, which can be large if you need sudden repairs. You shouldn't have to worry about paying your bills even if they turn up unexpectedly. The only thing that should concern you is cash coming in. That is plenty to worry about. You cannot afford to start your business until you are sure that you have enough money to support both your family and the business for at least six months to a year without relying on what you're bringing in from events.

Budgeting skills are also necessary. Once you have a financial cushion, you can't afford to see it shrink because of poor budgeting. It is definitely a skill you can learn. You know if you already have it. Have you survived so far in your personal life by bringing in more than you spend? If so, chances are, budgeting in your catering business will not be a problem.

2.5 Dealing with seasonal highs and lows

Seasonal highs and lows are difficult to deal with in small businesses. The smaller the business, the harder it is hit by a month or two of little income and negative cash flow.

In your catering business, the seasonal highs and lows will vary with the type of catering you do. If much of your business comes from industrial catering, the holiday season will not affect you very much; it might even reduce volume. But most caterers are in great demand around the holiday season, with up to one-half of their annual gross income earned in two and a half weeks. Caterers who specialize in weddings will be very busy in May, June, August, and September, the traditional wedding months. But they will have slumps during the early and late months of the year. Corporate catering is fairly even throughout the year, though it tends to dip somewhat during summer vacation months.

These are just broad generalizations to give you a concept of what to expect. In reality, the highs and lows are very difficult to predict from year to year, even by caterers who have been in business for a long time. No one knows why. For example, most caterers expect to have slow months in January and February. But the same months could be very busy if corporations decide to expand their employee training and schedule classes right after the holiday season in January. If they want you to cater breakfasts and lunches for their classes, you'll be swamped with work.

If you have planned your finances adequately and have a comfortable cash flow, you can also take the seasonal highs and lows without losing your peace of mind. You will simply have to dip into your bank account during lean months, while keeping your faith in the financially solid future. When money pours in all of a sudden, put some back into the savings account for those future lean months. Rely on your good budgeting skills, and invest in one of those pieces of costly equipment you've been wanting, but don't spend all the surplus.

Seasonal highs and lows are something you can live with, even enjoy, once you expect them. It is nice to be busy again after a period of being in the maintenance and house-cleaning mode, but it is even nicer to anticipate a few weeks of very little to do after a busy schedule. This is one characteristic of catering that distinguishes it from other food service fields.

2.6 The holiday season: Beyond a rolling boil

Catering is busiest during the Christmas holiday season, when both individuals and corporations are expected to invite guests and employees to lavish and elegant parties. Many, many catering clients are only going to call you once a year, during this time. Your year-round clients expect to have you cater their holiday affairs, too. This is the time when you have to be very careful with scheduling events. You can schedule up to your maximum capacity of your equipment and staff, but no more, no matter how tempting it becomes to bring in even more income. You may have many more requests for catering than you will be able to take.

PLAN SOME TIME FOR RELAXATION, MASSAGE, OR ANY THERAPY TO RELIEVE TENSION AFTER A BIG JOB.

The stress and pressures of working at maximum capacity for 16 hours a day for a little over three weeks can be tremendous, emotionally and psychologically. You are in the limelight during your events, sometimes several times a day, after an extremely demanding time in the kitchen. It is not uncommon to start in the middle of the night and end late the next night. Then it starts again a few hours later.

If you can take the pressure and stress, you will be handsomely rewarded. If you cannot, schedule just a limited number of events, with reduced stress and income. You cannot afford to fail to deliver what you promised to your clients. Doing so will cost you much more than you'll earn from turning down one more event. Just knowing how much you can comfortably take on for those three weeks will reduce or even eliminate this problem. You'll learn a lot from your first holiday season, and future ones will be much more under your control.

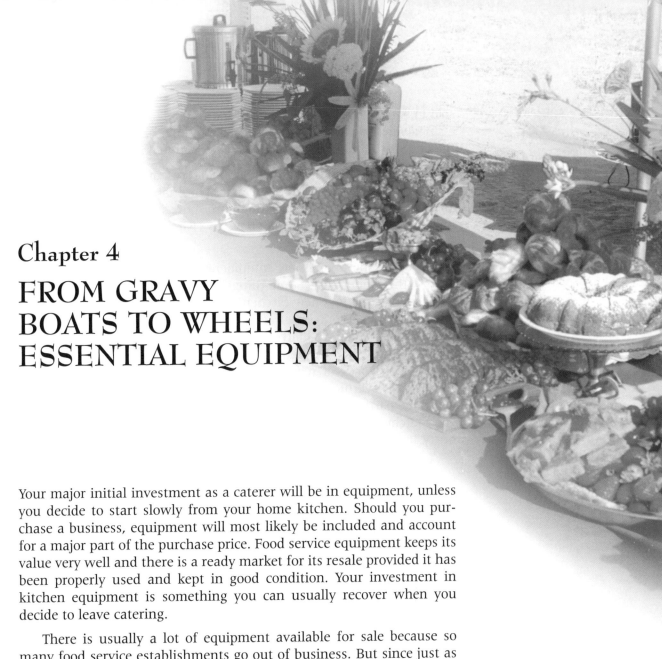

Chapter 4

FROM GRAVY BOATS TO WHEELS: ESSENTIAL EQUIPMENT

Your major initial investment as a caterer will be in equipment, unless you decide to start slowly from your home kitchen. Should you purchase a business, equipment will most likely be included and account for a major part of the purchase price. Food service equipment keeps its value very well and there is a ready market for its resale provided it has been properly used and kept in good condition. Your investment in kitchen equipment is something you can usually recover when you decide to leave catering.

There is usually a lot of equipment available for sale because so many food service establishments go out of business. But since just as many people think that the food service business is so easy, the same number open new restaurants, and the kitchen equipment remains in circulation.

Buying used equipment makes sense and can save you money. In most larger cities, restaurant equipment auctions are common. Attend them even if you are not currently in the market for equipment; it will give you an idea of the prices and condition of equipment being auctioned off. You will learn, too, that it is hard to find individual, smaller items — the type of things you most likely need. Lower-priced items are

FOR EQUIPMENT,
BOTH NEW AND USED,
EBAY IS A WONDERFUL
SOURCE AND FUN IF
YOU LIKE AUCTIONS.

sold in batches, or in a collection of many small, unrelated things with a single auction number. You may have to buy a box of utensils to get the one spatula that is the shape you've been looking for.

Secondhand restaurant equipment stores are a good source for small equipment. Their prices are more reasonable than auction prices, and you can buy a single item no matter how small. If you are searching for specific items, you may have to visit several stores before you find what you want.

If you decide to buy new equipment, weigh the value of your time against the higher cost. Some things, of course, you have to buy new. The best place to buy new kitchen equipment is on the Internet. Try a few sites for small purchases and stick with the ones that offer reasonable prices and quick delivery. The best companies ship your order either the same day or the next day, and if you live in North America, chances are you will receive the order as fast as fermenting crème fraîche (i.e., overnight). Often it's worth the extra delivery cost to save you time, particularly if your business is located some distance from a good kitchen equipment store. If you need a piece of equipment in a hurry, buying it via the Internet is a blessing from cyberspace.

For equipment, both new and used, eBay is a wonderful source and fun if you like auctions. eBay has absolutely everything for auction, including professional kitchen equipment, and if you are lucky and there are not many bidders for an item you want, you may get it for a good price. eBay does not screen buyers and sellers, but it is easy to check on a seller before you bid on an item and pay for your purchase. His or her rating is right there on auction page. You must establish an account before you use eBay, and any transactions you enter will affect your eBay rating.

Your current domestic kitchen equipment can be used for your initial catering work, provided you start with smaller events. In this initial stage, it is possible for you to book a larger event than you can comfortably cater out of your home kitchen. Your best choice is to rent a commercial facility for that specific event. Investigate what is available in your area.

Generally, church kitchens are the best bet for a beginning caterer; churches can use a little extra income and the kitchens are usually only used on weekends. Many caterers start off in church kitchens, sometimes with an agreement that they can use the kitchen with the ongoing use of storage, refrigerator, and freezer space. It is far from ideal, but may work temporarily. Church kitchens are also notorious for having equipment and tools disappear. You may be ready to put together an event and discover an essential ingredient or piece of equipment has disappeared, a costly nuisance since you have not scheduled time to replace what is missing.

Let's discuss the specifics of what you will need in a small catering business.

To collect unusual serving equipment, browse thrift shops and flea markets.

1. FACILITIES AND MAJOR EQUIPMENT

1.1 Kitchen facilities

Let's assume that you are over the initial stage of using your own domestic kitchen and its equipment. Commercial kitchen facilities that are suitable for a small catering business are very hard to find. They have to be approved by the health department, and regulations governing what is required to approve a kitchen vary depending on where you live. They range from lax to reasonable to overly strict. Local health departments will usually have a pamphlet stating the requirements necessary for the kitchen to be approved. Obtain a copy and be familiar with it before searching for a facility. Anything approved already, such as a former restaurant kitchen, is suitable. Beware of old restaurant kitchens located in older buildings; they are notorious for pest control problems. Starting a brand new kitchen is by far the most difficult initially, but the most convenient for you in the long run.

Your kitchen facilities need to have three major areas: a kitchen with large work areas and at least one work table, a good-sized storage space, and an office. In addition, there should be a bathroom large enough for you and your staff. You'll need to freshen up before you depart for your event after ten hours of prep work and cooking in a hot kitchen. A shower is highly desirable, if not essential.

The kitchen must be at ground level, preferably without steps, for easy loading and unloading. Ideally, the storage room is on the same level as the kitchen. The storage area should have very sturdy commercial shelves to hold your equipment and supplies.

Both gas and 220-volt electric wiring are necessary. In addition, you need an exhaust fan, preferably a built-in one. Plumbing must conform to health department regulations, and good lights over the work areas are essential. There should be electrical outlets everywhere and enough circuits to run equipment without blowing fuses, as well as several telephone jacks.

BE FAMILIAR WITH
YOUR LOCAL HEALTH
DEPARTMENT CODES
AND REGULATIONS.

Even if health codes don't require light-colored, glossy paint on the walls, it is very desirable. It will look and stay cleaner longer. The floor should be smooth and easily washable. Molding should seal the joints between the floor and the walls to keep bugs out. All doors and windows should be sealed tightly for the same reason, especially the space under doors. (Leave only enough space, marked by an arrow, for clients to slip their checks under the door when you are not there.)

Garbage disposal service is a must. Liquid waste garbage disposal for a food service business is regulated by the local municipality. Check with them and the local health department to ensure you are operating within the regulations. For a small caterer, the smallest dumpster available is sufficient. The dumpster should be located near the kitchen, but not close enough to attract insects. The indoor garbage can must be kept tightly closed when not in use and emptied frequently. All these precautions will help prevent insect problems.

A good, well-equipped first aid kit should be part of your kitchen, but hopefully never needed for more than an occasional aspirin, something you should always keep in good supply.

1.2 Refrigerators and freezers

You will need at least one refrigerator and one freezer. Both must be of adequate size for your business. To determine what that size should be, try to visualize the minimum storage capacity you would need for a good-sized event, then at least double that capacity. If you don't have enough space, you cannot keep adequate supplies and will have to shop for perishables more frequently.

You will need space for usable leftovers in the refrigerator and freezer. Many perishable items are only good for immediate consumption by you and your staff, but many other food items, such as cheese, baked goods, and hors d'oeuvres, keep very well and can be served later or used in future dishes.

A large refrigerator space is needed to store finished platters that need to be chilled. An ordinary household refrigerator is not big enough for such items. Ideally, a large commercial refrigerator should be part of your equipment.

The same applies to freezers. You need space in your freezer to store food for short-notice events. Keep a supply of frequently used items, such as butter, bread and rolls, and juices in your freezer. It is a good idea to keep a limited supply of extra meat or chicken on hand, too.

Having extra space for cold storage will make your catering life more manageable.

The health department requires a thermometer in both freezer and refrigerator. You must know what the local code is for maximum temperatures and adjust your appliances to conform. Once adjusted, they will keep steady temperatures for a long time.

Nevertheless, problems can develop in your freezer and refrigerator and you should have an emergency plan for such times. Hundreds of dollars worth of food in your freezer may be at stake. Keep a smaller household freezer around for emergency use and for an occasional overload (e.g., during the holiday season).

A second refrigerator is also a blessing, but consider the total cost of your utility bill. You can save money by turning off extra appliances for weeks or months when they are not in use. Remember, the more cooling appliances running in your kitchen, the more heat is being generated — something you rarely need when your kitchen is in full swing.

1.3 Ranges and hot plates

Ranges can be gas or electric, but commercial kitchens favor gas. Gas ranges are expensive but are available secondhand. Since not much can go wrong with a gas range, it is worth your time to investigate the possibilities. You can, however, get away without a range for a long time by relying on commercial hot plates and convection ovens. As a matter of fact, they have a lot of advantages over ranges. Many catering kitchens have no ranges at all. They take up a large amount of your capital and kitchen space. As well, fire codes in most municipalities insist on a hood over any range in a commercial operation. Hoods are very expensive, require an automatic built-in fire extinguisher (for grease fires), and an externally vented system away from anything combustible, which can be costly to install. Fire codes also require range inspections about every six months (depending on your local code).

One way to avoid the huge expenses of a hood and ventilation system is to be licensed as a "cold" kitchen. What defines a cold kitchen varies with local health and fire codes. Basically, in a cold kitchen, frying is not allowed, since accumulated grease is the most frequent source of kitchen fires. If you don't have a range or fryer, you presumably cannot fry, and therefore won't accumulate grease in a filter or run the risk of hot oil catching fire. You can use hot plates up to a certain maximum wattage per plate (again, the code varies), and you can use any size of convection oven without a hood or built-in exhaust system. Some localities require that the convection oven be vented, but that is a fairly simple matter compared to a hood. Large unvented convection ovens are used in many shopping malls for baking chocolate chip cookies. You can smell the chocolate from all over the mall — a deliberate attempt to lure you to buy some — so you know the oven is unvented. (Fire codes in shopping malls are extremely strict.)

Almost any catering event can be accomplished with a good-sized convection oven and inexpensive hot plates. When the health inspector asks you what you do with the hot plates, tell him or her that they are for boiling water, blanching and cooking vegetables, sautéing, but never for frying. Hot plates come in all sizes, and single and double burner models. You'll want to buy the largest one allowed by your local code. It will probably be wired for 220 volts with a special plug so you cannot carry it along to sites. However, you should also have a second set of hot plates that are wired for 110 volts with conventional electric plugs. The maximum wattage of a hot plate that is wired for 110 volts is not very high, but such plates are light, easy to carry, and great for keeping things warm. They are ideal for light cooking at sites with no stove.

1.4 Ovens

If you opt for a range, you also get a built-in oven. Depending on how large it is, you may or may not need another oven. The additional one should be a half- or a full-sized convection oven, either gas or electric. If you want to cater small- to medium-sized events, the built-in range oven may be sufficient.

If you have no range yet, start with a half-sized convection oven, which can accommodate six hotel pans or three large turkeys. You don't even have to rotate them during baking because of the principle of convection heat. A fan distributes heat uniformly throughout the oven. Because of the convective heat, baking temperatures are generally 50°F (10°C) lower and baking time is 15 percent to 20 percent shorter than in a standard oven. The only disadvantage is the lack of a broiler, but that problem can be overcome to some extent. Many of the newer and more expensive domestic ranges also create convective heat when you turn on the fan.

Convection ovens also come in smaller sizes that are light, portable, and great to use on location where no kitchen facility is available. You should have at least one. Though they are small, you can prepare a fairly large number of hot hors d'oeuvres, or 20 to 25 boneless chicken breasts at a time. If you use larger pans, you can bake even more.

Ovens and hot plates intended for domestic use are not allowed in a commercial kitchen. A health inspector probably will not approve a kitchen for commercial operation if there is a domestic stove in it. Small domestic hot plates that are used off-premise are acceptable, but keep them in the storage area, not in the kitchen.

1.5 Dishwasher

A dishwasher is another essential but expensive piece of equipment that you will need. It is probably required by your local health code. Even the smallest commercial dishwashers are expensive, but they are very sturdy and reliable. Even if a domestic dishwasher were acceptable by your local code, it would not be satisfactory for a catering kitchen unless the operation was restricted to small events.

A COMMERCIAL DISHWASHER REQUIRES HIGH WATER TEMPERATURES, AND CHLORINE IS AUTOMATICALLY ADDED TO THE RINSING CYCLE TO STERILIZE THE LOAD.

A commercial dishwasher requires high water temperatures, and chlorine is automatically added to the rinsing cycle to sterilize the load. (The chlorine level in the feed bottle is an item the health inspector invariably checks.) The total cycle is very short compared to a domestic dishwasher — one and a half to two minutes. The loads come out hot, and dry in minutes. Dishes are loaded on shallow trays or racks, and as soon as one load is clean, the next one is put in and started. By the time the first rack is dry, the second one is clean.

You will need several racks, each made for different types of loads — flat-bottomed for silverware, and racks with spikes for holding glasses or plates. You can manage with two racks, but it saves a great deal of time when you load dirty glasses on special dishwasher racks. When the glasses come back from a job site already loaded into the rack, they slide directly into the dishwasher (though you do have to turn them upside down before loading them into the dishwasher since you carry dirty glasses right-side-up in their racks to avoid dripping coffee and wine all over). You remove the rack with the clean glasses from the dishwasher and put the rack directly on the storage shelf.

The dishwashing detergent used is a high-potency chemical. For a small dishwasher, only one tablespoon per load is used.

1.6 Holding oven

A holding oven for a catering business is a portable, double-walled warming oven that is used to keep food hot during transportation and setup. They come in different sizes, and your business can get along without one if you don't plan to serve more than 50 people at a time. For a larger event, you must have a way to keep food hot (it is a health department requirement) from the moment it is cooked until serving time, which is usually at least one hour after you leave your kitchen but could be much longer.

The holding oven has a thermostat control that can be set to keep food from barely warm to hot, but it only goes up to about 250°F (120°C). It is great for dinner rolls, roasts, turkeys, hundreds of chicken breasts, or any hot food you are transporting to the site.

The most efficient way to use the holding oven is to put it on your truck, plug it in with an extension cord, preheat it for about an hour before departure time, load the hot food directly from the kitchen oven, unplug the holding oven, and go. If you need to hold the food for a longer time before serving, plug the oven in again at the event site to keep things warm. Even if it is not plugged in at the event site, it should keep the food quite hot for several hours. A holding oven is ideal in some catering situations, such as a Thanksgiving dinner at a hospital for 100 interns, residents, and their families. In this situation, dinner might be a drop-in affair over a four-hour period, eaten whenever the guests have a free half hour.

1.7 Transportation equipment

Once you have prepared and stored the food, you need equipment to transport it to the event. There are many kinds of catering trucks. You and your business will dictate the truck you will need. In the beginning, you may not want to put out a large expenditure (or make long-term commitment, if you decide to lease) that bites heavily into your budget. If the funds are available and you're sure catering is your cup of tea, go ahead and purchase a vehicle. If not, your car will do as a means of transporting equipment and food to smaller affairs, especially if it is a small van or station wagon.

Eventually, however, you will need to commit yourself to a more professional-looking and practical vehicle. Your vehicle should reflect your company image. You will be the first one to arrive and one of the last to leave, so your vehicle will be in clear view of the host, hostess, and all the guests. It will be their very first impression of your business. An old, sad-looking vehicle does not communicate an image of elegant food, sparkling-clean serving equipment, and neat staff dressed in impressive, formal uniforms. The familiar proverb, "You cannot judge a book by its cover," simply does not apply in business, particularly in show business, which is what catering is. A somewhat aged vehicle is acceptable provided it looks clean and well cared for.

Small businesses need a small delivery truck, whether it is a van (what most small caterers favor), a large station wagon, or a pickup truck with a large camper shell. It depends on the business you are running and the volume to be carried. No matter how much you anticipate carrying, your vehicle will always seem too small. So if you have to purchase a vehicle to transport your equipment and food, get the largest size possible.

Bear in mind that larger vehicles are harder to park, maneuver, and store on your lot, and ensure your staff can drive your vehicle without problems. Also remember to budget for the higher costs of insurance, maintenance, upkeep, and gas for a larger vehicle.

If your vehicle cannot carry everything, you have several choices. Have staff members transport some of the food and equipment that won't fit into the company vehicle and reimburse them for their costs. You can rent a second vehicle for a day or two. You can also hire a driver with a truck for a day just to transport, load, and unload your catering food and equipment (don't forget the insurance coverage for that vehicle). Whichever option you choose, your extra cost will be small compared to the income from the event.

The best arrangement inside the vehicle is a set of fixed shelves for small- and medium-sized items and plenty of floor space for large equipment. Use a carrying trolley with brakes on the wheels, so it won't roll around the truck with food stacked on it. Shelving will probably need to be custom-made and fitted into the vehicle. That is a problem you must either solve yourself or rely on a carpenter with a creative touch. For a smaller vehicle, a single shelf across the front or on one side is the best solution. It has to be accessible and easy to load, even when you are balancing something heavy such as a marble board filled with cheeses. The shelves must be very sturdy and they should have a lip or barrier of several inches all around to prevent anything from sliding and tumbling down in transit.

The interior of the vehicle should be easy to clean, which is required by most health departments. Spillage is inevitable, especially on the return trip when everyone is rather tired and loading is less careful. Carpeted floors or walls are completely unacceptable. Surfaces should be kept as clean as your kitchen.

BEAR IN MIND THAT LARGER VEHICLES ARE HARDER TO PARK, MANEUVER, AND STORE ON YOUR LOT, AND ENSURE YOUR STAFF CAN DRIVE YOUR VEHICLE WITHOUT PROBLEMS.

YOU WILL ALSO WANT
A STEAM IRON FOR
TOUCHING UP
TABLECLOTHS, SHIRTS,
AND OTHER ITEMS.

1.8 Washer and dryer

These are not essential, but very useful to have. If you have space and a little money to invest, I highly recommend a washer and dryer. There are towels, aprons, and uniforms to wash regularly, and the tablecloths and napkins also need to be cleaned. Services to pick up and drop off linens and towels are available, but many have a minimum charge that doesn't justify setting up an account for your small business. By far the cheapest solution for a small caterer's linen needs is on-site laundry facilities; if possible, budget for a washer and dryer. Domestic models are fine, but choose the large capacity and heavy-duty models.

You will also want a steam iron for touching up tablecloths, shirts, and other items.

2. KITCHEN FURNISHINGS

As far as kitchen furniture is concerned, there are three important items: work tables, sinks, and shelves. First, you need a very large, heavy, and solid work table. It can be a butcher block, solid plank, steel, or any material that is acceptable to the health department and easy to clean. It needs heavy wooden or metal legs that are braced in every direction, and stools around it for you and your staff to sit. In a small catering operation, two work tables are preferable. A foldable banquet table is acceptable for your second work table.

Second, you must have two (in some municipalities three) sets of stainless steel sinks with hot and cold water. The washing-rinsing sink has two or three compartments and must be connected to the dishwasher. The vegetable sink must have a main sink and a floor sink. The floor sink is a small additional sink either at or below floor level that is not directly connected by a drain to the main sink. There is a gap of a few inches in between; the drain pipe of the main sink hangs over the floor sink. The purpose of this configuration is to eliminate any possibility of sewage water coming up into the vegetable sink and contaminating it. Should sewage water back up for any reason, it will flow out onto the floor and your vegetables will remain uncontaminated. The third sink, if required, is the mop sink.

Third, you'll need as many shelves around the walls as you can fit in, up to the ceiling. Like table space, you can never have too much shelf space. No food material, even when it is in a closed container, can be stored directly on the floor. For larger containers, you will need to build a low shelf at least six inches above the floor. This guarantees that when mopping the floor, the mop cannot touch food containers or serving and cooking equipment.

Finally, you are required to have a proper-sized fire extinguisher that is fully charged, inspected and refilled annually, and approved for kitchen fires.

Any other furniture in the kitchen depends on your own needs and space, although chances are there is no space left for even an umbrella stand. It is pleasant to have some decorative items on the walls and shelves of your kitchen to soften the image of a dry, plastic commercial operation.

3. OTHER ESSENTIAL CATERING GEAR

Each time you transport your food and equipment to a job site, you and your staff will face the unpleasant task of unloading and transferring everything to the reception or dining area. This can be a considerable distance, especially in office buildings. Downtown areas are usually the worst for parking problems. If the building has a loading dock, use it. Many older, smaller office buildings don't have one, so you will have to find a place to park on the street. You may be able to pull your truck close to the door and park temporarily in a restricted zone just to unload. Unloading can take a full hour if the situation is really bad.

To make the job as easy and quick as possible, you will need a trolley and a handcart. There are many types of trolleys available for the restaurant trade but not many have been designed specifically for catering. Restaurant trolleys have fixed trays. In catering, you'll want to be able to change the spacing between trays to accomodate different-sized loads. Also, the small rubber wheels on restaurant trolleys won't suit your purposes. A good catering trolley must be able to roll over rough, decorative cobblestones and bricks in front of office buildings and deep plush carpets in corporate boardrooms, and bounce over high thresholds, and in and out of elevators that never stop level with the floor. Make sure your trolley has large, good quality rubber wheels with brake levers for all four wheels.

You'll want more than one trolley if you plan to do several simultaneous events. The most useful trolleys are stackable. The bottom half has the wheels; the second story has spikes that fit into holes on top of the lower trolley. These can be custom-made. Each cart is just a frame with six lips for sliding trays into. An amazing amount of food can be carried with the two stories stacked, but they must be loaded with care.

YOU'LL WANT MORE THAN ONE TROLLEY IF YOU PLAN TO DO SEVERAL SIMULTANEOUS EVENTS.

On the delivery truck they sit separately and double as shelves during transportation. They are made of aluminum, which is lighter than stainless steel but not as easy to clean and keep shiny.

A good, sturdy, collapsible, preferably not very heavy two-wheeled hand dolly is also very useful for transporting crates of china and glass, convection ovens, and other heavier items. Again, you need fairly large, good quality rubber wheels. A dolly will save a lot of backache. Make sure you get one with a long carrying tongue on the bottom so it is suitable for your large dish racks. The tongue should fold in to save space in your truck, and even better, the handle should telescope down into the body.

There are hand dollies that easily convert into four-wheel push carts. These are heavier and more awkward to use, but once you know your own transportation needs, they may be preferable for your business. Try for the lightest and sturdiest dolly you can find. Expect some drain on your equipment budget; a good one is expensive and rarely available secondhand.

It is usually not a good idea to invest in a large supply of chairs and tables for your clients to rent. They take up a lot of storage space and it is hard work to load and unload them. A big catering business is more likely to own a supply of tables and chairs. However, you do need a few folding tables of six- or eight-foot lengths for buffet and bar setups. You'll get requests for them fairly often. Depending on the size of your delivery vehicle, you may not want to keep more than two or three in your kitchen.

You will need equipment to transport both hot and cold food. For hot food transportation, a holding oven is ideal for large events. For smaller luncheons and dinners, smaller-capacity hot boxes are more suitable, though they do not maintain temperature as well as holding ovens. They are meant to be used for relatively short transportation and holding times. Hot boxes are made of various insulated materials and are fairly expensive. Each one should be large enough to accommodate at least two full-sized hotel pans and keep food hot for at least an hour.

You can make your own hot box by lining a wooden box with thick styrofoam insulation and fitting it with guide rails to hold the covered hotel pans.

Cold items are a little easier to care for. You need several coolers, from the largest available to smaller, family-sized ones. The largest will carry chilled, poached whole salmon while the smaller ones are just right for a bag of ice for the punch. Choose coolers with smooth, easy-to-clean outside and inside surfaces.

You will want to have a couple of beverage tubs available for serving chilled drinks. Depending on your style, they can be fancy or basic. Clean bussing tubs or galvanized steel tubs will serve the purpose. If you want a more elegant presentation, wrap your beverage tub in a clean white sheet or even a worn tablecloth no longer suitable for the buffet table. A simple trick is to spread the cloth on the floor, set the tub in the middle and fold all corners into the tub. Add alternating layers of ice and beverage cans, topping with plenty of ice. Now you have a neat-looking beverage container.

You will also need a good-sized carving board for your buffet table. A wooden board will do, but it must have a drain gutter on all four sides to save your tablecloth.

Finally, you will need to keep a supply of disposable plates, cups, and utensils for events where china, glass, silver, and linen are not called for. The quality of disposables you supply depends on your catering style and your client's budget. Make sure you have an adequate supply of everything you use on a regular basis. It is annoying to run out of disposable ware just before an event.

One or two portable gas stoves, which run on bottled gas, are a nice addition to your catering gear, especially for outdoor events where fresh hot food is to be served. You can do without them to begin with, so try to find secondhand ones at a cheaper price. Make sure they are clean, neat, and in good working order. The same goes for the gas bottle. Before you use gas stoves for an event, try cooking on them either at home or at your kitchen facility. They heat more slowly and do not get as hot as the hot plates. Their burners are smaller, so you have to allow extra cooking time.

Portable barbecues are great to have if they are fairly large and you expect to use them often. It is up to you to decide whether you want the comfort of bottled gas or the more down-to-earth charcoal with its enticing smell, causing hunger pangs in the guests soon after you light the fire. A small barbecue is of limited value to a caterer: it has to be big enough for you to feed at least 20 people. If you don't expect to use it very often, it may not be wise to invest in one. You can rent a large barbecue when you need one; you can pick it up or it can be delivered directly to the site. The client pays the rental fee. A very large one can be towed. If you are expecting to barbecue a lot, it is worthwhile to purchase a large one or even several of varying sizes.

A SMALL BARBECUE IS OF LIMITED VALUE TO A CATERER: IT HAS TO BE BIG ENOUGH FOR YOU TO FEED AT LEAST 20 PEOPLE.

Caterers who specialize in barbecues are often large businesses that cater for company picnics and larger outdoor gatherings, often with hundreds or even thousands of guests.

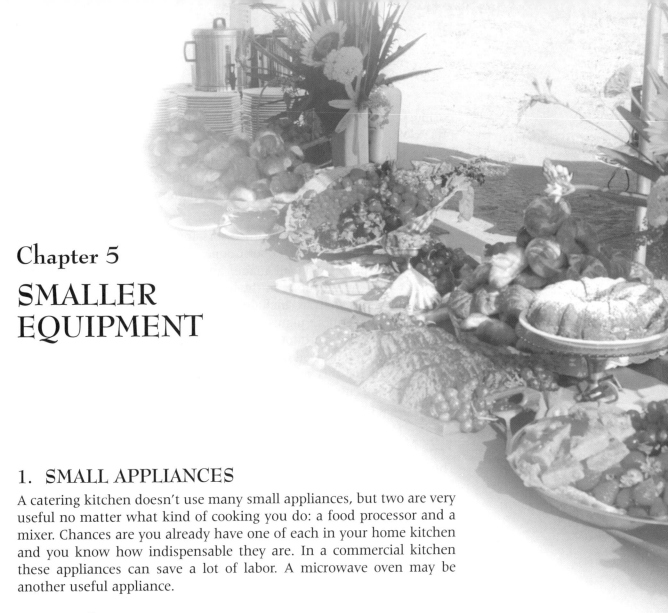

Chapter 5
SMALLER EQUIPMENT

1. SMALL APPLIANCES

A catering kitchen doesn't use many small appliances, but two are very useful no matter what kind of cooking you do: a food processor and a mixer. Chances are you already have one of each in your home kitchen and you know how indispensable they are. In a commercial kitchen these appliances can save a lot of labor. A microwave oven may be another useful appliance.

1.1 Food processors

Many chefs say that they can chop, grate, or slice just as fast as the machine, if you include the cleanup time for the machine in the entire job. That may be true if your knife technique is good and you are preparing a dinner for eight or ten guests. You can do a more even, more appealing job by hand than by machine. Certain types of cuts cannot be done with a machine at all. However, in a catering kitchen where you are usually chopping for 50 or 100 or more people, cutting up that many vegetables by hand is a considerable job no matter how good your technique is. It is much easier to use a food processor. In addition, the long-term repetitive motion with your knife can eventually injure your wrist, muscles, or joints, which you cannot afford if you plan to stay in the business. Even for relatively small jobs, it may be better to use your food processor.

The most commonly used, most powerful, top-of-the-line food processor in well-equipped domestic kitchens is the Cuisinart. It may do well for a start-up business, too, but for commercial operations it is too small and underpowered.

The next step up in food processors for smaller operations is the Robot Coupe. The smallest Robot Coupe is expensive (about US $700) because it is powerful, well made, and not mass-produced like the Cuisinart. You can get along in the beginning with the two most popular cutting plates that are included with the machine. Eventually you will want to have more plates: two slicers with different slicing thicknesses, a grater, and perhaps a julienne cutter. The plates are expensive, so hold off until you need one for a lot of work. Currently, there are 25 plates offered for this processor for all kinds of specialized, unusual, and interesting cuts — just what a caterer wants. Before you buy a commercial food processor, investigate your options.

1.2 Mixers

The food mixer market for domestic kitchens is dominated by KitchenAid. They are fairly expensive, top-of-the-line, well-built machines with power to spare. The largest one available will do fine for your kitchen for years. KitchenAid also makes a mixer approved by National Sanitation Federation (NSF) for a small commercial operation. It is just a little more powerful than the largest domestic machine, with rating at 350 watts (about two-fifths horsepower), compared to the domestic one at 325 watts (about one-third horsepower). It is sturdy and can be operated a longer time without overheating.

If you are planning to make and mix a lot of dough, the domestic KitchenAid may be too small. You can do the dough in batches, but that wastes your time. You may have to step up to the smallest commercial machine.

1.3 Microwave ovens

A microwave oven is useful to have but not essential. I personally dislike microwaves and find them useful only for quick defrosting or to heat up your personal lunch. You are probably at a point in developing your kitchen art by now that you can decide for yourself about the usefulness of a microwave. If you have an extra one around somewhere, put it in your commercial kitchen. If not, decide if you really need to buy one.

2. MISCELLANEOUS ELECTRIC EQUIPMENT

2.1 Coffeemakers

Coffeemakers are essential in the catering business. You will need at least two or three with different capacities. The most commonly used ones are percolators, not because they make the best coffee, but because they are convenient for making a large volume with a minimum of effort. Fill it up with water, add the coffee, plug it in, and it's ready in 30 minutes to an hour, depending on the size.

Drip coffeemakers make stronger, better flavored, more full-bodied coffee but they are much less convenient than percolators and require constant attention. They are versatile because you can make decaffeinated and regular coffee, and hot water for tea with the same machine, but they produce 12 cups at a time at about five-minute intervals and someone must monitor the machine and refill the baskets. This may be slow if you are catering a large party at a prime coffee-drinking time (e.g., breakfast and brunch).

Keep on hand one large, 100-cup percolator, one or two smaller ones with 50-cup capacity, and perhaps one or two 30-cup percolators. (It's nice to have two so one can be used for decaffeinated coffee.) Keep several drip coffeemakers for smaller events.

Almost every kitchen already has a coffeemaker, but don't count on it even when the hostess says she has one you can use. Take your own so that you know you will have a reliable machine that is an adequate size for the number of guests. (Most coffeemakers in client kitchens are too small for a party of 12 to 15 guests.)

Although you should have a variety of coffeemakers in your storeroom, for the occasional event when the requirement is beyond your capacity, renting a coffeemaker is no problem.

2.2 Electric kettles, heating trays, and crock pots

A two-quart electric kettle is nice to have but not essential. It can be used to heat up water quickly for tea and for supplying hot water for the chafing dishes. The hotter the water, the faster your food will heat; boiling water may not be available on some job sites.

An old-fashioned, large electric heating tray with a thermostat control is great to carry along to keep things hot that won't fit in ovens or on chafers. Two or three smaller ones are also useful. Since microwaves came in, heating trays are not used in homes much anymore, so they are readily and cheaply available in secondhand stores.

If it fits into your style of catering, crock pots are very useful, though not very stylish. They keep food at the right temperature either on or off the buffet table.

3. KITCHEN EQUIPMENT

As you know, there are literally hundreds of pieces of kitchen equipment and gadgets on the market. Most of these items are toys and no more. Everyone has his or her opinion of the usefulness of kitchen gadgets, but most professionals agree that only a few are really needed in the kitchen.

3.1 Knives

Your single most important consideration for kitchen equipment is your collection of knives. I cannot advise anyone else on how many and what kinds of kitchen knives should be part of their equipment. Personal opinions vary a great deal. But a basic collection might include several "French" (also called "chef's") knives, a carving knife or slicer, a large serrated (notched or toothed on the edge) knife, small paring knives, and a steel knife sharpener and sharpening stone. You can add more knives for special purposes as the need arises. For example, a boner and a fillet knife are nice to have if you do either of those tasks. Neither your French knife nor your paring knife will bone a chicken or fillet a fish with ease.

It is essential that you know how to sharpen your knives and do it often. With a very sharp knife, cutting is faster and easier, and there is less chance of slipping and cutting your finger instead of the food. Insisting on using a sharp knife proves you're a professional in the kitchen. A good chef sharpens his or her knife many times a day — not major sharpening with a stone, but just rehoning the edge for 10 to 15 seconds. Try it and see what a difference it makes in your food preparation. For more on sharpening, see Chapter 14.

3.2 Cutting boards

The second most important piece of equipment is a cutting board. Actually, you should have a number of them. You need at least two small ones and two large ones. How many you need depends on how many people will be preparing food at one time. Most cutting boards are made of either wood or high-density polyethylene (HDP), commonly called plastic. Any odor or stain on an HDP board can be removed in five minutes with a chlorine soak. The only complaint I hear about them is that they dull knives much faster than wood does. That may be true, but sharpening your knives a little more often is a small price to pay for a more hygienic, safer surface. In some municipalities, wooden cutting boards are no longer allowed by the health department and eventually this may become the general health code. So when you are buying cutting boards, look for the high-density polyethylene.

3.3 Scales, pots and pans, and strainers

You will need two or three kitchen scales: a standard, accurate, and sensitive portion-control scale that can weigh a cinnamon stick accurately and anything up to two or three pounds; another, less accurate scale that will weigh anything up to five or ten pounds, and a larger scale to weigh at least to 25 pounds. Comparable metric scales are also an option if you prefer to use metric measurements.

A few heavy-weight, domestic saucepans will be useful, but you will also need a good collection of industrial-weight pots of all sizes from two quarts to five gallons. You can start out with four, but as your business grows so should your pot collection. Most should be the regular stockpots, but you also need at least one wide, shallow pot. Your collection should include saucepans with handles, at least five with two-quart to two-and-a-half-gallon capacity, and a few smaller ones, down to butter-warmer size. Sauté pans should also range from a couple of very large ones (at least one to start with) down to a tiny one.

You will need four colanders: one huge colander, one large one, and a couple of regular-sized ones. Several strainers, from a tiny fine tea strainer to a small but coarser strainer, and one or two larger ones, should also be in your collection. You will need at least one deep strainer basket with handles for blanched vegetables, which should be fine enough not to lose the finely cut vegetables through the mesh.

The food industry favors heavy-gauge aluminum pots and pans simply because they are the best available for industrial kitchen work. Don't even think of buying light- or medium-weight aluminum — it won't hold up. Heavy-gauge, industrial-weight pans are the only suitable ones, and they are expensive compared to domestic pans. You can find them in used restaurant equipment stores, but for a complete collection you'll have to buy some new ones as well.

You will also need baking sheets: at least six or eight large ones made of heavy steel or aluminum that will fit in your oven, and several smaller ones for baking small amounts and using on-site because your larger ones won't fit in a domestic kitchen oven.

Regular 9" x 13" domestic baking pans and muffin tins are also essential. You will have to determine the number according to your expected needs. You will always need more than you think. A collection of bread pans in different sizes will complete your basic baking pan needs.

Other essential requirements include the standard stainless steel hotel pans or chafing dish pans that fit into chafers. They can be used for baking, refrigerator storage, and serving on chafer stands. You will want at least six or eight full-sized pans to start with, as well as four half-sized pans (two of these fit in a chafer stand), and perhaps even three one-third-sized pans for small parties. You will need covers for serving as well.

4. SERVING EQUIPMENT

4.1 Serving ware

Unless your catering business serves entirely on disposable platters, you must have a substantial collection of serving platters, baskets, and bowls. You'll want all kinds, shapes, and sizes. They can be china, pottery, glass, stainless steel, silver or gold, aluminum or copper, as long as food, especially acidic food, will not chemically react with the material and as long as their appearance fits the image your company wants to project. In addition to price and appearance, consider weight (the lighter the better for you, since you have to carry them around the reception room loaded with food), and durability (after a 14-hour day you and your staff can get pretty careless packing up the truck to head home). Glass punch bowls are pretty but very difficult to pack and carry. If they break before you get to your event, you have a problem. A false cut-glass bowl made of plastic is a nice compromise if it is acceptable to your standard and your event. Sometimes, of course, it is not.

It is entirely up to you to select serving equipment; you know the style you want and the money you can afford to spend. Secondhand platters and bowls are available, but you have to hunt for them in secondhand and antique stores and flea markets.

You will also need good-sized water pitchers and coffee servers, preferably the thermos type. They should look nice since they will be displayed on the buffet table, or your servers will be using them to serve beverages at the dining tables.

4.2 China, glassware, and linen

Clients often want you to supply china, glass, silver, and linen. You have three choices: rent everything from a rental company and pass on the cost to the client, buy your own set of everything and charge a rental fee to the client, or buy enough supplies for small events and call a rental company for the larger events. Choose what is most logical for your catering style.

All three choices have advantages and drawbacks. If you have nothing in the way of tableware, you have to run to the rental agency all the time. That may be fine if the agency is just around the block. If not, it can be time consuming. On the other hand, at the end of an event you don't have to deal with the dirty dishes or maintain a large inventory that ties up both capital and storage space.

Even if you choose not to have your own sets, you will still need a nice collection of table linen for your buffet tables. Choose the colors and styles that fit your business image. Be sure that they are easy to wash and stain resistant. Sometimes these tablecloths come back from events in sad shape. Do some research on how to get rid of the stains or you will be buying new linens all the time. Having them dry-cleaned is just too expensive.

4.3 Baskets and other decorative items

An extensive collection of baskets from tiny to huge is in virtually every caterer's storeroom; the prettier the better. They are inexpensive if you find the right source. You will also want pretty napkins in various colors to use as inserts and covers.

Less essential and more personalized decorative items include candleholders, vases, and decorative table pieces of all sorts. You'll accumulate them as needed. Besides standard table decorations, you may want to collect special items for specific events, so that each client has the impression that the decor was designed specifically for his or her event.

5. NONESSENTIALS AND OTHER SMALL TOOLS AND EQUIPMENT

In a small catering business, you are on your own. You equip and furnish the kitchen to suit yourself, the way you feel it serves your purposes best.

However, assuming that you have few tools and equipment at this time and you want a general concept of what an average small caterer might use, here are the nonessential and specialized tools and equipment my catering business uses:

- 2 large polyethylene cutting boards
- 2 small polyethylene cutting boards
- pastry bags (two different sizes) with tubes and tips in assorted sizes and shapes; buy the easy-to-clean plastic instead of cloth bags
- 8 tube or bundt pans, several sizes
- 10 quiche pans with removable bottoms (7 to 11 in. or 18 to 25 cm)
- 6 torte pans with removable bottoms (6 to 10 in. or 15 to 25 cm)
- 6 cake pans (8 to 10 in. or 20 to 25 cm)
- cake carriers
- French baguette pans
- 2 sifters: one large, one small
- 5 wire whips, variety of sizes
- 7 icing grates (wire racks), from small to 28 in. (70 cm)
- rolling pin
- set of stainless steel measuring cups and spoons (flour and sugar bins each have their own set that stays in the bins), one 8-cup and one 2-cup glass measuring cup
- 3 kitchen timers
- meat thermometer, oven thermometer, and an accurate digital kitchen thermometer
- 5 brushes, different sizes, the largest 3 in. (8 cm) (to spread melted butter on phyllo sheets), one reserved for brushing pastry only

- 4 icing spatulas from small (great for spreading sandwich fillings) to large
- baster
- 3 pairs of tongs
- large spoons, both solid and slotted, and carving forks
- skimmer
- 2 mashers, one small, one large
- 5 dishers (like ice cream scoops) with release wires, 0.5, 1, 2, 4, and 6 ounces (15, 30, 60, 120 and 180 ml), respectively
- apple corer
- pineapple corer
- dough cutter and scraper
- pastry blender
- 2 funnels
- cookie cutters
- pastry and pizza roller
- cherry and olive pitter
- vegetable peelers
- kitchen shears
- pruning shears (for flowers and to cut up bunches of grapes)
- zesters
- grapefruit knife
- tiny scoops and ballers
- can and bottle opener
- juicers
- 3 ladles, different sizes
- egg slicer
- butter cutter
- hand chopper
- 2 hand graters, 1 tiny for spices like nutmeg

- 6 wooden spoons
- 3 rubber scrapers
- spaetzle maker
- 1 pair swimming goggles (for cutting onions)
- 16 bowls, from tiny to huge
- pizza wheel
- large salt and icing sugar shakers
- mortar and pestle
- spice grinders, small hand and larger electric (formerly coffee grinder)
- 10 bussing tubs
- six 13 in. (30 cm) rectangular plastic tubs
- 2 electric tea kettles
- 2 electric fans
- fly swatter

Chapter 6
MENU INGREDIENTS

1. FINDING AND DEALING WITH SUPPLIERS

1.1 Retail versus wholesale outlets

Suppliers present a formidable problem for a small caterer. Large caterers and restaurants have all types of food and other supplies delivered on a regular basis. If you are a small caterer, the large suppliers are not particularly interested in dealing with you unless they are desperate for business. They usually have a minimum purchase before they deliver — most of them set it at several hundred dollars. Some of them even require a minimum order before you can purchase anything from them. You can order and do the pickup yourself at many suppliers' "Will Call" departments and pay cash until you establish credit with them. Some suppliers require a minimum purchase of about $100 even at "Will Call"; others will let you pick up a single item such as a large fresh salmon worth $40. This sometimes works out fine, but many suppliers are located out of town where warehousing is cheaper, and you sacrifice your time by picking up. Call suppliers and find out their policy regarding small accounts.

Some large suppliers treat your tiny account fairly well, but many don't hide the fact that they would prefer you to go somewhere else. Your purchase of a large salmon or one case of Roma tomatoes is just not worth the paperwork. Often they will save the top-quality merchandise for their regular clients, so you get second choice.

As for prices, it is not necessarily cheaper to buy from the large suppliers. When you buy small amounts, you don't get their discount or case prices, so you are paying virtually retail prices. They are unwilling to break cases for many items — for example, produce. They will sell you vegetables by the pound or kilo but charge so much that you are better off shopping at the nearest supermarket.

So what can you do? The first step is to decide what quality of food you need and then start working out a source for each type of ingredient you will buy. If you live in a large community, there should be a number of choices for you. In small communities, the choices may be very limited, and you may even have to depend on delivery service from central distributors.

Often, your best source for many items is regular retail outlets, while for some things wholesalers are your best bet. You must have your entire line of suppliers worked out before you start booking events. Assuming you have been cooking seriously for quite a while and have lived in your area for some time, you probably already know many good retail sources for the types of food products you will be using.

The large warehouse-style discount stores where you can get a business membership if you have a state or provincial seller's permit are a blessing for small caterers. Business members often receive certain privileges, such as lower membership fees and designated hours when only business members can shop. These warehouse stores started off in the mid-1980s with low prices and medium quality. Over the years their focus changed and they began to stock many high-quality food items, as good as what most wholesale suppliers carry. You will readily find most of your catering supply needs in these warehouse stores — meat, seafood, poultry, cheese, produce, bread, and disposable items, as well as some equipment. If you are a business member with a seller's permit, you are exempt from paying local taxes on your purchases. It pays to join as soon as you start your business.

1.2 Establishing relationships with suppliers

Here are the main food areas in which you will have to establish your source of supplies:

- meat, fish, and poultry, including cold cuts

- dairy products

- fresh produce

- dry and canned goods

- bakery products

- specialty products, such as vegetarian raw material, organic produce, gourmet items, unusual and exotic items

- food trade products, such as one-gallon cans of Sterno and disposable items

SMALL WHOLESALERS OFTEN PROVIDE BETTER SERVICE TO SMALL CATERERS THAN LARGE WHOLESALERS.

You have two sources for each: retail or wholesale. To buy from a wholesaler, you must have a resale license. Whether you can get any of the above from a wholesaler depends on the quantity and frequency of your purchase. Some things you will have to purchase from a wholesaler, such as a large baron of beef, or a case of frozen croissant dough, or four cases of portion-controlled boneless chicken breasts. These items would be hard to obtain through most retail outlets, although your butcher may be able to order any meat item for you. And more and more, warehouse stores carry such large items specifically for small businesses.

Consider three factors when looking for a source for each of the above categories: price, quality, and reliability. The larger warehouse stores have the lowest prices, often lower than wholesale. This source is also somewhat unreliable. Three weeks ago you purchased large rounds of Brie from them and when you are looking for the same item today, there is no Brie in sight.

To buy wholesale, the best bet for a small caterer is a small wholesaler. They appreciate your account even though it is small, and often they don't charge for delivery if you are close to their regular delivery route. They may have no minimum order or minimum delivery requirement. They compete with the big food distributors by providing far better service. Once you establish a relationship with them, they tend to treat you well, provided you pay their bills promptly. They need quick cash flow just like you do.

1.3 Ready-made versus half-ready items

You need to think about how much food you want to buy ready made or half ready, and what you will prepare from basic ingredients. If you are in low-end or medium-quality catering, you have a wide variety of choices available from ready-made, commercial products that can be served with a bare minimum of preparation on your part. If you are planning to operate a medium-quality or high-end business, ready-to-serve food items of the quality you need are less easy to find.

Ready-made foods you can use include frozen products such as meatballs, cookies, or cakes, that just need defrosting and warming up. Partially prepared items include frozen cookie or croissant dough that needs to be baked before serving. Some of these products are poor and some are very good quality, but none are very cheap. You're paying for the labor of preparation, which is what you saved by buying these products in the first place.

There are caterers who buy ready-made products almost exclusively and resell them to their clients. There is minimal kitchen preparation work involved. Other caterers prepare everything, or nearly everything, from basic ingredients. Your best compromise is to try some of the ready-made products and calculate how much profit you can make by buying them versus making them yourself, including the cost of labor. Of course, you must compare quality as well.

1.4 Buying produce

For produce you need a source that is not only relatively inexpensive, but also has a good variety for your catering needs, and a quick turnover of food so you can count on fresh produce. If there is a farmer's market near you, visit it regularly. First of all, the produce is fresh, and sometimes even cheaper. Second, you can find unusual fruits or vegetables that supermarkets won't carry. Small produce wholesalers stay in business to serve small restaurants and food markets. They will sell you anything by the pound or kilo at near-supermarket prices, and they want your small account. They often have good quality, very fresh produce, and a good wholesaler picks the top of the crop from the distributor. These products are often better than those available from an average supermarket. The best of wholesalers' produce is often reserved for restaurant suppliers, their most discriminating customers.

1.5 Keeping tabs on prices and quality

For finding your sources, you will need to know two things: prices and quality. Keep a complete list of all food prices in your files, in a notebook, or on your PDA (Personal Digital Assistant) that you can carry with you on all your shopping trips. This is not only for comparison shopping but also to calculate the cost of the final products you are preparing.

You must keep track of prices. Devise your own system if you prefer. For example, you could use a small, palm-sized electronic system in which you input all food and related items with their prices per unit (in ounces, pounds, gallons, kilos, or liters) or per piece, and the quantity of the container the item comes in at what price. Perhaps even enter your own codes for the suppliers where you can purchase each item.

Your little price book or electronic system should list everything you use in your kitchen, from almonds to yogurt. Don't carry this pricing to extremes. Surely you don't want to figure out how much a teaspoon of salt costs! If you feel that keeping track of everything is too much trouble, keep track of only the major ingredients or expensive items. Seasonal items (such as produce) are a little more difficult to track because their prices vary so much. Nevertheless, you should have some idea of the cost so you can add it when you are pricing seasonal items on your menu.

2. FOOD QUALITY

Learn how to choose the best quality at your selected price level. Since you are at least a reasonably good cook, you probably already pay attention to the quality of food you buy, much more so than the average shopper. Just watch people shopping at the produce section. Most will pick up the first pineapple they see and put it in their basket with no thought given to ripeness, freshness, or quality. Others are more discriminating and take the time to look at the leaves, feel the flesh for soft spots, and smell the pineapple near the stem end to judge its ripeness.

Never take things from the top of the pile because those are the oldest in the bin. Have you ever watched store clerks replenishing produce? They take all the old stuff off the shelf and put it on their cart. Then they pile up the fresh produce on the shelf and put yesterday's produce on top. This is called rotating the stock: "first in, first out." Let other shoppers take the older produce; you want the fresh ones, so dig down for them.

Make deliberate efforts to be an expert on judging the quality of food items you buy, especially produce, dairy, meat, fish, and poultry products.

And remember to look for the expiration or pull date. Grocers say that the product you buy will be fine for quite a while after the expiration date. Don't believe it. For dairy products, for instance, they say it will be fresh tasting a week after the date. That may be true if the dairy item was stored and transported under ideal conditions; however, this

GROCERS SAY THAT
THE PRODUCT YOU
BUY WILL BE FINE FOR
QUITE A WHILE AFTER
THE EXPIRATION
DATE. DON'T
BELIEVE IT.

is rarely so. To be on the safe side, consider the expiration date the last day you can still use that aging product.

Should you buy brand name, or generic (store brand or private label) products? This topic is discussed in Chapter 17.

3. SUBCONTRACTORS

For most catered events, your business will be the only one that supplies food and services to a client, and no other suppliers are involved. These are the routine catering jobs — receptions, grand openings, corporate luncheons, dinners, or breakfasts. But other catered events involve a number of other contractors or subcontractors in providing services and other products. These are the festive, more elegant, lavish events, with substantial budgets to spread among several service businesses.

You can be part of these more elaborate events in two different ways. Either you are one of the subcontractors or you are the main contractor responsible for hiring everyone else. In the first case your responsibility is minimal and your income is less. An event coordinator often hires your services, and he or she is your client rather than the host or hostess. You will be paid by the coordinator who is responsible for the smooth running of the entire event. Menu planning and all details are done with the event coordinator, who gets approval from his or her client on your food and prices.

In the second case, you run the show. The host or hostess is your direct client and the person who writes out the check. You subcontract for any services you don't provide. You have far more responsibility and work, but your income is larger because each subcontractor pays about 10 percent of his or her gross to you, or you add a 10 percent surcharge to your invoice for the subcontract. This is not free money. You are not only entitled to it, you earn it. It takes many phone calls, much running around, negotiating, and paying of deposits to schedule the whole show.

Some high-budget events have many subcontractors. Here is an example of a birthday dinner party I catered, organized by an event coordinator. The main vendor was the caterer. Other vendors included a florist, an ice sculptor, two musicians (one inside, one outside), a decorator, a chocolate-dipped-strawberry supplier, a birthday cake baker, a rental agency, a photographer, a limousine service, and a magician. When an event is that complex, it is common practice to hire an event coordinator.

However, you should keep a list of all subcontractors available for various services, especially cake bakers, musicians, and florists. Keep track of their prices, the quality of their products, and most of all, their reliability. It is bad business if the baker delivers a mediocre cake, but it is worse if he or she does not deliver at all.

Make sure it is understood by both you and the subcontractor what your commission is and how it will be paid. Subcontractors routinely give you a 10 percent discount and you charge full price to your client, or the subcontractor charges a so-called wholesale price and you add a commission of about 10 percent to that.

It is important to establish a good relationship with a rental agency whose services you use often. You want to be familiar with everything available for rent, including tents, podiums, dance floors, various outdoor structures, artificial turf, and so on.

It also pays to forge links with local event and wedding coordinators. If you provide the type of service and food their clients want, you could be a preferred vendor, which can mean good business for you. There is often an association of local wedding coordinators in cities. Think about inviting them to an open house at your facility and provide a lavish food table so they can see your presentation and sample your products. If you have enough space in your facilities, you could offer it as a regular meeting place with a luncheon thrown in. Most hotels, banquet, and reception halls hold these events routinely to lure the event coordinators and their clients.

Finally, you should have a list of all reception halls available in your market area that allow outside caterers to provide services. You'll use it and share it with clients once they have committed to using your services. Most clients reserve a hall before booking a caterer, but occasionally there are people who ask your help in finding a place. This is when you will need a complete list that gives details of everything about that reception hall: size, how many it will accommodate for a stand-up and for a sit-down party, how much it costs, whether the kitchen is included, liquor restrictions, security, safety of guests late at night, parking lot size, equipment in the kitchen or staging area, condition, and the upkeep of both the reception hall and kitchen. You can make this list and visit the various possibilities during slow periods when there aren't enough events scheduled to keep you busy 18 hours a day.

WORKING WITH A GOOD WEDDING OR EVENT COORDINATOR CAN BE MUTUALLY BENEFICIAL.

Chapter 7
TOO MANY COOKS

1. SELECTING YOUR STAFF

While your business is in its initial, negative cash flow stage, you will not only be the sole proprietor but also the sole employee nearly all the time. If you have a partner, the two of you will be marketing the business and waiting for phone calls. Unless, of course, you start by fluke when a bride walks through your door and asks you to cater a wedding for 125 guests.

As long as your business is based on relatively small events, you can handle all the work by yourself. By small events I mean meals for 20 to 30 people, or receptions with hors d'oeuvres for up to 50 guests. You can manage these kinds of events by yourself if they are self-service buffets. For full-service events, you will need help with anything over ten guests. If your experience is limited, you may feel the need for help even on smaller events, and you will be wise to hire staff.

Because catering is a service business, find good, reliable people to help you prepare and serve your food. This is a often a challenge. As I mentioned in Chapter 3, the biggest concern caterers have is finding reliable staff. As soon as you are in business, seek out at least half a dozen trustworthy people who can be on-call for you. Don't offer them only minimum wage. Make it worthwhile for them. Even if they cannot count on a steady income from you, they can count on taking home a reasonable reward after an event.

1.1 Part-time or full-time staff

Most catering companies, due to the unpredictability of the business and constantly changing workload, rely on on-call staff rather than hiring permanent part-time or full-time people. The larger companies have some permanent, full-time staff positions — chef, kitchen manager, receptionist, and sales and marketing personnel. The medium-sized companies may have one or two full-time or part-time permanent staff members. You and your staff will have irregular hours: 12 to 14 hours one day, off for several days, and then working all weekend.

Your motto should be "short list of personnel and long hours of work." The latter part applies to you, not the hired help. Initially, cash flow dictates that you keep the payroll low. It will eat up your meager profits. Your overhead is likely to be high enough and difficult to trim; your food costs cannot be cut very much without sacrificing quality or quantity. The cost of labor is your only flexibility. Once a positive cash flow has been established, you can relax a little, cut down on your working hours, and add extra staff hours to replace your own.

Small caterers often have no full-time permanent staff. If they have enough business, they may be able to afford a permanent part-time chef or a sales and marketing representative. They rely extensively on their list of on-call staff. This list is exactly what you will need to build up.

Depending on the state of the economy and your location, you may have a relatively easy time finding staff. There are many people, young and old, with solid food preparation or serving experience who want to earn a little extra money. For on-call catering staff, you will need people who want to earn extra income and have a flexible schedule. They could be students, mothers with young children at home, or other small-business people who have flexible hours and the time available to work in catering. Try to avoid the unambitious, the ones who simply don't want to work more than a few hours a week. They are not suitable staff for your catering business.

If you live in a community with a college or university, students make good on-call staff, and they often have some food experience. Your friends may refer people interested in working for you. You can even call other caterers and ask to share available staff for a particular time slot.

1.2 Presentable, hardworking, and reliable

Select your staff extremely carefully; they have to be almost as good as you and be exceedingly reliable. You want to hire staff who represent your catering business, arrive on time, work hard, and present themselves well. The people you hire for kitchen work must be experienced, good with food, able to follow instructions, efficient, and diligent. In a small catering business you often take the kitchen personnel to the job site to serve at the event. They arrive in your kitchen in work clothes and must change into serving clothes before departure.

The staff's attitude and physical appearance should, if possible, be compatible with your style of catering. If it is upscale or high-class catering, your staff should be comfortable serving food in a wealthy home or a plush corporate boardroom. Industrial catering requires a different style of staff. For example, a subservient waiter in a tuxedo would look out of place in a "roach coach" and would intimidate the customers. An outdoor barbecue demands still a different character. Your selection of staff needs to conform to the style of catering and the surroundings.

Catering an event is physically draining. Carrying equipment, food, and supplies in and out of the job site, setting up and serving, standing for several hours, cleaning up, packing up, loading, unloading, putting the food away, and stacking dirty pots and pans all adds up to several hours of demanding physical labor without much rest and certainly without sitting down. Often this is on top of several previous hours of food preparation.

Not many people can or will undertake such "hard labor," so you must select people with strong backs and legs and explain in detail what they can expect. Unless you know the prospective hire personally, make sure you check his or her references. Your staff is crucial to the success of an event. You cannot afford to keep no-shows, poor workers, or incompetents on your list.

Until you know your staff well and can rely on them, overstaff your events in case someone fails to arrive. It will cost you an extra $50 to $100 but it is a reasonable insurance policy against an unsuccessful or difficult party due to a missing staff member.

1.3 Your relationship with your staff

How you treat your staff is very personal, an art that has nothing to do with catering, just simple knowledge of how to deal with people. Some

CATERING AN EVENT IS PHYSICALLY DRAINING. NOT MANY PEOPLE CAN OR WILL UNDERTAKE SUCH "HARD LABOR," SO YOU MUST SELECT PEOPLE WITH STRONG BACKS AND LEGS AND EXPLAIN IN DETAIL WHAT THEY CAN EXPECT.

MANY PEOPLE
CONSIDER PREPARING
AND SERVING
ELEGANT FOOD TO
CLASSY GUESTS
GLAMOROUS WORK.

of your on-call staff will also be on-call for other caterers, which is fine as long as they don't give your trade secrets and cherished recipes away. When any staff member talks a great deal about working with other caterers and how they do things in their kitchens, you should be suspicious of whether he or she is talking about your business while working for the other employers. Talk to your employee and explain that it is a poor policy to openly discuss the competition's kitchen. If that fails, find another employee.

Since you will have a small number of employees, your relationship with them is particularly important. Let your staff try new techniques and be open to seeing their ways of presentation and preparation, provided it does not clash with your style of catering. You may learn a lot from your staff.

Give your staff feedback on their performance. Food preparation can be monotonous — for example, when you need to fill 600 phyllo triangles with spanakopita. Have them take turns on the phyllo preparation and let everyone have a chance to do something more interesting, such as preparing a platter that requires patience and creativity.

One thing in your favor when searching for catering help is that many people consider preparing and serving elegant food to classy guests glamorous work. It can be and often is. Even though a lot of the work is routine and tiresome, your workers will rarely do a monotonous type of preparation for more than an hour before they move on to another task. It is unlike restaurant food prep work where mountains of the same vegetables must be peeled day after day, hour after hour, to be served on the same routine menu. Working with food itself is an added incentive for many. In general, finding help for your catering operation is rarely a problem.

1.4 You make the rules

Set up the house rules early and enforce them. Don't allow food sampling, but be generous with any extra food after the event. For long days, you may want to set aside some extra or leftover food for your staff, or assign someone to prepare a pot of wonderful soup from all the vegetable and chicken trimmings. Your satiated staff will leave the client's food alone. It doesn't matter how you do it, but make sure everyone understands and respects your house rules.

If you have employees who work for you regularly, you need to have a written manual of company policies. The manual should cover a broad range of personnel matters. Hire a professional to make sure everything is covered to avoid lawsuits. Both new and old employees, as well as you, the employer, should be familiar with the company manual. You must adhere to it as closely as possible regarding your employees' rights and other matters. As business consultants say, the only thing more damaging to a business than not having a manual is to have one and ignore it. For more information, see *Employee Management for Small Business*, another title in the Self-Counsel Business Series

GIVE YOUR STAFF PLENTY OF ADVANCE NOTICE WHEN YOU WANT THEM TO WORK A PARTICULAR EVENT.

2. PAYING YOUR STAFF

Most food preparation staff get very little money, with wages hovering at or slightly above minimum wage. The work they perform often reflects the money they earn. Give your staff the best wages you can afford. You will have more satisfied employees and a better chance of getting them on short notice when a last-minute event comes up.

If your catering business is low- or medium-class, your staffing requirement is much larger and you can pay less to produce food on a production line. For high-end catering, you need staff with better qualifications and the only way to get them is with better pay. A good policy for a small business is to pay a little more than the average for your industry. Staff turnover is reduced and your staff has an incentive to work for you instead of the competition.

Give your staff plenty of advance notice when you want them to work a particular event. Reserve them at least 10 days ahead of the event. They will appreciate it and you can relax about staffing needs. The only problem is that the number of guests expected at an event is often overestimated. The number tends to go down during the last week before the event and a drastic reduction may force you to cut your staff. Canceling reserved staff is a poor practice because it jeopardizes their trust in you. It may be better to reserve fewer staff than needed and add an extra person the week before the event. Or if you must cancel, compensate the staff person with a small cancellation fee of say $20.

Now, what about your sales and marketing person? How does he or she get paid? Compensating sales staff is more complicated than it is for food prep people. Follow general guidelines of sales staff in other industries. A salesperson can be paid an hourly wage, a salary, or a commission, or any combination of the above. A full discussion of this issue is outside the scope of this book, but here is a brief summary of how it is handled by caterers.

MAKE SURE PAYING
COMMISSIONS AND
BONUSES WON'T EAT
UP A SIGNIFICANT
PART OF YOUR
PROFITS.

Catering is a seasonal business and many catering sales personnel prefer to be on salary so their paycheck doesn't fluctuate with the seasonal highs and lows. Salary is the easiest to deal with for your business, too. As long as your salesperson produces results without being on commission and he or she prefers a salary, agree readily to that means of compensation.

Commissions reinforce productivity. If the salesperson sells more, he or she earns more money, and with higher catering volumes you can afford to pay more. There is little doubt that a person will work harder for you if the compensation depends directly on performance. The problem is that the commission is only paid after you receive payments for the events, which means a delay in paying the salesperson.

Many caterers pay a combination of salary and commission. For a part-time salesperson this is a good method of compensation. An hourly wage combined with a modest commission may be a good way to start someone off in your business. How much those figures should be is difficult to determine since the rates vary from area to area and from small communities to large cities. Commission in the catering business is generally between 5 percent and 10 percent. Large caterers can pay less commission because the salesperson makes enough by the sheer volume of business. Smaller businesses pay closer to 7 or 8 percent with little or no additional salary. Then there is the draw account method, a somewhat complicated method of compensation not suitable for any but the largest companies. It is guaranteed advance pay for future sales in some businesses. In others, it is not guaranteed, so the salesperson has to pay back anything drawn against the account from future sales.

Commissions are based on any item in your invoice that you make money on, excluding delivery, rental charges, gratuities, service charges, and so on. Generally, a commission is paid on gross food and beverage charges. When discussing potential earnings with a new salesperson, show him or her the amount of monthly total food and beverage charges you have been billing and calculate the potential earnings from that, using the agreed-upon commission rate.

Bonuses also encourage higher sales. In most sales situations, bonuses are given if certain predetermined levels of sales are reached or surpassed. A lower bonus may be given if the goal is nearly reached by your salesperson; for example, 90 percent of the goal.

Make sure paying commissions and bonuses won't eat up a significant part of your profits. Offering commissions and bonuses requires a profitable operation. Make sure you have a written contract with your salesperson. You can write one yourself or use your lawyer's help in this area. See Sample 1 for an example of a sales contract.

3. HOW MANY STAFF?

You will need food preparation personnel who work directly under a chef, a kitchen manager or you; serving staff who may be the same people; and a cleanup crew. For smaller events, the initial cleanup can be done by the serving staff. For larger events, it is cheaper to pay someone a lower hourly rate just to clean up after the event. That person (or crew) could come to the job site near the end of the event and take care of the cleanup: stacking and loading equipment, china and glass at the job site, and washing the china and glassware in your kitchen either the same day or the next morning. If the china, glass, and silver are rented, they need to be rinsed and stacked into crates, ready for pickup at the job site. Your higher-paid staff can go home an hour earlier, satisfied to earn one hour less to avoid cleanup duties, especially after a full day of tiring work.

You'll also need some bartenders on call. You often need more than one and if so, someone should be in charge of all the bar duties, supplies, cleanup, and related work. Then you have one less thing to worry about, and you can concentrate fully on food catering. Bartenders demand a little more hourly pay than serving staff, but it depends on supply and demand in your area. Be sure to be familiar with local regulations (they vary widely across North America) regarding who is responsible for guests' drinking and driving, and who is liable if a guest causes an accident on the way home. Discuss these regulations with your clients who request bartending service. If the liability is yours, hire a bartending service instead of your own bartender so that they are responsible for monitoring guests' drinking.

How large a staff do you need for a specific event? For a self-service buffet meal, as a rule of thumb, for every 50 guests you need one person to set up and attend the serving table, replenish food, help when needed, clean up, gather plates, glasses, and silverware, change courses on the table, and be polite to the guests. Another person should be working with the food in the kitchen, keeping things hot, and making up new platters. For a reasonably simple menu, a team of two experienced staff can serve up to 70 to 80 guests. As the menu gets more complicated or the length of the event becomes shorter, you should increase the number of staff accordingly.

SAMPLE 1
LETTER OF AGREEMENT

This letter of agreement is between John Dough, John Dough Catering, and Jane Pastry, 415 Piecrust Canyon Drive, Sourdough, an independent sales and marketing representative. It is agreed that Jane Pastry will be employed as a freelance, independent agent to sell and market John Dough Catering services. Compensation shall be $10.00/hour for approximately 15 to 20 hours a week. Working hours shall be determined by Jane Pastry, who will be working predominantly from her own office. Pay for her services shall be twice a month, on the 15th and last day of the month.

In addition to hourly wages stated in the previous paragraph, a commission of five percent of the net sales of all events catered by John Dough Catering and directly attributable to Jane Pastry's efforts will be paid by John Dough Catering to her after receipt of payment from the client. The net sales will be the total of all billed items that include John Dough Catering's principal services, i.e., food and directly related services. It will exclude rental charges, catering service charges, delivery charges, and any charges that are included for subcontracting part of the event. However, if John Dough Catering provides services, even if they are not directly food related, such as bartending and flower arrangements, such services will be included as items for commission.

Frequent telephone or personal contact will be maintained between John Dough and Jane Pastry regarding progress. A brief weekly summary of Jane Pastry's sales and marketing progress, including hours worked, will be submitted in writing to John Dough Catering.

Day-to-day expenses directly related to work will be compensated by John Dough Catering. Expenses greater than $75 must be preapproved by John Dough.

This agreement will be in effect for 60 days, but either party may request any change that seems necessary or desirable. Such changes will be in effect as soon as both parties agree to them in writing.

This agreement may be renewed for another term, or the parties may decide on a new long-term agreement as they both see fit.

Jane Pastry shall start work on _____ and this agreement shall begin on the same day.

Dated:_____   Dated:_____

_John Dough_____   _Jane Pastry_____
John Dough,   Jane Pastry
John Dough Catering

You also need one person in the kitchen for every 100 guests. For full-service meals, you need about one person in the kitchen for every 30 to 40 guests and one server for every 20 to 25 guests, depending on how complex the menu is, what the facilities are like, and how far the servers have to walk from the kitchen to the dining area. Staffing requirements change somewhat with the menu; they go down with simple meals and go up with more complex ones. For example, for a dinner party for 150 guests, served buffet-style, reserve your chef and a helper in the kitchen and three more staff members on the floor. For a full-service dinner for the same number of guests, schedule five helpers in the kitchen and six servers in the dining area. For simpler, lower-budget meals, reduce the kitchen staff. When each plate must be garnished and presented beautifully, increase the kitchen staff.

For reception food, one person can take care of 50 guests; with a very simple lower-budget menu, 70 to 80 guests; or in low-end catering, 100 guests.

For bartending, the requirement depends on the bar service requested. For a simple bar of wine, beer, and nonalcoholic drinks, one bartender can serve 70 to 80 guests. For a full bar, reduce the ratio to 50 guests per bartender. If the bar is for a reception or open house over a relatively short period of time, you should figure even fewer guests per bartender. The guests will probably want to down at least a couple of drinks over the short period and the bartenders will be inundated. For a longer open house (three to four hours), the pace will be more leisurely, so a bartender can take care of more guests without being overworked.

4. DRESS CODE

Dress code for you and your staff is something you have to decide on and stick to. Whenever you hire someone, explain the dress code and make sure the new person has the necessary clothing to look like a presentable member of your crew.

The more formal your catering business is, the more dressed up your staff should be. A uniform is a good idea for several reasons. The client appreciates having uniformed staff serve. It looks professional and businesslike to have everyone in the same uniform. Many businesses recognize this fact. That is why so many restaurants, bakeries, garages, and gas stations dress their staff in uniforms. It is also good for the staff. They don't have to worry about how to dress for the occasion and they have a sense of belonging to an identifiable team.

WHENEVER YOUR
STAFF IS SERVING, NO
MATTER WHAT TYPE
OF CATERING THE
EVENT IS, UNIFORMS
ARE WORN.

At the very least you should have aprons printed with your company's name, logo, or even a motto. The most classy outfit for catering staff is a white tuxedo shirt, black pants or skirt, and a bow tie. The bow tie could be black or your company's chosen color. Most companies that require a uniform ask employees to pay for it. Your catering company should use the same policy. Either have your new staff buy the necessary garments if they don't have them, or buy a supply yourself, give a set to each new employee, and deduct it from their paychecks. You will find that many who have worked in the catering business already have the "black and white."

Whenever your staff is serving, no matter what type of catering the event is, uniforms are worn. What about events when all you do is deliver, set up, and leave? Or when you just deliver the food? In general, it is always a good idea to wear the uniform. It represents classy service, and even if none of the guests will see you, the receptionist or the executive assistant who is in charge of the event will be impressed. It pays to keep up your company image. This is the way to get the contact person to remember you and your company for events in the future.

As the owner and manager, you have the choice of wearing the same uniform as your staff or something that indicates you are the "big boss" at a larger event. If you are part of the working staff, it may be a good idea to wear the same uniform. If you are acting as the chief supervisor, you may want to wear a somewhat different outfit, such as a fancier tuxedo or a different colored one, a red cummerbund, or a different-colored bow tie.

Make sure everyone's uniform and appearance is acceptable before you go to an event. Have a few extra tuxedo shirts and pants available for emergencies. When a staff member forgets to bring his or her black and white and there is no time to go back for it or there is a last-minute spill, you will be grateful for your foresight.

Make up a short list of your company's dress code requirements and hang it in plain view to remind your staff. Insist on their compliance. Here is a sample dress code to use as is or modify to your needs:

John Dough Catering Dress Code

- Black slacks or skirt

- White tuxedo shirt

- Black or dark shoes, clean and shiny

- Long hair pulled back (neat and clean)
- No large or dangling earrings
- Natural-colored hose worn with skirt
- Black socks for men
- Conservative makeup
- Well-kept hands (nails short and clean)

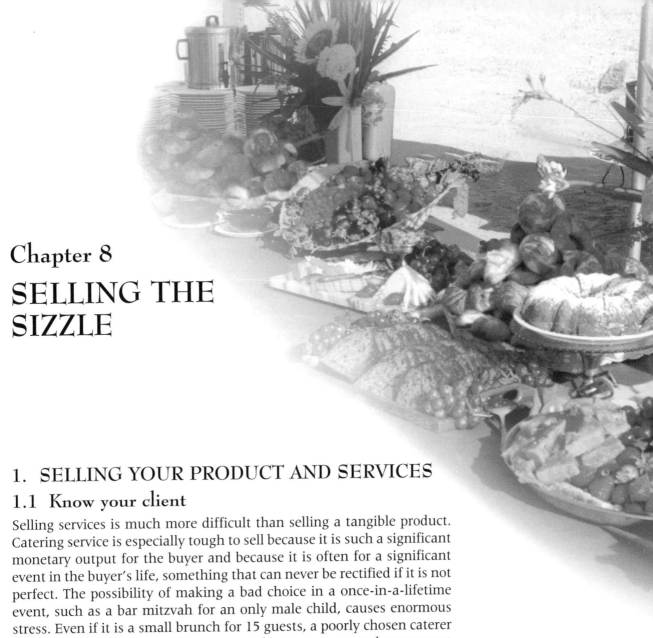

Chapter 8
SELLING THE SIZZLE

1. SELLING YOUR PRODUCT AND SERVICES

1.1 Know your client

Selling services is much more difficult than selling a tangible product. Catering service is especially tough to sell because it is such a significant monetary output for the buyer and because it is often for a significant event in the buyer's life, something that can never be rectified if it is not perfect. The possibility of making a bad choice in a once-in-a-lifetime event, such as a bar mitzvah for an only male child, causes enormous stress. Even if it is a small brunch for 15 guests, a poorly chosen caterer can turn the event into a disaster, or at least, an acute embarrassment to both guests and host.

In other services, such as shoe repair, the biggest consequence of a bad choice is annoyance for poor service. The fault is usually easy to remedy and a relatively small amount of money is at stake. For catering even the smallest event, hundreds of dollars are on the line, and for larger events thousands are at stake. To add to the pressure, the merchandise cannot be returned or exchanged.

Whether you decide to do your own selling or hire a part-time sales representative, the average scenario for a typical sales transaction in catering is the same:

ASSEMBLE AN
IMPRESSIVE
COLLECTION OF
YOUR PHOTOGRAPHS
IN A PROFESSIONAL-
LOOKING PORTFOLIO.

(a) At your first contact with the potential buyer, you determine qualifications (a quick personal assessment of the person and a few questions will tell you if you are in the same ballpark.)

(b) At the first or a subsequent meeting early on, you discuss the proposed event in detail: the type of menu, service, and available dates.

(c) There is often further discussion with the chef, kitchen manager, or you about specific menu selection, service required, and the other particulars.

(d) At this point, you prepare a written proposal for the client. (You may have to adjust this proposal after the client's initial approval.)

(e) The client confirms the event and hands you the deposit.

You or your salesperson should determine a number of selling points for your specific catering business. Chances are, you have a niche — an unusual or unique angle that makes your business different. You may have a number of unique "signature" food or beverage items or an outstanding way of presenting food, or you may be known for serving the healthiest food or using the freshest ingredients in town. Any of these selling points can help you convince the buyer that you are the best caterer for his or her event. Stress that the guests will be impressed by having you as a caterer because no one else in town can do it as well as you can. Every host or hostess, business or social, wants to impress the guests. After all, that is one reason to hire a caterer. (The ones who don't care to impress buy a large deli tray at the supermarket at a fraction of the cost of catering.)

Sell your catering service from your own office. You are on home territory. You can impress the potential client with your office, sample food, photos, and a clean and neat kitchen. You feel at ease and you can concentrate on selling. The client should see your working facility. Whenever possible, set appointments in your office to save you travel time. However, for a larger or more complex event, you will want to visit the client's facilities. When making an appointment, point out the advantage of the client seeing your operation.

1.2 Create a photo portfolio to show clients

Assemble an impressive collection of your photographs in a professional-looking portfolio. Large, high-end caterers tend to display glossy, four-color, Madison Avenue-style brochures and professionally produced commercial photos of their events. Smaller caterers want to give a less expensive look, something that does not scare prospective clients away with a "too expensive" look. But the other extreme, printing menus very inexpensively on cheap paper and with an unimpressive layout, is equally unacceptable. Your client may think your brochure matches the quality and care you put into your food and service. It is best to aim somewhere in between. Your decision should be based on the type of catering you want to develop, the type of client you want to please, and current trends at the time you open your business.

UPDATE YOUR PHOTO PORTFOLIO ON A REGULAR BASIS.

Recently, marketing experts have favored good quality snapshots for caterers as the best selling tools. (See examples included on the CD-ROM enclosed with this book.) The photos should show your uniformed staff at work, some of your food displays, and guests munching away. The better dressed the guests, the more suitable the photo. Limit the number of photos in your portfolio so anyone can page through within half a minute. Letters of appreciation are also good additions, as well as anything else you feel you should include. Don't crowd the pages and don't make the portfolio overwhelming. The photos can be different sizes, neatly mounted, with or without labels, with your own personal touch. The clients should not feel that the portfolio was produced by a commercial enterprise, but that it is a simple collection of snapshots of your typical events.

It is best to produce two or more copies of your portfolio — one for your office, and one for each salesperson. You may not need more than one copy, but a spare may come in handy from time to time.

Scan a few good snapshots of your events to make digital copies and keep them in a folder on your computer. When you e-mail proposals or notes to clients, you may want to attach one to your message for a quick visual presentation of what you can do for the client.

1.3 Business cards and menus

There are two other essential selling tools: business cards and catering menus. The choices in each are very personal and it is not easy to give suggestions on styles and how much to spend on them. For caterers, they range from simple to lavish. Naturally, the more high-end your business is, the more elaborate your printed material becomes. In times of economic hardship, clients may not be impressed by four-color glossy menus, which suggest high-cost catering.

Recent trends favor simple yet tasteful business cards and menus. The best approach is to collect your competitors' business cards and menus and see what they produce. Have a friend call around to ask for the information if you don't want your name to be known to the competition. That may help you decide what sort of literature you want for your business. Besides business cards and menus, you need some general information that very briefly tells the prospective client what sort of food and services he or she can expect from your catering company. The help of a marketing expert would be useful in writing this information. If you have a website and e-mail address, display them prominently on business cards and brochures.

1.4 Choose your clients well

I have to caution you about one pitfall many beginning entrepreneurs won't escape: taking all the business that comes your way. Be discriminating, even if things are extremely slow. There is nothing less rewarding than working with an impossible client. Start evaluating your clients immediately. At first, many clients can be tense and too demanding, acting as if they know more about cooking, food, and catering than you do. But slowly they ease up when they see that they can trust you and that you are sincere. Some, however, will never soften up. They keep telling you how to run your business and that your prices are unreasonable, and they insist that you provide such and such a menu in spite of your explanation that fresh sautéed fillet of catfish is not only impractical for 95 guests, but virtually impossible. Do not waste your time with impossible clients. It may be best to refer them to your competitor.

Other potential clients you don't want to spend a lot of your time on are the ones without sufficient funds to pay for your services. Try to qualify them right away, even though it can be tricky. If you are a good salesperson, you can do it in no time. As soon as the budget looks questionable, send them politely on their way to a budget caterer. If you are already a budget caterer, send them to the supermarket.

As you work more and more with potential clients, you will develop gut feelings about which clients you want and which ones you don't. Be suspicious when a client drastically changes a previously agreed-upon arrangement, when the promised deposits are not paid in spite of several phone calls or letters, or when the client appears to be unhappy with you. These are occasions when it is best not to accept the event and even refund the deposit.

If you already have a heavy commitment during the time of the proposed event, refuse, no matter how good a client it is. Don't ever overcommit yourself and your staff, no matter how lucrative it appears.

Even though catering is difficult to sell, one powerful advantage you have over other businesses, as well as a good selling tool, is the food you can offer to visiting potential clients. If you are visiting the client, take a little plateful of samples. It is a very convincing selling argument.

Of course, there are numerous sales gimmicks, techniques that apply to any business and those that apply to catering only. This is an area where you or your salesperson can benefit from books or seminars on selling techniques.

2. RESPONDING TO REQUESTS

Most of your first contacts with potential buyers will probably be telephone requests for information. If you have a display ad in the Yellow Pages, you will get many calls. Most of the callers from this source are price shoppers who call every business with a display ad. Some of them are blunt enough to say that all they want to know is how much a catered meal costs. These calls are generally a complete waste of time and money for you; many caterers won't even bother to send out the requested literature to such callers. Of course, before you disregard a caller, question him or her a little further. You can quickly get enough information to decide what to do with the caller.

If you have a salesperson, pass the information on and delegate him or her to take care of it. If you are your own salesperson, get the caller's name, address and preferably an e-mail address and fax. Send out a menu, which may be a fixed or a sample menu, by e-mail or fax (cheap, quick, and effortless), or by snail mail, with either a cover letter addressed personally to the buyer, or a prepared information sheet about your business.

Certainly a personal letter gives a better impression, but e-mail or fax is perfectly acceptable; in fact, often more desirable because it is instant. Companies often request electronic transmission so they can act at once. Whatever way you are sending the information, it should explain everything about the company: the type of catering you do, the kind of food you serve, the serving staff, and anything else to convince the buyer to become a client. It is best to have at least two standard letters, one for corporate clients and one for social clients. (Have versions of the two ready for e-mail or fax transmission as well.) The two types of clients may be convinced by somewhat different approaches. Right now, testimonials are in vogue in selling and marketing, so you may want to include the kind and complimentary words of a client who wrote a letter of appreciation to you.

Cover letters are very individual and I advise you to make up your own. However, the examples shown in Sample 2 may help you start the process of writing yours. Selling and marketing trends do change with time, so stay alert and change your letters when necessary. You probably receive a lot of unsolicited mail, like everyone else, and it is a good indicator of the latest promotional approaches.

Form letters on your computer should not be sent out unaltered. It is a good idea to include something in them that refers specifically to your telephone conversation with the buyer. That way, the letter does not look quite so cold and impersonal, even though everyone knows that it is reproduced at the touch of a few buttons.

How should you handle price requests? Most experienced salespeople say you should never, ever give out prices on the telephone. Anyone who is calling for prices is simply a price comparison shopper. You don't want their business unless your focus is on large, low-budget catering. These callers have little potential to use your services. You can answer a request for prices by offering to spend a complimentary half hour with the buyer in your office to discuss the upcoming event. Explain that once you gather more information, you will be glad to give him or her a proposal or a price. Tell the caller that you feel the telephone is not a satisfactory medium for discussing the event. If the buyer is willing to meet with you, it is worth a half hour of your time to pursue the matter further.

3. MARKETING YOUR BUSINESS

3.1 Identify your market

Marketing runs parallel to selling, and both are essential to continued success. If you are fortunate, your salesperson is good at both selling and marketing. But some salespeople don't like to market and some marketers are not much interested in selling.

Many, but by no means all, standard marketing techniques apply to catering. Some unique marketing approaches are needed to increase the chance for success in selling your services. For example, it is generally agreed by most caterers and their sales/marketing personnel that media advertising is of little value except when targeting very specific markets.

August 3, 20--

Ms. Ginger Prosciutto
Spiced Ham Distributing Company
100 Clove Street
Tarttown

Dear Ms. Prosciutto:

Thank you very much for your interest in John Dough Catering's services. We are proud of our reputation for quality food and service since 1995 and our prices make us indisputably the area's finest catering value! As Joe Clam from the Barrister Club put it:

"The participants were quite complimentary and you and your staff prepared great food and handled the occasion in a very professional manner."

In catering you get what you pay for. At John Dough Catering our prices insure many things such as fresh, high-quality foods, sanitary preparation, on-time delivery, generous portions, and many small extras. And John Dough Catering is the only caterer in town approved by the Great Plains Heart Institute's Dine Right program.

Our client list includes both large and small corporations with one thing in common: demand for fine food and good service.

Please call us at 55C-ATER.

Sincerely,

John Dough

John Dough, Chef/Owner
John Dough Catering Company
35 Batter Road
Crepeville, CA 94066

Mr. Chuck Roast
100 Beefy Way
Lone Loin

Dear Mr. Roast,

Thank you very much for your interest in John Dough Catering's services. We are proud of our reputation for quality food and service since 1995 and our prices make us indisputably the area's finest catering value! Joe and Nancy Smith put it best when they wrote us after their wedding:

"Thank you and your crew for a job well done. You made our day very special indeed."

Our very talented chefs have a wide range of creativity and skills. The food we prepare represents many years of recipe testing. We are quite conscious of the current need for lower cholesterol, fats, less sugar, and salt. That's why we are proud that we are the only caterer in town approved by the Great Plains Heart Institute's Dine Right program.

In catering you get what you pay for. At John Dough Catering our prices insure many things such as fresh, high-quality foods, sanitary preparation, on-time delivery, generous portions, and many small extras. We are aware of the current recession worries and if your catering budget is not what you would like to have, we can suggest more economical ways without cutting corners in quality.

I will do everything I can to make sure you are absolutely satisfied with our services. Call me at 55C-ATER.

Sincerely,

John Dough

John Dough, Chef/Owner
John Dough Catering Company
35 Batter Road
Crepeville, CA 94066

To verify this, scan your local newspapers or magazines. Rarely, if ever, do you see a caterer advertising in these publications. The only exception is a restaurant or deli whose sideline business is catering. Banquet halls and hotels often advertise their facilities with a word about their superb catering. Pure off-premise caterers put their marketing dollars into more productive areas.

There are innumerable marketing ideas in catering. Some ideas apply only to specific kinds of catering. Clients who want catering fall into these five areas:

(a) Corporate

(b) Social

(c) Contract

(d) Wholesale

(e) Budget

Focus your marketing dollars on the particular area(s) you want to target. No matter what type of catering you do, you will likely market to more than one of these basic categories. Most caterers will do both social and corporate catering. A few will do contract only and a few will focus on budget only. Both contract and budget catering are usually done by very large caterers whose food is produced in mass quantities. An example of contract catering is doing the food service for an industrial cafeteria, where the contract is of several years' duration. In budget catering, food is prepared at the lowest possible cost, packaged inexpensively, and distributed. Large volume is necessary to realize profits since the profit margin is small. Making hundreds or thousands of sandwiches for the lunch trade is an example. It can be profitable, perhaps even very profitable. There are a number of books that specifically address this segment of the catering industry.

As a small caterer, you can market to the corporate, social, and wholesale segments. Corporate and social catering are the best mix. It is a good idea to do some wholesale catering (i.e., selling to a retailer). This business, though not very profitable, is steady and fills in the gaps between events. However, it does sometimes interfere with more profitable business if you overcommit on wholesale catering. Keep it to a reasonable level or at least have a fair degree of flexibility with the client on delivery schedules and amounts you supply.

In addition to these major marketing areas, there are certain catering niches that are suitable for a small caterer. These are discussed in

As a small caterer, you can market to the corporate, social, and wholesale segments. Corporate and social catering are the best mix.

Chapter 1. Any of the niches listed can be targeted for your business, but don't attempt to target too many of them. Each needs a specific body of expertise.

3.2 Be sensitive to your client's needs

When marketing your business, you should keep in mind why your clients buy catering services from you. Let's look at the two major types of clients. Corporate clients buy mainly out of necessity and for convenience. Food is needed for a working luncheon, for instance. If the budget is really tight, they send out an assistant for deli trays, bread, packaged cookies, chips, and cold drinks. Unless you can compete with supermarket prices, you don't want to target this type of business. Some companies call in caterers to impress clients during open houses, grand openings, groundbreaking ceremonies, and other festive occasions when the budget is generous enough to provide high quality catering.

Finally, corporations use catering services to reward their employees. This is usually only once a year, during the holiday season. Some also provide company picnics in the summer. These tend to be fairly traditional events and the budget varies a great deal, depending on how the well company is doing and how generous the boss feels toward his or her employees. Picnics are relatively low-priced, very casual affairs where standard picnic fare is expected. When caterers are called in for this service, it is for convenience and to save time and work, not for prestige. Holiday season events are much more festive, and caterers are relied on because a festive meal is not easy to prepare.

Social catering clients have a variety of needs, too. Caterers save time and work, and guests are impressed with the presence of uniformed servers, perhaps a chef in the kitchen, and the presentation and quality of the food. Many of the clients who demand elaborate and lavish cuisine want to compete with their friends and relatives to show who can afford to provide this luxury and who can afford a more elegant service. This is especially true for bar mitzvahs, bat mitzvahs, and weddings. But some social clients are only looking for convenience and necessity in hiring a caterer.

Your targeted clients' needs should be the focal point of your marketing strategy. You and your marketing person should spell out and emphasize that your company will satisfy these needs when you are hired to cater a client's event.

3.3 Letters of appreciation and testimonials

If you provide excellent service and exceptional food, you will occasionally receive unsolicited letters of appreciation. These are wonderful to have, both for your ego and for promoting your business. Occasionally, you can mention to an especially pleased client that letters of appreciation are very welcome. It provides you with excellent fuel for your marketing efforts. Use quotes from these letters as testimonials.

Advertising testimonials are in vogue. You see them in newspaper and magazine ads, on billboards, and in television commercials. Marketing experts say that testimonials sell products. Use this marketing tool to promote your catering service. Notice that the name of the person being quoted is always mentioned. You may or may not need to ask for permission to quote from a letter in your promotional material. Use your best judgment in each particular situation, but err on the side of caution. The letters should definitely be a part of your sales portfolio.

4. PROS AND CONS OF ADVERTISING IN THE YELLOW PAGES

What about advertising in the Yellow Pages? This is a controversial issue among caterers. Opinions differ, which shows you that this type of advertising is not a sure way to develop new business. You cannot imagine a locksmith, a plumber, or a restaurant without a prominent Yellow Pages ad. When someone is looking for a locksmith or a plumber, chances are the first place he or she will look is in the Yellow Pages. Not so for caterers. Someone interested in purchasing catering services tries to remember a catered event he or she attended or the name of someone who deals with caterers who can recommend one. Checking the Yellow Pages is a last resort.

People who are price shopping may go to the Yellow Pages and call up every caterer listed for the type of event they have in mind. Those calls are a nuisance for all the caterers who waste time and money sending the menu off to the caller and don't get the job. Many callers will use up more than five minutes of your time on the phone. They want a free consultation, asking numerous questions about how you would do the event, what is included, and the cost of each part. You have to decide how much time you can take to educate the general public in the proper use of a caterer. Because of the numerous shopping-for-price calls, many caterers choose to be listed inconspicuously in the Yellow Pages.

Since you must have a business telephone, you will get a listing in the Yellow Pages with the price of the phone. This listing includes only your telephone number and street address. To direct the price comparison shoppers to your website, you need at least a small display ad. A well-designed website eliminates many of the price shopper calls.

However, some sales and marketing people claim they can get business out of Yellow Pages callers. If you employ one of these people, maybe you should run a larger ad. But remember, a business-card-size display ad in a US metropolitan Yellow Pages costs you $750 annually for a very simple display and up to $2,400 for the same size that includes graphics and color. Can you get enough business out of the Yellow Pages to break even? Or can you find a marketing tool that gives you a better return? This is your decision.

The general feeling among caterers in my community is that the more high end they are, the smaller the Yellow Pages ad should be. A caterer's reputation travels best by word-of-mouth. As well, very few of the callers who see an ad will have the budget for or interest in high-end catering.

Low-end and medium-quality caterers will benefit more from the large display ads. They need volume. They are also the type of caterer most callers are looking for.

The Yellow Pages Association reports in 2006 that catering is 95th on the list of most frequently called classifications in the Yellow Pages. If you do decide on a display ad, it is important to know which style will result in more sales with fewer calls. An advertising specialist can help you with this decision.

Slowly but steadily, Internet advertising is replacing Yellow Pages ads. The projection is that before the year 2010, Internet ads will equal print ads and eventually Internet ads will be the primary form of ads. YellowPages.com is now available, so one account can take care of both promotional media, print and online.

5. CLIENT FEEDBACK

A good way to get feedback from your clients is by conducting an annual survey. It is a strategy many businesses use, no matter how large or small. It is especially good when you really don't know why your business takes a sudden downturn. You'll find out if clients don't like your product, or if your prices are too high, or if the competition is cutting into your market share. You may find it is simply that the economy has declined and the first things your clients cut from their budgets are nonessentials, including catering.

The cost of a survey is relatively low. Make up an intelligent questionnaire and send it to a small number of your clients along with a self-addressed, stamped return envelope. For your clients with e-mail, send the survey by e-mail as an attachment. You can send a single e-mail to all the recipients, but be sure to use an option that the recipient receives the message with "Undisclosed Recipients" on the "To" line. You enter the actual e-mail addresses on the "BCC" (or blind carbon copy) line.

For those who don't respond to your e-mail request, follow up by snail mail. Expect a return rate of 15 percent to 20 percent from the survey.

The number of surveys you send out could be a dozen, or hundreds, depending on your client base. It costs you no more than your time. The answers your receive in these surveys are very useful in identifying any problems, especially if you allow clients to return them anonymously (not quite so easy with e-mail). If the results point to your service or product, correct the problem quickly.

Surveys must be brief. Most clients will not take them as intrusions; on the contrary, they feel that you care about their needs and requirements, and that you want to serve them better. To emphasize this point, you may want to start with the phrase, "In our continuing effort to serve you better … "

Sample 3 shows a cover letter that accompanies the questionnaire and Sample 4 shows a client questionnaire.

6. COMPETITION

Caterers are as thick as flies in most communities, particularly larger cities. There is plenty of competition. Catering is a business that a lot of people think they want to get into, until they discover how tough it is.

Your competition is going to be intense. If you have found your niche, then you eliminate a great number of those listed in the Yellow Pages who don't specialize in that same niche. But your competitors will still number in the dozens. To learn more about your competition, look at their brochures and menus. Pretend you are a client and have an event coming up, and ask for their literature, even a price list or proposal, if that is the only way you can get it. Having that information for comparison is invaluable. Or offer to give your clients a small added service in exchange for proposals they gathered from your competitors.

Dear Client:

In reviewing our accounts, we noticed that we have not received an order from your company for some time. We hate to lose a good client.

We feel it's important to keep informed of our customers' responses to our food and service so we can continue to serve them well. It is particularly important that we learn why old clients no longer order from us.

Won't you please help us by completing the following questionnaire and returning it to us in the enclosed stamped envelope? It will only take a minute and your answers are invaluable to us.

Thank you, and we hope you'll be placing an order with us soon.

Sincerely,

John Dough

John Dough, Chef/Owner
John Dough Catering Company
35 Batter Road
Crepeville, CA 94066

JOHN DOUGH CATERING

Questionnaire

Why did you stop ordering from us? (Check all that apply.)

❑ Dissatisfied with quality of product

❑ Prices are too high

❑ Dissatisfied with service

❑ No longer using catering services

❑ Other (Please explain) _____

_____

_____

_____

What will it take to get your business back?

_____

_____

_____

_____

_____

_____

Friendly cooperation among caterers is very desirable but difficult to achieve. It is particularly ideal when two or three caterers complement each other's services; for example, one can only do smaller events, the other is set up for larger ones. These two caterers can refer business to each other without hurting their own, and at the same time solve a caller's problem, which is the goal if you're tuned into marketing techniques.

Call up the owners of a few catering companies and suggest a mutual visit to each other's facilities with a friendly coffee and chat. Something like this can be beneficial to everyone, not only for referral business, but also for shared equipment, expertise on a specialized subjects (e.g., How do you make black pasta?), exchanged operational information (e.g., Where do you get your specialty produce in town?), and kitchen, bartending, or serving help in an emergency.

Friendly cooperation may or may not be possible, but try it. You may find one or two caterers in your neighborhood who agree that cooperation can be mutually beneficial. Most, of course, will consider you a competitor and refuse to talk.

Any catering association in town may be worthwhile to join if the meetings provide you with useful information. It is a good way to meet other caterers, get a feel for what is going on in catering in the area, and monitor trends and problems in the field. However, catering associations are generally geared to help and serve the large caterers — those in huge hotel chains, institutions, banquet halls, and large-volume caterers. Most small caterers will learn little, if anything, from their meetings and large caterers tend to disregard you anyway.

If you live in a small community, your competition is much more limited but so is the available business. With a dozen or fewer caterers there is not much chance of forming an association, but inquire about a local restaurant association. If it exists, join. Many potential clients ask restaurateurs to recommend caterers, and the first one that comes to mind is the caterer they know.

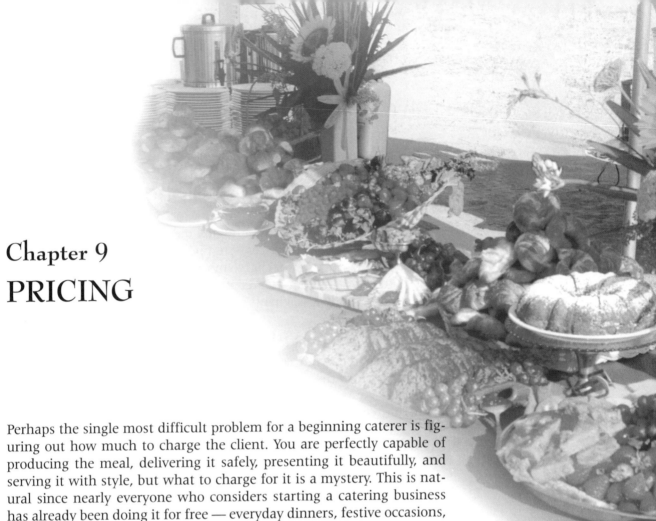

Chapter 9
PRICING

Perhaps the single most difficult problem for a beginning caterer is figuring out how much to charge the client. You are perfectly capable of producing the meal, delivering it safely, presenting it beautifully, and serving with style, but what to charge for it is a mystery. This is natural since nearly everyone who considers starting a catering business has already been doing it for free — everyday dinners, festive occasions, and receptions for guests and family. But money rarely changes hands except maybe as reimbursement for ingredients.

As a professional, if you've thought about this in advance, you'll tell your potential clients that the meal has to be priced out and you'll get back to them. This gives you some time to research pricing. If you give an answer on the spot, your price is usually too low, barely enough to cover your costs. This is a typical scenario and if you are in the process of converting from a cook with a reputation to a caterer, the time will come when you are confronted with this situation. Start doing your research now so you won't be at a total loss later. And remember, never give a price right away unless it is a standard item you are familiar with, and you know a reasonable charge that will include an acceptable profit.

1. DECIDING HOW MUCH TO CHARGE

There are several ways to arrive at the price you want to charge your client for your products and services. As a small caterer in a small business, use the simplest calculation, which considers two factors:

(a) How much your competitors charge for the same or similar products and services

(b) What your costs are to produce the food items

1.1 What does the competition charge?

Start collecting your competitors' menus and proposals, especially competitors who are selling a similar quality menu to yours. These will give you an idea of what your prices could be. If your quality of catering is about the same, you cannot charge more. If you want to underbid those caterers to carve out your market share, charge less. But beware: if you charge significantly less, clients get suspicious.

1.2 What are your costs?

The second factor, your cost, is not difficult to calculate either. If you paid attention to the advice given in Chapter 6, you are already carrying around and entering the prices of everything you use in your kitchen in your notebook, Palm Pilot or PDA. Using these prices, you can calculate the cost of the ingredients for a dish. Sample 5 is a typical chicken recipe with prices.

A few notes of explanation: unless they are major ingredients, prices of spices, herbs, salt, sugar, and flour can be disregarded. Just add a few cents to the total, based on your guess, since these amounts are insignificant compared to the total. It is not worth your time to figure out their exact cost. In Sample 5, paprika is used in a relatively large portion and its cost was calculated as 28 cents. Usually spices, herbs, thickeners, and salt amount to a few cents per serving, which is of no significance compared to the cost of meat, chicken, or cheese in that dish.

For the chopped green pepper, the price varies depending on the season and also on the quality of the dish you want to present. You can use lower-priced green peppers, but if you want it to look prettier, using a mixture of green and red peppers will cost more. The flavor remains the same. When you calculate your cost, calculate the presentation considerations, too.

It is a good practice to add a cost calculation to all your recipes. Note the year you figured the price to indicate how current it is. Decide if it is still valid or if prices have gone up (they rarely go down). Having this information on your recipes will make pricing a good deal easier.

PRICING A RECIPE

HUNGARIAN CHICKEN PAPRIKA

20 portions

	Unit price	Cost
20 8-oz (550 g) boneless chicken breasts	$3.00/lb	$30.00
24 oz (700 g) chopped onion	$0.25/lb	$0.38
5 Tbsp Hungarian paprika	$3.65/lb	$0.28
4 tsp salt		$0.05
24 oz chopped green pepper	$0.75/lb	$1.13
8 oz tomato paste or 1 lb (450 g) chopped tomato	$0.30/6-oz can	$0.40
½ c sour cream	$0.60/cup	$0.30
¼ c flour		$0.02
Total cost		**$32.56**
Cost per serving		**$1.63**

Using one of the catering software programs that I discussed in Chapter 3 makes your food cost calculation a snap — just click on the right buttons and your price is on the digital display faster than you can blink.

Another manual method that sidesteps these calculations, which is commonly used in catering, is to multiply the material cost by three.

2. CALCULATE YOUR OVERHEAD

Now that you know the total cost of all your raw ingredients for a particular recipe, it is time to calculate your overhead and labor costs. Don't let this intimidate you. A simple way to figure these costs is to add up a year's total costs (not including food and related expenses): fixed and variable expenses including rent, insurance, business taxes, utilities, depreciation, and so on. From this total you can derive your daily overhead expense. Do the same for labor costs. One advantage of being a small caterer is that you don't need to be exact on your calculation.

3. PREPARATION TIME

The total cost based on raw ingredients, overhead, and labor still needs to be modified. If the preparation of an item is very simple — chicken wings browned in an oven with a barbecue sauce, for example — you can charge less than three times your material cost and still make a good profit. If the item being served is bite-sized spanakopita that requires a labor-intensive preparation of small phyllo dough squares individually filled with the mixture, the multiplier is closer to four times the cost of raw material, partly because of the amount of labor and partly because ingredients for spanakopita aren't cheap.

To return to our example of Hungarian Chicken Paprika, let's say we serve it with a side dish of poppy seed noodles and sautéed mixed vegetables. The cost of these two items is about 65¢ per serving. Add a bread roll and butter and another 35¢. The chicken dish is $1.62 per person, which makes the total material cost $2.62 per person. The preparation of all these items is simple, so if we multiply the figure by three, the price you charge will be $7.86 per person, a fairly reasonable price for a main meal. Add a salad for $2.00 each and dessert for $2.50 each, and the total for this meal is $12.36 per person. Now think about this individual client's expectations and what quality he or she expects. If it is a fancy meal, you inflate the price because you need garnishes for the plates or the table, and fancier salads, breads, and vegetables.

4. NUMBER OF GUESTS

Another consideration is the number of guests. If it is a small party, your price per person should be higher. If it is for a large event with 100 or more guests, you can easily afford to reduce the price and still make a good profit on volume. Consider also the state of the economy, your booking calendar, and how much you need the business. These factors influence prices, too. If your catering business is running at close to capacity, losing a job because it is too expensive for the client is not as crucial as when you're facing a near-empty month.

Take another look at the price you arrived at. Can the client get a similar dinner in a better-quality restaurant for that price? If so, your prices are too low. The price of a delivered catered dinner should be more than a comparable restaurant meal. Then look at similar items in your competitors' menus. If their prices are comparable, your price is about correct.

5. PERCEIVED VALUE TO THE CLIENT

The price also varies according to its perceived value by the client. A whole poached salmon on the buffet table is very impressive with an elegant presentation. The total cost of materials is not very high and the labor cost for preparing this item is moderate. Because of its high perceived value, you can charge a higher price for it. Another example is a chilled sour cherry soup laced with cabernet sauvignon. It is easy to prepare and the ingredients are not expensive, yet you can charge extra because it is unique and elegant. That is why restaurants come up with fancy names for otherwise simple dishes; the perceived value is higher. You cannot charge the same price for "spaghetti with meatballs" that you could for the identical "angel hair pasta with ground round smothered with fresh herbed Italian tomato sauce."

As you can see, pricing is very subjective. The factor of three is something to remember as a useful tool, but only to give you a starting point for pricing. Lately, caterers have switched to using a higher factor than three, because of the constantly and rapidly rising costs of insurance, labor, utility, energy, and rentals.

This discussion has considered only a basic price for the meal. The total price might also include charges for chairs, glasses, tables, china, and so on. Caterers differ a great deal in how they quote on these extras. Many include the price of china, glass, and silver in the basic meal, and quote separate prices for tables, chairs, and linen as needed. Sometimes a separate price is quoted for the serving staff. Another way to give a total price is to list each item separately — food, beverage, rental, flowers, serving staff, and taxes.

The cost of serving staff can be by the hour or as a percentage of the food charge. Caterers commonly use both methods. Some caterers charge by the hour and add a percentage for gratuities. Some use gratuities only to pay for serving staff. A 15 percent charge is commonly added to the cost of food and service as a gratuity. To avoid the sometimes unpleasant sound of a compulsory gratuity (North Americans, unlike Europeans, have never felt comfortable with this), you can label it a "catering service charge."

6. RECEPTIONS AND BUFFETS

What about reception food or self-service buffet items? Basically, you derive their price by a similar method, but the final price can simply be the total of the prices of individual items. For instance, if the client chooses six items from your hors d'oeuvre selection for 35 guests, you simply add up the prices of the individual six items and use that as the price per guest for food.

Let's suppose that another client has a similar reception for 35 guests but wants to make it really lavish, so she orders 12 different items. Will your charge still be the sum of the individual items? That would be too expensive. Guests can eat only a finite amount. If there are six items, they will eat the equivalent of 3.5 ounces of cheese and meat combined (a realistic figure). If there are 12 items, they will still only eat 3.5 ounces of meat and cheese, so will eat less of each item. Even though it is much more work to prepare twelve items than six, you have to prepare a smaller quantity of each of the twelve items, so you can afford to discount. How big a discount is really up to you. There is no good guide or formula for it. Make up a guide for yourself, a figure of 10 percent or 15 percent, and see how it works out for you profit-wise, then adjust if needed.

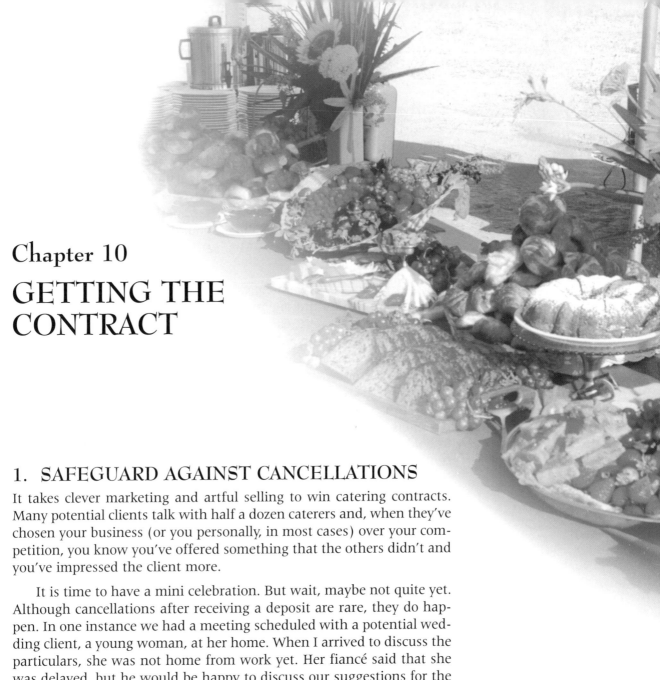

Chapter 10
GETTING THE CONTRACT

1. SAFEGUARD AGAINST CANCELLATIONS

It takes clever marketing and artful selling to win catering contracts. Many potential clients talk with half a dozen caterers and, when they've chosen your business (or you personally, in most cases) over your competition, you know you've offered something that the others didn't and you've impressed the client more.

It is time to have a mini celebration. But wait, maybe not quite yet. Although cancellations after receiving a deposit are rare, they do happen. In one instance we had a meeting scheduled with a potential wedding client, a young woman, at her home. When I arrived to discuss the particulars, she was not home from work yet. Her fiancé said that she was delayed, but he would be happy to discuss our suggestions for the wedding.

The discussion took an hour. He was impressed with our food and service, we selected the menu that fit their needs and budget, and he wrote me a check for 50 percent of the estimated bill for a wedding scheduled in two months. I marked our event calendar in ink, but it turned out to be too soon. When the bride arrived home, she was furious that the discussion and selection of food had taken place place without her. The next morning she called and demanded her money back. She canceled the contract, no reason given.

1.1 Always ask for a deposit

Once the buyer decides that you are his or her caterer and becomes a client, the haggling over details is over. You have joined each other on the same side, and you are both fighting for the same cause: a successful event. There is no more mistrust. Once the client has decided to hire you, quickly assure him or her by saying something like, "Mrs. Pat, you made the right decision. We will make your daughter's wedding a most memorable event!" And now, if Mrs. Pat hasn't offered it yet, it is time to ask for the deposit.

Deposit policies vary among caterers. Some want to have one-third when booking, one-third one month in advance, and the final balance on the day of the event. Others want a nominal amount on booking (about 10 percent), half of the expected total (less the earlier deposit) a month in advance, and the balance on the day of the event. These are the most commonly used schedules. If the event is within five or six weeks from the day of the decision, ask for half of the expected total. If the event is scheduled far in advance (which is commonly the case for weddings and larger events), ask for about 10 percent or at least $100 to hold the date. Mention that you will require the rest of the 50 percent deposit a month in advance. Be sure to figure rental, taxes, gratuities, and all subcontractors' fees and charges into your estimate.

Some caterers are willing to refund the full deposit if the client cancels at least a month before the scheduled event. This is a good policy, especially if you use it as a selling point when the client is trying to decide. They know the door is still open to switch to another caterer. But that virtually never happens. In my business, with a full refund policy, it may happen once in two or three years.

A deposit is something that you must have, no exceptions, unless you are dealing with regular corporate clients. Any time you do not receive a deposit, you are in danger of cancellation — even at the last minute. We booked an event early on in our business for a graduation party for a small gathering of about 40 guests. We didn't insist on a deposit. Sure enough, they called a week before the party and said they would have to postpone the event because of illness in the family. If we had insisted on a deposit, the party would have been held, illness or not. That taught us a lesson — never reserve a date without money down.

There are so many unforeseen circumstances that may result in cancellation. There are many more questionable reasons, and a deposit at stake can influence the final decision. If the computer crashes and everyone must stay at work to rectify the crisis, or important guests at the wedding party are delayed because of tornadoes in Texas, or the family cat dies, the party will still be held if there is a deposit. If nothing is at risk for the client, the attitude is, let's postpone, to heck with the caterer. The deposit is also necessary to cover any expenses you have already incurred.

Soon after you receive the deposit, you may want to get the competition's proposals from the client. This information is of no value to the client anymore and probably will end up in the trash. For you it is invaluable. You want to know what you were up against and how your prices and menu look in contrast to the other bids. Offer the client something in return for the other proposals, perhaps a free coffee service or upgrading the disposable hors d'oeuvre plates to china at no cost. Offer something that will not cost you very much but will add an extra touch to the client's party. It is a win-win situation.

A few clients may consider your request for competitors' proposals unethical. In that case, drop the subject. Others are delighted with your cleverness in learning about your competition and will readily agree.

1.2 Always confirm the engagement

As soon as you receive the deposit, reconfirm the party with a letter stating all details: the price of everything, what you will supply, and what the host or hostess will supply. If you have already done so in a formal proposal, stating these details may not be necessary. If your correspondence has been by e-mail and fax, send the confirmation letter by mail. If the client is a regular, a simple e-mail or fax is sufficient to confirm, and for some frequent clients who know and trust you, verbal phone confirmation is sufficient ("Thanks for your order, we will be in the boardroom with a luncheon for 12 at 11:30 Wednesday morning.") State clearly that you need to know the guest count, or a guaranteed minimum number of guests, at least five days before the event. A small change after that date may be acceptable up to two or three days before the event, but a significant change (more than 5 percent) should incur extra charges, depending on the specific situation. Caterers customarily add a 15 percent surcharge over the regular per person charge for additional last-minute guests. Explain to your clients that this is to cover the extra cost of having to buy small amounts at retail prices to provide for the added guests.

A written record of what you agreed upon — menu, prices, type of service — is essential for most events. For regular corporate events,

AS SOON AS YOU RECEIVE THE DEPOSIT, RECONFIRM THE PARTY WITH A LETTER STATING ALL DETAILS.

such as routinely scheduled luncheons, dinners, or breakfasts, this is not necessary. Even for a small social catered event, a telephone or e-mail confirmation is often sufficient. Putting it in writing can be handled in two ways:

(a) A simple letter of confirmation which you write and send to the client in duplicate. The client signs and returns one copy to you.

(b) A contract that spells out the legal aspects and is signed by both you and the client, with original signature copies to each. In addition to the contract, a letter or a standard form spells out the details of the party. A typical event contract and standard order forms are shown in Sample 6.

During the main discussion with your client, you must resolve the following details:

(a) Menu. Agree on the menu in as much detail as possible, but leave some options open so you have enough flexibility. If the event is a reception, the food items should be decided exactly since you will be calculating the price per person or total price according to the agreed-upon menu. If the event is a main meal, decide on the entrée and a side dish, the first course, and the dessert. Where seasonal items are to be considered — salads, vegetables, fruits — you and your client can decide tentatively, but keep the freedom to change according to what is available on the market and what looks best (and for your own benefit, what is priced the lowest). Most clients will understand this and let your chef do the final selection. Some are very particular and insist on specific items: "I want cauliflower because my husband loves it, but I also want green beans because that is Aunt Mabel's favorite and she will be the guest of honor." Agree to special requests, particularly if they are easy to satisfy. If it is creamed and puréed spinach the client insists on, don't agree. Explain that the honored guest will simply love your chef's creamed spinach but it is a questionable choice for the rest of the guests. Suggest a vegetable acceptable to more palates.

(b) The date of the event.

(c) The place it will be held at.

(d) Timing for the event. You need to know when the guests will arrive, when food and beverages should be served, and when the event will end.

SAMPLE 6
CONTRACT AND ORDER FORMS

EVENT CONTRACT
JOHN DOUGH CATERING CO.

CLIENT: _____   EVENT DATE: _____

GUEST COUNT CONFIRMATION:

John Dough Catering is reserving for _____ guests. This estimate will be used as a basis for purchasing, scheduling, and preparation with a final guarantee to be given to John Dough Catering five days prior to the event. Thereafter, the number may be increased at the quoted rate per person, but not decreased. An increase in excess of 10% may incur additional cost.

DEPOSIT AND PAYMENTS:

If the proposal meets your approval, please sign this agreement and return the original copy with your deposit by _____ to reserve the date and confirm the event. Deposit of 50% of the expected total bill is required, including rental and other charges.

A final invoice detailing all actual charges will be mailed to you shortly after the event. Payment is due upon receipt. Unpaid invoices will be charged at the rate of 1.5% (18% APR) per month after 15 days.

CANCELLATION:

If you cancel the event before _____, your deposit will be refunded. If you cancel the event after the above date, 75% of your deposit will be refunded or the difference between actual costs incurred and the amount of your deposit if in excess of 25%.

EQUIPMENT:

A count of silver, china, linen, glassware, and other equipment will be taken after the event and you will be charged for any missing items.

TAXES:

Local laws require that sales tax be charged on all food and beverage order items. If you are tax exempt, your tax registration number and a certificate of exemption must be returned with this agreement.

THE ATTACHED PROPOSAL AND THESE TERMS AND CONDITIONS ARE ACCEPTABLE.

By _____   By _____
    John Dough Catering   Client

Date _____   Date _____

EVENT ORDER FORM
JOHN DOUGH CATERING

Date of order _____

CLIENT

Name: _____

Address: _____

_____

_____

Phone: _____

Fax: _____

E-mail: _____

EVENT

Date: _____

No. of guests: _____

Place: _____

_____

Time: _____

Occasion: _____

What service?: _____

MENU/PRICE

_____

_____

_____

Total price/person _____

Total price: _____

CSC (15%): _____

Tax: _____

Delivery: _____

Rental: _____

Flowers: _____

Bartending: _____

Others: _____

OTHER SERVICES

Beverage: _____

Tablecloth: _____

Napkins: _____

China, glass, silver: _____

Disposable: _____

Flowers: _____

Others: _____

STAFF

_____

_____

_____

_____

SPECIAL NOTES

_____

_____

_____

EQUIPMENT REQUIRED

_____

_____

_____

❑ Deposit received   ❑ Bill Out   ❑ Paid

Date: _____ Amount: _____ Date: _____ Date: _____

(e) Approximate number of guests. Let the client know the final date on which you need a guaranteed minimum guest number. Also inform the client of your policy about last-minute guest number changes.

(f) Style of service. Will it be self-service, full-service, or a combination? Let the client know the price of each style.

(g) Rental items. Decide on whether china, glass, and silver, or disposable ware is to be used. Also, discuss linen and anything else that will need to be rented, such as tables, chairs, and so on. Let the client know the exact price of each of these rental items. Even if you get a discount from the rental agency, make sure you charge enough to cover your costs and the extra time you spend on getting the rental items. Also, the rental agency may charge a delivery and pickup fee, and you may have to pay for broken or missing pieces that are very difficult to charge to the client when it is only a small amount, such as a few broken glasses. In addition, when dealing with china, glass, and silver, you will need staff to rinse and stack them back into the crates at the end of the event. With disposable ware you can save several staff hours on the event. Include the extra staff cost in your rental charges, either by stating a certain number of hours for a cleanup charge or simply charging a little more for rental per person. If your client cannot decide right away, give him or her a deadline so that you can reserve the necessary rental items.

(h) Beverage service. Decide who will provide the beverages, the beverage service, the glasses, ice, fruit, mixes, and all other bar paraphernalia. Your client's needs may fall under any one of the following situations:

    (i) Full bar service, where the caterer provides everything and charges the client. You may or may not need a liquor license.

    (ii) The client supplies all beverages and the caterer supplies the bartending service at either a fixed price per bartender or an hourly rate.

    (iii) The client supplies the alcoholic beverages and the caterer supplies the nonalcoholic beverages. Include these details in your letter of confirmation. Spell out who is supplying what, including glassware, ice, table, or a more formal bar for the service.

(i) Miscellaneous. Discuss any other options such as flowers, a special cake, music, favors, and table decorations both for the guest tables and serving tables.

(j) Contact person/liaison. For some events, particularly weddings and other large events, you have to ask the client for a contact person at the event. The client, whether it is the bride, groom, a parent, or a host or hostess, will be far too busy to answer questions during the event. A contact person should be agreed upon, usually a close friend or relative, who knows what is going on and who is available for quick questions or decisions. These questions could be little details such as where the garbage can is, should we cut the cake or wait another half hour, should we cut off alcoholic beverages since there are some serious drunks among the guests, or what should be done with the extra food. It is useful to the have the contact person's phone and cell phone numbers in case you need to contact him or her shortly before the party when the client may be too busy to discuss last-minute details.

2. ESTABLISH A REFUND POLICY

What about a cancellation policy for when the party could not be held for a valid reason? There are no definite guidelines here. Use your best business instinct or wing it. If the event is far in advance and you have not refused other events on the same date, the best policy is to refund the deposit in full. If the event is scheduled within a month of the cancellation, it is best to discuss it with the client personally. When the client calls to cancel on less than a month's notice and you are not sure how to handle the cancellation, postpone your decision. Tell the client that you have to check first with the kitchen manager (whether you have one or not) about what was already ordered for the event, how much money and time has already been put into it, and what commitments you have made to subcontractors and your staff. This gives you time to calculate a reasonable amount to pay for costs you've already shelled out. Then refund the rest. It pays to be fair: there is a possibility of future business from this client.

If you made the mistake of not asking for a deposit, chances are excellent that you will not be reimbursed by your client for any charges you already incurred on behalf of the event. That is a business loss, an expensive lesson that teaches you to insist on a deposit in future, no exceptions.

Another type of refund that some caterers recognize is called "the embarrassment refund." This is initiated by the caterer. If you run out of a food item early on at an event or a server drops a whole tray of food that can't be reassembled, you must apologize to the client. Offer to adjust the final invoice to compensate for your error. This occasionally happens and it can be costly. Your invoice adjustment should be sufficiently high to console the client, so avoid it whenever you can.

Sometimes an embarrassment refund is not voluntary and not a "refund" at all. If the client finds something unsatisfactory at the event, he or she may not want to pay all or part of your full invoice. In this case, there is not much you can do. If the amount involved is a large sum and you feel that the unpaid balance is not fully justified, you can argue your case with the client or even go through legal procedures if all else fails.

A GENEROUS REFUND POLICY HELPS TO GAIN YOUR CLIENT'S CONFIDENCE.

Chapter 11
IT TAKES MORE THAN A HOT OVEN

1. PLANNING AND ORGANIZING AN EVENT

The entire infrastructure of a catering business, including marketing and selling, exists for the sole purpose of executing a successful event. Nothing else really matters as long as both the client and the caterer are satisfied.

One of the issues when planning an event with a client is determining who will provide all the food for the event. Inevitably, some clients will suggest that you bring some of the food and the rest will be supplied by various other people. This happens mostly in low- and medium-budget affairs, particularly weddings, and is always a headache for the caterer. There are two reasons a client may want to do this:

(a) your price will be lower because you are supplying only part of the meal, and

(b) because Aunt Mabel makes the most wonderful dips and providing them will be her gift to the bride and groom.

Your answer should always be a gentle but firm no. Explain the reasons why such mixing of the food cannot be done. One of them is legal liability. You are fully responsible for the food being served, but when all

NEVER ALLOW A
CLIENT TO MIX YOUR
CATERED FOOD WITH
OTHER FOOD
BROUGHT BY GUESTS.
YOUR REPUTATION IS
ON THE LINE.

the food is not brought by you, your responsibility isn't under your control. Besides, your insurance policy will not allow it. Another equally good reason is quality and presentation. Aunt Mabel's dip could be one made with packaged powders and sour cream. As far as the guests know, everything on the table was catered. You cannot afford to have second- or third-rate food mixed with your own high-quality food. Your reputation is on the line. Never accept such compromises.

Once the client has reserved a date with a deposit, the caterer's job is to successfully execute the event. There still may be changes in the menu or in the number of guests or rental requirements, but these are usually minor and easily handled details. From now on success depends on the caterer's ability to plan and organize the event.

None of the three phases — planning, organizing, and executing — is difficult for an experienced caterer. The prerequisite for successful execution is planning and organizing in advance. Without this step, an event is unlikely to be fully successful. However, no matter how much time was spent on careful planning and organizing, if the execution is not done exactly right, the client is not likely to be pleased. All three phases are equally important.

There are additional complications when several events are being planned and organized simultaneously, especially if they are large, complex, and difficult affairs. Smaller events are less of a problem. As a matter of fact, several smaller events can be planned and organized simultaneously in less total time than it takes to plan and organize each one individually.

2. THINKING AHEAD

How far in advance you should plan an event depends on you, the type of event, and the type of catering you do. Determine this by experience and eventually you will come up with a reasonably comfortable schedule for when to start planning an event. Until you get comfortable and secure in your planning ability, start very early so that you aren't frantic the day of the event.

If you need hard-to-find ingredients or items you must order in advance, schedule the searching and ordering at least two weeks before the event. There's always the problem of the exact number of guests changing significantly, even a week before the event, but that is a chance you have to take. Compensate by over-ordering a little. It's low-priced insurance and the extra food is good to have even though it bites into your net profit. Give the extra food to the client at the end of the event, if possible. The payback in good relations justifies the extra cost. (Regarding extra food, see the discussion in Chapter 12 about storing food, and Chapter 14 about contaminated food.)

When planning several events with dates close together, try to have similar menus for them, or at least some duplicate items. If you or your salesperson played the cards right, the menus will be identical.

Plan the menu using ingredients that are freshest and lowest priced at that particular time of year, or something you over-ordered the week before because you could get a case at a lower unit price. Use it for the next corporate luncheon. It should not mean that you sacrifice quality, of course. All it means is that you are using up the available ingredients or that you are taking advantage of seasonally low-priced products.

For a second or even a third event spaced closely in time, the same menu means much less labor. Some things can be prepared or partially prepared at the same time — for instance, spanakopita filling for cream puffs. For other items that must be prepared fresh, time can still be saved. For example, if at Thursday's luncheon you serve pasta salad, you can serve the same salad at Friday's luncheon if you mix the salad fresh on Friday from ingredients premade the day before. On Thursday morning you cook the pasta, cut up and blanch vegetables for both salads, then divide it into the Thursday and Friday portions. Friday's salad ingredients go into the refrigerator for storage. (Toss the pasta first with a little oil.) On Friday morning you combine the salad ingredients with the dressing and it's ready to go.

Again, the decision about how much you can make ahead is yours.

3. CHECKING THE SITE BEFOREHAND

Should you plan to visit a new client's facilities before the event? Some caterers feel that you definitely should at all times, no matter what the event is. Others feel it is an unnecessary waste of time. My own policy is determined by the event. For a larger party with several food stations and bars, and a complex menu, a preview visit is advisable. This is the time to scout out the following:

- Nearest door you can park at to unload; where you can leave your truck so it won't be blocked by the guests' cars (they love to do that)

- Shortest, easiest transportation route from the truck to the party site

- Kitchen facilities — if there are none, a staging and storage area (sometimes an empty office is fine)

- Availability of tables for preparation

- Refrigerator, freezer, and oven facilities (don't count on space in the refrigerator or freezer unless you arrange it ahead of time)

- Where to set up food and bar tables

- What the logical traffic flow is

- Availability of electrical outlets

- Water sources and cleanup areas if there is no kitchen

- Trash disposal

Check the electrical outlets both in the kitchen and serving areas whenever you have several appliances you are planning to use. Most heating appliances use high wattage and older circuits are not wired to deliver the amount of electric current needed to run them. The circuits blow when you overload the wiring — a real nuisance when you can least afford the time. You have to find the host or someone to reset the circuit and that can cost you 10 to 15 minutes in an office building. It could be even worse on a Saturday evening when no maintenance person is around. An alternative is to carry your own multi-plug strip with an overload reset button between the appliances and the wall outlet. If the wiring is too weak, your circuit breaker will be tripped. Before resetting, you can take one of the appliances to a different part of the house or use the equipment one at a time. Carry a multi-plug strip with you to all events.

We learned our lesson on a Saturday morning workshop for judges and lawyers in an old courthouse. The building was nicely remodeled and modernized, except for the wiring. We only had two coffeemakers and an electric tea kettle, and when it was hard to find an electric outlet, we should have thought about the fact that the original wiring in the building was not meant for 21st-century appliances. We had to run an extension cord from a bathroom socket, the only one we could find near the buffet table, an outlet that was designed for the power of an electric razor. As soon as we plugged in one of the coffeemakers and an electric kettle, the circuit blew.

We moved our equipment downstairs and cautiously plugged in both appliances on two widely separated outlets, praying that they were on different circuits. It worked and soon after that, the maintenance person reset the tripped circuit upstairs. Since that event, we have always carried our own multi-plug cord with built-in circuit breaker.

Coincidentally, there was a second lesson to be learned at that courthouse breakfast. To get into the building, we had to go through a metal detector that immediately got all excited by our metal equipment. The guard would not, under any condition, let our knives through. We needed those knives to cut the freshly baked walnut-date bread, one of the items on the buffet table. In the end we had to send someone back to the truck with the knife, a cutting board, and the breads to finish the job.

For a smaller, simpler event, an advance visit is usually unnecessary. If you feel better about looking the place over, by all means go. With experience, however, you will learn how to quickly evaluate every new situation and in no time work out all the particulars of the site within minutes after arrival. If you have not visited the site previously, you should allow an extra 20 or 30 minutes to work out the details on the day of the event.

Sometimes the client asks you to visit the facilities. If you feel that it is an unnecessary trip, say so. If it makes him or her feel better, visit the place anyway.

4. THE SUPPLY LIST

The first stage of planning is to prepare your shopping list. If you personally use your kitchen a lot, you know how much you have of most items. If you always replenish items as they run low, your list will only include fresh and special products for that particular event. If you don't do the cooking in your business, work out a schedule with the chef so that you have the list far enough in advance to complete the shopping comfortably.

A good, efficient shopping list is not at all what most people carry into the supermarket. A professional list is well organized to save you shopping time. Even if you use a catering software that produces your shopping list, you must recheck it manually to eliminate even the possibility of error. Whether the software does it for you or you do it manually, divide your list into at least four parts: meats, dairy, produce, and other items. Then, by color coding or some other visual means, mark items according to where you expect to purchase them. Or if you prefer, make separate lists for different sources you expect to get your supplies from. Cross each item out as you get it, and before you reach the checkout counter, take another close look to make sure nothing has been

EVEN IF YOU USE A CATERING SOFTWARE THAT PRODUCES YOUR SHOPPING LIST, YOU MUST RECHECK IT MANUALLY TO ELIMINATE EVEN THE POSSIBILITY OF ERROR.

NO MATTER HOW
GENEROUSLY YOU
ALLOW TIME FOR
CONTINGENCIES ON
YOUR SCHEDULE, IT
IS NEVER ENOUGH.

forgotten. The goal is to cut your shopping time to a bare minimum. Occasional forgotten items are inevitable, but the better organized you and your kitchen are, the less likely a second trip will be needed. A forgotten but essential bunch of parsley can cost you a half hour, provided there is a store nearby! Work at making those forgotten items a rare occurrence.

For smaller events, one shopping trip can take care of all necessary supplies. For large events you often need at least two trips — one several days in advance to purchase ingredients for items that hold well, such as dressings, stocks, marinades, pastry crusts, concentrates for punch, fillings for quiche, and so on. Items that must be defrosted have to be bought in advance, too: chicken, shrimp, some vegetables, and juices.

The second trip should take place either the day before or on the day of the event. Shop for the fresh items that don't hold well: vegetables, fruits, pastries, bread, and dairy products.

If your business is large enough that suppliers will deliver to you, your shopping is reduced but not eliminated. The planning is about the same. Your lists will consist of items that you can order from different suppliers, and your job is to coordinate the deliveries so they arrive when you need them.

5. THE WORK SCHEDULE

5.1 Minimize preparation time

Now that you have your supplies, you can make up a schedule of what to prepare and when, either manually (only a few minutes' work) or using a catering software. The idea is to have as little left to prepare at the last minute as possible but still have everything as fresh as possible. This isn't always easy but it can be worked out. If you planned well with your client, the menu won't include too many items that must be prepared either at the last minute or on location. Many items can be partially or fully finished days ahead. Some items are better prepared in advance.

Eventually you will devise your own system of mapping out a schedule. In the meantime, here is one efficient way to do it. Start at the day of the event. List all items that absolutely must be prepared that last day. Then list jobs that can be done the day before and continue listing backwards a day at a time until all jobs and items are taken into account for that specific event. Your motto should be to prepare as much in advance as possible. Check your refrigerator, freezer, and storage to make sure you are not preparing some things unnecessarily.

When your schedule of food and beverage preparation is completed, checked, and rechecked, assign an approximate preparation time for each item. The daily total will give you the food preparation time required for that day and will tell you how much labor is needed. Add extra time for cleanup, breaks, telephone calls, and miscellaneous contingencies.

The actual preparation of the food is just one of the many things that takes up the total preparation time, though it is by far the most time consuming. Another important part of preparation time is the presentation. You will have to think about how the food is going to be presented, how the table will look, and what you will need to acquire and purchase to follow through on your presentation plan.

If you have a simple catered event with a modest budget, the presentation should match it. It is always nice to have a few items to adorn or garnish your tables or trays. They don't have to cost a lot: a few radishes trimmed into flowers, the tender inner leaves of celery, sliced scallion greens, even lemon slices and a few flowers can add a great deal. Whatever you choose, you have to plan and add these items to your shopping list.

Be sure to schedule time to collect all the required equipment for the kitchen. For this you need a checklist (see the event checklist in Sample 7). Without a checklist, the chance of forgetting something essential is much greater.

5.2 Organize your equipment

It is a good idea to have a separate list of items that should come out of the freezer and refrigerator for loading at the last minute. Since in most kitchens both freezer and refrigerator are quite full (often more than full), cold and frozen items needed for a particular event cannot be isolated easily. It is best to list them separately and check them off as they are loaded on the truck just before leaving.

It is also good to have a catering box permanently loaded with items and equipment that may be needed at any event. This box is carried to every event, like a life vest on a motor boat. Here is what I carry in mine:

- extra menus, business cards
- business card holder for the buffet table

- disposable plates, containers for food left for the client
- oven mitts
- extension cord
- multiple outlet strip with circuit interrupt on it (so you don't blow the circuit that supplies all the electricity to kitchen outlets on-site)
- cutting board
- chef's knife, paring knife, serrated knife
- salt and pepper shakers
- dish towel
- wiping cloths
- roll of plastic wrap or aluminum foil
- rubber spatula to scrape used plates
- matches
- corkscrew
- champagne bottle opener (it's hard to open dozens of bottles by hand quickly)
- champagne bottle stopper
- oven thermometer
- rubber bands, wire twists
- tape, thumbtacks, string
- pocket timer
- small calculator (when the invoice needs adjustment)
- cake cutting chart

Note: A cake cutting chart is a useful thing to have if one of the servers must cut a cake. Cakes have to be cut by different methods to produce nice, even-sized pieces and to keep the cake from collapsing when the support is removed. Sample cake cutting diagrams are included on the CD-ROM that accompanies this book. Ask ahead what shape cake has been ordered and decide how it should be cut.

EVENT CHECKLIST

LUNCHEON

- ❏ tablecloths, napkins
- ❏ plates, cups, glasses
- ❏ flatware
- ❏ serving platters, chafers
- ❏ serving utensils
- ❏ trays
- ❏ electric kettle (to quickly heat water for chafers, tea, etc.)
- ❏ hot plates (to keep extra food hot in kitchen or on buffet table)
- ❏ extension cord
- ❏ circuit breaker (always use it when plugging more than one electric appliance into a socket)
- ❏ water pitcher
- ❏ coffee server, carafe
- ❏ ice, ice bucket, and scoop
- ❏ oven mitts
- ❏ chef's coat and hat
- ❏ aprons, serving jackets
- ❏ extra bow ties
- ❏ can opener
- ❏ corkscrew, bar equipment
- ❏ cutting board, carver, serrated knife
- ❏ colander, strainer, bowls
- ❏ vegetable peeler

- ❏ measuring cups, spoons
- ❏ wooden spoons, whisk
- ❏ candles, matches, Sterno
- ❏ salt, pepper
- ❏ sugar, cream, their containers
- ❏ disposable containers and wraps for extra food and drinks
- ❏ trash bags
- ❏ dishwashing detergent, dishcloth, sponge, wash-up bowl
- ❏ dish towels
- ❏ food umbrellas (small umbrella-like food covers made of gauze-like material to cover food outdoors; they come in different sizes and can be found in Asian variety stores)
- ❏ beverage tub
- ❏ water bucket
- ❏ bus tub
- ❏ disposable wine glasses (to exchange wine glasses of reluctant-to-leave guests at the end of the party so you can go home)
- ❏ invoice
- ❏ business cards, menus
- ❏ catering box

ONE MORE
IMPORTANT ITEM:
TAKE SOME CASH
WITH YOU FOR ANY
EMERGENCY
SHOPPING.

5.3 Coordinate your staff

Next you will need to schedule your staff. You may be able to do smaller events, for instance, a buffet business luncheon for 20 guests, by yourself or you can assign the whole event to one staff person. For larger events you have to calculate the number of staff needed and reserve them sometimes weeks ahead of the event, especially in a traditionally busy season. Reserve the food preparation and cooking staff, serving and cleanup crew, and bartenders and their helpers.

For larger events or several simultaneous small events, you may also need a kitchen manager, someone who is experienced and knowledgeable enough to direct the kitchen operation in addition to being part of it. During the busy holiday season it is often essential to have a kitchen manager. You may also need a cleanup crew to come in right after the event or the next day.

5.4 Other details

Reserve rental items as far in advance as possible. Also book florists, musicians, ice sculptors, limousine services, and any other subcontractors whose services you are responsible for well in advance.

Another thing you should remember is to check the client's address if you or your event manager don't know exactly where it is. You cannot afford to be searching for a location when you're on a deadline. Print out several copies of the map and directions from the Internet that show the exact location of the event and how to get there, and give copies to staff members who are driving on their own.

This is the place where cell phones are of tremendous help, either to check on staff arriving on their own or to communicate with other vehicles.

Finally, prepare an invoice to take with you to the event. Have a folder or briefcase ready for your paperwork: invoice, notes for the event, staff schedules, staff work assignments, and telephone numbers of your staff, rental agencies, subcontractors, and anyone else who is scheduled to deliver anything to the job site. And one more important item: take some cash with you for any emergency shopping. It is embarrassing to send someone out for another bottle of vodka and no one has enough money to pay for it.

6. TRANSPORTATION

Your carefully prepared food, gleaming glass and china, shiny silver and brass have to arrive at the event site in the same condition as they left your kitchen. This also takes some careful planning, a good transportation system, and plenty of experience. Many catering disasters occur in transportation, where the vulnerable food and equipment are in the most danger of damage.

Use boxes or crates to transport equipment efficiently. Organize the packing systematically — serving equipment is separated from plates and flatware; kitchen and cooking equipment are separated; and garnish, greens, and table decorations are all together, and so on. Assemble as much of this as possible the day before the event.

When you are transporting raw or partially cooked food to be prepared on site, the danger is much less. For many events, especially receptions where kitchen facilities are not available, food is transported ready to be served. A sudden stop or an unexpected bend in the road can send the food skating across the truck.

There are some types of food that transport easily, provided they are well secured on the truck and well wrapped on their serving dish: fruits, vegetables, breads, pastries, and anything in chafing pans. Other foods are harder to transport, such as stuffed eggs or other stuffed items without a flat base, any food on an unstable pedestal server, and large arrangements of fruits or vegetables. To transport these items, you have two alternatives: start preparing them in your kitchen and finish them on the event site, or prepare them fully and devise ingenious, accident-proof ways to carry them in your truck.

Often the first alternative is better, provided you have some time and space to finish them at the party site. If it takes 20 minutes to finish the food, that means arriving 20 minutes earlier, which also means that other menu items need to be held an extra 20 minutes outside of your own safe holding facilities. When planning how to transport items, keep in mind things like the refrigeration or warming facilities at the party site, how much labor you have available, and the difficulty of transporting your fully-prepared food items safely.

For example, stuffed cherry tomatoes are really hard to keep from sliding around in transit. One way to prevent them from moving around is to set them in a bed of chopped parsley. Even if they slide around a little, they will remain undamaged. Or, hollow out the cherry tomatoes and transport them in a carrying container. The filling is in a pastry bag, which is also easy to transport. On arrival the tomatoes are put on their designated serving platter, the filling is squeezed into them from the pastry bag, and the platter is ready in minutes. You won't need to do them all, just a first batch as a starter. A little later, when the pressure of setting up is off, you or one of your helpers can fill the rest in your spare time.

Liquids are easy to transport. Just make certain they are in tightly closed containers. Sauces, juices, or liquids that are part of cooked food are more of a problem. They spill easily if they are in chafers since these cannot be closed airtight. Covering the chafers with aluminum foil seals them reasonably well, though they can still spill a little. Another possibility is to pour most of the liquid off (or drain it off with a baster) into a tight container for transportation and pour it back in when you arrive. This is for cooked or baked dishes. If you plan to prepare the food on site, then don't add the liquid until you arrive.

Finally, remember to fill up all gas tanks a day before the event. You cannot afford to lose valuable time waiting at the pump on the way to the event.

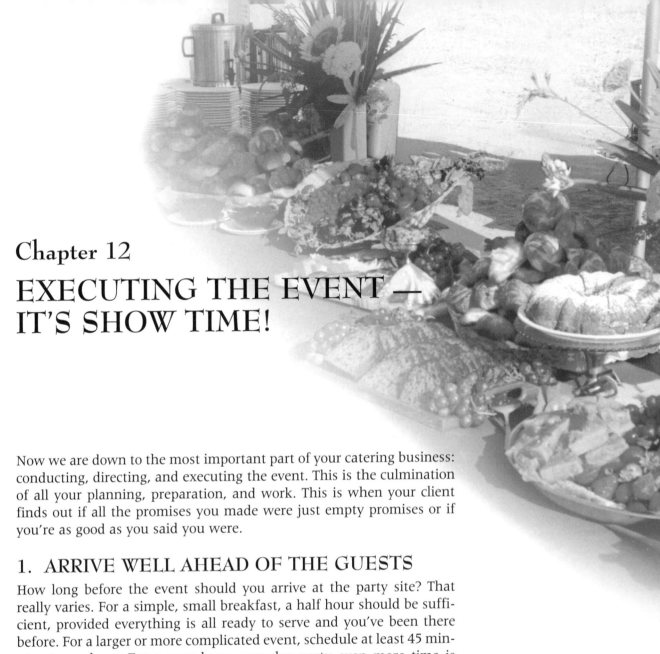

Chapter 12
EXECUTING THE EVENT — IT'S SHOW TIME!

Now we are down to the most important part of your catering business: conducting, directing, and executing the event. This is the culmination of all your planning, preparation, and work. This is when your client finds out if all the promises you made were just empty promises or if you're as good as you said you were.

1. ARRIVE WELL AHEAD OF THE GUESTS

How long before the event should you arrive at the party site? That really varies. For a simple, small breakfast, a half hour should be sufficient, provided everything is all ready to serve and you've been there before. For a larger or more complicated event, schedule at least 45 minutes to an hour. For a very large, complex party even more time is needed.

If you have to set up tables, chairs, china, silver, glasses, etc., an advance crew can be sent to handle that part. The food and the rest of the equipment can arrive later but still at least 45 minutes before the first guests arrive. This assumes that there is little or no food preparation being done on site. If food is being prepared on site, schedule the arrival so everything can be comfortably prepared and cooked by serving time.

A GOOD CATERER PLANS TO ARRIVE EARLY ENOUGH TO SET UP, PREPARE FOOD, THEN TAKE IT EASY BEFORE THE GUESTS ARRIVE.

How the event is executed differs with the various types of functions. The three most common varieties are reception catering, self-service, and full-service meal catering. These are discussed in detail in this chapter.

2. RECEPTIONS

Reception catering is generally of three different styles:

(a) Full-service meal with staff in attendance

(b) Meal delivered and set up but no staff in attendance, pick-up later

(c) Delivered on disposable ware, no staff in attendance, no pick-up

Full-service is most commonly used for better quality receptions. Many medium or high-end caterers will not do anything but full-service receptions. The logic is that reception food cannot be left unattended and still look presentable.

For smaller events where food can be delivered, do the setup on quality, nondisposable platters. Since the equipment is picked up later, no serving staff is needed; however, menu items are limited to food that holds up well or needs a minimum of preparation and no replenishment. This type of service is limited to events with simple food and no more than 25 to 30 guests.

Reception food delivered on disposable platters along with an invoice is not common in better-quality catering. It is akin to pizza delivery with advance reservation. This type of food cannot be presented quite as well as the same items on china, glass, silver, baskets, or wood. However, very good quality disposable ware is available and is perfectly acceptable for certain types of events, such as a picnic. High-quality disposable ware is fairly costly and you have to consider that when pricing the event. Ordinary, inexpensive disposable ware can also be used if it is completely covered with layers of greens, chopped parsley, paper, or even cloth napkins. For low-budget catering, you don't even need to cover the platters. The client gets what he or she pays for.

2.1 Setting up

Let's assume that you, your staff, the food, and the equipment have arrived at the job site safe and sound, on time as promised. First, take a quick look inside the truck to make sure that no problem has occurred as a result of transportation. Survey the facilities if you haven't done so previously. Take ten minutes, if necessary, and plan where everything goes. Where will the serving and bar tables go? How well can you manage in the existing kitchen facilities? If there is no kitchen or dining room, set up your staging area in an empty office or another room. In a private home you often need a small storage area as well, such as a laundry room, office, or even a garage where you can stack the extra equipment, food, and transportation crates. Watch out for cats. They adore your jumbo shrimp or poached whole salmon and can wreak havoc in a very short time.

There are clients (mostly in social catering) who hover around you and your staff during the entire setup period, making you feel uneasy. Or they sit down near the reception table and just quietly watch you working. Try to ignore the client's presence. The worst, of course, are the clients who not only sit down next to your work but also chatter nonstop, asking you questions while you are trying to concentrate on making their event a success. Or they criticize and disapprove of arrangements, color, the order of platters, and so on.

2.2 Unloading

Let's assume that all went well with your planning, and you and your staff are left alone. Now comes the time to do the most unpleasant task: unloading. Unloading is a thankless job. It is also physically taxing, particularly when cases of liquor, china, glass, tables, and other heavy equipment are involved.

Offices are easier to set up than homes. There are no stairs involved, so you can use your cart and dolly. There are almost always stairs or steps in a private home, so you often have to carry everything by hand. You can sometimes park your vehicle close to the kitchen and reduce unloading time.

Planning and organization are still critical, but you can slow down on your worrying. If your planning and organizational skill got you this far without any obvious problems, you can execute the event as well.

When unloading, try to arrange things in an orderly fashion right away. Food items go into the kitchen or staging area, anything that belongs to or near the buffet table is carried to that area, and so on. The idea is to lift each piece only once and put it down where it will be used. China, glass, and silver for a buffet dinner can stay near the table in their boxes and be unloaded later directly onto the table. At a full-service dinner, plates are taken to the kitchen; glasses and silverware are deposited in the eating area ready for table setting.

ALLOW 10 TO 15 MINUTES ON SITE TO CHAT WITH YOUR CLIENT AND HIS OR HER FAMILY — THEY LIKE TO DISCUSS THE PARTY AND THE WEATHER AT YOUR BUSIEST TIME.

As your staff carries the boxes, cartons, and crates in, the favorite place to deposit them is on counters, a poor practice. Eventually they need to be handled again to lift them off, and placing items that were sitting on floors directly on counters is unhygienic. Give specific instructions to avoid problems. Leave counters free for food and work space.

For a self-service event, the next step is to set up the food table as much as you can to eliminate some of the clutter of food and equipment. Plates, silverware, glasses, napkins, and some of the food items can go on the table. Anything that needs to stay cold should wait in the refrigerator or on ice until the last minute. Food to be freshly prepared should also wait. If the event includes hot food and it is ready, it can go in the chafing dish. Bring the water to a boil in your electric kettle or in a pot on the stove and pour it into the bottom half of the chafer, light the Sterno, put the pan of food over it, cover it, and forget it. Many caterers use hot water from the tap for the chafers. It will not keep the food as hot as when the water is boiled. When you see steam escaping from the bottom half of the chafer, turn the flame down a little to save fuel, especially if you have a long reception and your fuel must last several hours.

2.3 Staff pep talk

For a larger event, once the entire staff has arrived, it's useful to have a brief organizational meeting. Explain the event in a few quick phrases, emphasizing timing. Mention the name of the host and hostess and any other important guests, and where they will be seated, as well as the name of the contact person whom they can ask questions.

Go through your event plan briefly, outlining the various phases. Then assign each person to his or her specific role and tasks during the event. If you have new or fairly new crew members, mention again the various rules you want them to follow.

Mention the continuous cleanup mode during the event. Anyone who has any free time can collect dirty plates, glasses, and ashtrays to keep the site clean. Also make sure that equipment is not mixed up. There could be your equipment, the rental agency's, and the client's. They all must be in separate piles at the end of the event. It is time-consuming to return someone's china and flatware, and costly to lose yours.

Make sure everyone knows the name of every food item. The meat in the chafing dish is not "meatballs" but "Latin albondiguitas." And the other chafer holds not "chicken wings" but "chicken drummettes."

Scrutinize the crew to make sure everyone looks up to your standard. Always be pleasant to your staff. They will pass on your pleasant attitude, and ultimately, your business will benefit.

This meeting should not take more than ten minutes, possibly much less, and it is a very useful exercise. The crew will appreciate knowing their exact roles and having the event clarified. You may also get some useful feedback and questions from your crew, often about things you have not considered or may have overlooked.

HAVE THE SERVING STAFF LEARN THE CORRECT NAME OF THE DISHES SERVED AND THEIR KEY INGREDIENTS.

2.4 Keep everybody busy

While you or one of your staff is working on the food table, someone else should be busy in the kitchen finishing the food that still needs preparation.

Next, bring all food in the kitchen as close to finished as possible, but never sacrifice quality by preparing too early. It is better if the guests have to wait a little longer. A little waiting is usually acceptable at leisurely evening or weekend social occasions. At corporate lunch functions or any other function with a tight schedule involving speakers or similar programs, waiting should be kept to the absolute minimum. Some sacrifice in quality is even acceptable rather than keeping the guests waiting in these situations.

Reception food is ideally small, bite-sized finger food. For lower-budget and simpler events it could be only two to three items, such as the popular (because they are cheap to prepare) fruit and vegetable platters, cheeses, and cold cuts. More extravagant events will include at least six to eight different items, some hot, some cold. Cold items are the easiest for the caterer, not only to transport but to serve and maintain on the serving table. If hot items are served, the easiest are those served in chafing dishes kept hot by steam. The most difficult are those that must be served fresh out of the oven.

2.5 Hot and cold foods

Let's assume that we are catering an event with a mix of hot and cold food. After unloading from your vehicle, the cold food can be placed directly on the serving table. The hot food served in chafers can be

REPLENISH PLATTERS
SO THEY ALWAYS
LOOK AT LEAST HALF
FULL. IF YOU ARE
NEARLY OUT OF AN
ITEM, REMOVE THE
PLATTER.

transferred and kept warm on the table. If an oven is available, hot food should be held in the oven to save the Sterno fuel for later.

The buffet table should be the most visible part as soon as guests arrive, so set it up as fully as possible. Many guests arrive quite early. The table should look good by the time the early guests arrive, even though the preparation is not quite finished.

There is a nightmare story a caterer told us about an elegant, high-priced, lavish reception. The table was set up, looked gorgeous, and had a huge crystal chandelier over the center. The first guests were just arriving. The bartender walked over to admire the table while opening a bottle of champagne. The exploding champagne cork hit the chandelier and broke many of the crystals, and the shattered glass pieces dusted most of the table and freshly uncovered food. I don't know the ending to the story, but it could not have been a happy one.

Anything to be baked or broiled is kept aside, ready to go into the oven at the proper time. These foods are best brought to the event site fully prepared for the oven so there is no extra work with them. It is up to you to decide when to serve these hot items.

2.6 Keep small batches circulating

Food should not be served too early or the later guests may not get any. Few people eat right after arrival. Most will start at the beverage table, then socialize, and finally drift over to the food table.

The best way to deal with hot food is to prepare it in small batches throughout the reception. Don't attempt to bake everything at once and keep it hot. Prepare enough servings to serve half of the guests present; when you run out, announce to the guests that fresh ones will be ready in a few minutes. They'll anticipate your food. Plan the baking so that small batches of items come out of the oven every 10 to 15 minutes. Assign one of the servers to pass it out immediately. When everyone has been served once, wait a while with the new batches, perhaps 30 to 40 minutes. If this hot food item is one of the main foods on the menu, it should be served more continuously than if it is one of many items.

Someone should be in charge of ready-to-bake items, equipped with a small timer in his or her pocket. It is easy to forget that something is burning until the smell reaches you. People, especially the client, start sniffing and wonder what the caterer just ruined. Don't let that happen; carry a timer.

2.7 Replenish some items, ration others

Traditionally, in mediocre catering (often in hotels and banquet halls), what the first guests see are huge platters of food set up on large tables. The later guests see the same platters, now less than half full. The food is in disarray and looks much less appetizing than the original setup. Guests arriving late see even worse conditions: the food is beginning to resemble leftovers and has definitely lost its appeal.

Better caterers serve on smaller tables on small serving platters and replenish the food continually, carrying full platters to the table and taking the half-empty ones away. This type of service takes more staff time, but the last guests will find the serving table virtually in the same condition as the first guests. Plan to serve in this style if at all possible.

Certain food items may not need to be on the serving table all the time, such as hot, freshly prepared food that is carried around or items that need to be rationed. Steamed jumbo shrimp, for example, are devoured in huge quantities. Unless the budget is unlimited, these are best rationed. Serve them by carrying them around every 15 to 20 minutes or have them on the table so that half the time there is shrimp and the other half there isn't. Guests will ask you about the shrimp when it is not there. Politely inform them that a new plate is just being readied — they must be prepared absolutely fresh, you may add. Make sure that the host or hostess is offered the first choice from each freshly carried full platter of these rationed items. That way he or she will have the impression that someone is carrying a full platter around all the time and an unlimited supply is in the back.

No matter how you ration these very popular items, some guests will overindulge. It is horrifying to see a guest take a dozen large shrimp and add nothing else to his or her plate; there goes your estimate for two-and-a-half shrimp per person. There is nothing you can do except to stare that guest into shame, and sometimes even that won't work. Usually there are also a number of guests, however, who are either allergic to shrimp or dislike it, and they compensate for the greedy ones.

For the caterer, the pressure will be at its most intense during the first third of the event. This is when you are setting up and attempting to get everything on the table. Once the table is ready, you have a respite until the first few guests drift over to the serving table. Soon after, more come — the ones who are starving but did not want to be the first ones

YOU OR YOUR CHEF MUST KNOW ALL INGREDIENTS IN ALL DISHES TO ALERT GUESTS WITH FOOD ALLERGIES.

at the food. Then come the hordes. From this point on, you must constantly replenish platters, adjust garnishes, wipe up spills, add plates and napkins, and answer questions and requests. About halfway through, the pressure eases. This is the time to carry platters around the room, offering items to individuals. Doing so shows off your good service and extra attention. Always start with, or near, the host or hostess and any honored guests.

Guests will accept anything you carry around, so offer items that you have plenty of. Food that you're running short of should remain on the table. Encourage the guests to eat items that will not keep. Hold back food that can be used in the future. If you have anything that did not turn out as well as expected, don't pass it around. Leave it on the table.

The last third of the reception is the winding down period. An important part of your staff's job is to keep everything in beautiful order on the table until it is removed. If you calculated your food correctly, there should be enough left in the last third of the reception to keep the platters reasonably full and attractive. Near the end you may be running low on some items, so you cannot fill a platter completely. In this case combine two or even three items, or switch over to smaller serving plates. If you're combining items, they should complement each other. Don't combine the raspberry tarts with the pickled herring, or the fruit sticks with the pesto tortellini just because both are on skewers.

2.8 Clean as you go

As mentioned earlier, continuous cleanup is important. Pick up used plates, napkins, glasses, bottles, and ashtrays, and clean up spills.

Finally the hour approaches when the party is scheduled to end. Your instinct tells you that it is time to clear the food, clean up, present the bill, and head home. Don't listen to your instinct. Keep the table looking nice and leave the food there. Don't ever appear anxious to leave. Start the cleanup process in the back. If it isn't obvious to the guests, start carrying a few unneeded items to the truck. China and glasses can be rinsed and put back into their carrying cases or bus tubs.

Once the scheduled end of the reception is reached, assess the situation. If it looks as if your food is no longer needed, ask your client if you can start clearing the table and cleaning up. If there are still guests around (there almost always are), suggest consolidating the food on a few disposable plates for anyone who may want to nibble some more. Or ask if the client wants the food left in the refrigerator (or wrapped to take home if it is a reception hall). Most clients will agree that you can go ahead and clean up. Some may ask if you can stay for an extra half hour because they are still expecting a few late arrivals. Generally you should agree; there isn't much of a choice unless you can make a nice arrangement of your food on disposable platters. Some caterers simply charge an extra half hour for the staff time. Consider specifying this in your contract.

Once the client agrees that it is time for you to clean up, you can gather your equipment and leave. Some guests, particularly close friends or relatives and people who won't depart unless they are shown to the door, are still standing around with your wine glasses in hand. How do you collect them? A good plan is to carry disposable wine glasses with you and ask those guests to exchange their glass for the disposable. No one will object.

2.9 Leftovers

Finally comes the tricky question of the leftover food. This has always been a dilemma for caterers. There is no clear solution. The client may claim that it belongs to him or her, particularly when far fewer guests showed up than expected. You may claim that you prepared extra food not paid for by the client and for safety and legal reasons nothing can be left behind. The caterer is legally liable for what he or she serves and leaves behind. While the food is under your control, there is no problem. Once you leave it with the client, you don't know how it is going to be stored and taken care of. It may have already been sitting out on the serving table for an hour or two and if it is not eaten soon, its safety could be in question. If someone gets sick, you can still be blamed.

Here is a partial solution. Discuss extra food with the client while planning the event. Have the client understand that any food you deem safe will be left behind; other items will be removed.

But even though the food may still be perfectly safe, it is no longer very attractive. You hate to leave a bad impression. To avoid such a complication, leave extra food either on your truck or covered in the staging area. Remove everything extra from the staging area before the end of the event and the question of extra food may not come up at all.

If you donate leftover food to a nonprofit organization, remember that legal liability lies with the delivery person. If the organization picks it up from your kitchen, you are no longer responsible for it.

IF EXTRA FOOD HAS BEEN OUT TOO LONG, REMOVE IT AND PUT IT IN YOUR VEHICLE TO AVOID PROBLEMS WITH A CLIENT WHO WANTS TO KEEP THE LEFTOVERS.

IT IS IMPORTANT TO
HAVE CORPORATE
MEALS READY ON
TIME WHEN THE
SCHEDULE IS TIGHT
AND THEY EXPECT
TO EAT AT THE
APPOINTED TIME.

3. SELF-SERVICE MEALS

A full meal buffet is the easiest on the caterer. However, this form of service requires the least number of staff members, so whoever sets it up has the extra burden of loading and unloading alone or with a small staff. Arriving early is essential. Count on 45 minutes to a full hour to unload, carry everything into the work and serving areas, and organize and set up a small luncheon or dinner, depending on how much last-minute on-site preparation is needed. If the meal is at a previously unvisited place, allow a little extra time.

It is important to have corporate meals ready on time when the schedule is tight and they expect to eat at the appointed time. When meetings are scheduled with out-of-town visitors, this may not happen. There are often travel delays for guests. Plan ahead by bringing extra fuel for the chafing dishes and plan the menu with this eventuality in mind.

Like reception catering, the self-service meal is also of three different styles:

(a) Self-service with server in attendance to assist

(b) Delivered and set up, no server in attendance, pick-up later

(c) Delivered on disposable ware, no attendant, no pick-up

If an attendant is present to assist, the caterer has two choices: food that is brought in fully or partially prepared, or food that is prepared on the premises. Planning is somewhat different for each, as was discussed above, but the execution of the event is basically the same for both styles. When food preparation is required on the premises, you change your planned arrival time.

Most corporate functions are in the first category, where food is delivered almost fully prepared. This is because cooking and food preparation facilities are not commonly available in a corporate office. However, there are corporations with small, fully equipped kitchens (not cafeteria kitchens) next to the executive offices. These are meant for meal preparation for executive meetings, but they are often available for use at other corporate meal functions. If you are a permanent caterer with such a corporation for a client, you can set up, stock, and equip the kitchen for your convenience and cook meals there regularly for your client.

Self-service on disposable ware is not common in medium- and high-end catering. But from time to time, clients want to have a full meal delivered and ready to go into the oven. The client can take care of all food preparation after drop-off. For brunches and picnics this is acceptable, especially when all the food is served cold or at room temperature and no preparation is required to be done by the client except uncovering the disposable serving dishes. (Some clients will need instructions on how to do this.)

4. FULL-SERVICE MEALS

Full-service meals commonly have the highest per-person costs of any event. Clients ordering full-service meals have adequate or even unlimited budgets. These are your favorite clients. Cherish them, treasure them, nourish them.

The difference in price between self- and full-service is mainly in the labor costs. It takes one server for every 10 to 15 guests for full service, but one server can handle about 50 guests at a self-service event. You also need additional kitchen staff to prepare the plates individually for a full-service event.

Food costs remain the same, or are even less for full-service meals. When you preplate food, you don't need to prepare much extra food, just enough to serve the number of guests for the order and a little extra. For the preplated dinner, if you have learned to calculate accurately, you end up with virtually no food in the pots and pans when the last plate is served, so waste is nearly eliminated.

On the other hand, each plate is individually garnished for full-service meals. Preparation time and the cost of the garnish offset the reduced food cost.

There are five common styles of food service:

(a) American (or plate) — food is portioned out, garnished in the kitchen, and served.

(b) French — the food is partially prepared in the kitchen but the final preparation is done at the table as well as adding sauces, garnishing, and plating.

(c) Wagon — similar to French in that finishing is done at the guests' table, but requiring no cooking skill, such as carving meat or tossing salads; only the illusion of French service remains.

(d) Russian (or platter) — the finished food is served on platters and transferred to the guests' plates; it requires skill and practice to transfer the food properly.

(e) Family — large bowls and platters of finished food are placed on the table for guests to serve themselves.

In full-service catering, American-style food service is used almost exclusively. Very high-end catering may use other styles. Whatever you use, remember: food is served from the left, taken away from the right. Water, wine, coffee, and soup are served from the right and also taken away from the right.

4.1 Full staff

Unlike reception and self-service catering, full-service can only be done with a full staff in attendance serving guests individually. The only exception is a type of catering with a blend of full- and self-service, something that is used fairly commonly. In this case there is a partial aura of serving staff but not the cost of a full-service meal. An example is when the entrée is served buffet style but the salad or soup is pre-plated and placed at each place setting. Dessert can also be preplated and served or passed by a server from a tray to each guest. You do need extra staff, so calculate the cost and add to your price for this type of service.

4.2 Kitchen facilities

The food for the full-service event is prepared as much as possible in the catering kitchen, but naturally, final preparation, cooking, and baking should be done on-site if feasible. This is usually not a problem for smaller, more intimate meals, but it may be tricky for a large group, depending on what sort of kitchen facilities are available at the site.

Make sure you know what the kitchen facilities include. We had a holiday, full-service dinner party for 35 guests in a house with small kitchen facilities. I met the client at the house and inspected the site carefully. I told her that it would be tight for that many people but we could do it. She said she had two ovens. I went in the kitchen and, sure enough, there were two ovens. This was somewhat of a surprise because the house was older, from a time when putting in two ovens would have been very unusual.

I told the client that with two ovens there would be no problem. We could do the entire meal on location. When we arrived several months later, our fancy marinated chicken breasts were in pans ready to be baked. We were in no hurry to turn the ovens on; there were hors d'oeuvres ready to be served; the evening was going to be slow and leisurely. Finally the time arrived to heat up the ovens. This was when we discovered that even though the hostess had two ovens, only one worked. For the next hour we had a terrible time using one oven to bake two ovens' worth of food. By rotating pans every 15 minutes in and out of the oven, we finally cooked all the chicken breasts, though not to perfection. We were only a little behind schedule in serving. Our servers diligently kept serving wine, hors d'oeuvres, and bread to divert the guests' attention. No one noticed the difference, although the host did complain that his chicken was not quite hot.

With good planning, many things can be done ahead of time. For instance, all garnishes can be ready for the plates, salad ingredients cut up, blanched, or prepared ready for plating, vegetables partially cooked or blanched, meat cut up and perhaps browned or half-baked, hors d'oeuvres ready for the oven or ready to be passed, desserts half or fully prepared, and coffee measured out. All this early preparation will free valuable time at the event site.

The very busy high-pressure period is somewhat different at full-service functions. In a self-service meal most of the pressure is at the very beginning — before and during setup and the first part of serving. With the full-service meal the pressure comes later, mainly around the serving of the entrée. This is the most time-consuming part of the meal, the preparation of a garnished plate with piping hot food served to the guests with a minimum of time from stove top to table. Once the entrée has been served, the pressure eases somewhat. It will take a while before guests are ready for the next course, and since the main part of the meal is in front of everyone, the guests will have more tolerance to wait. In fact, they should be allowed to have ample time to finish the entrée, socialize, cleanse their palates, and digest.

IN A SELF-SERVICE MEAL MOST OF THE PRESSURE IS AT THE VERY BEGINNING — BEFORE AND DURING SETUP AND THE FIRST PART OF SERVING.

4.3 When to take the plate away

Don't start collecting plates until most guests at a table are finished. Often there is the problem of an overly talkative guest who forgets to eat. Or someone who has to leave for some reason and comes back to start the meal when almost everyone is finished. This is a problem with no obvious solution. The servers just have to wait as long as possible, but if it is obvious that there will be too much delay, it is best to clear the table and leave the last guest talking with the food getting cold.

Eventually he or she will get the message. Often such a person ends up sending the barely touched plate back. Don't be offended. For some people, talking has priority over food.

Before dessert and coffee are served, the table must be cleared of everything that was used for the previous courses, including china, glass (except what may be still used, such as wine and water glasses), and silver. The servers should clean off any serious spillage as well as they can or cover it with a napkin.

It is best to serve the hot beverages before the dessert. That gives the kitchen staff a little extra time for the dessert preparation and plating, but also, most people like to have the coffee or tea right after the meal and with the dessert.

If this is the last course, then the only service left is refilling the hot beverage cups and eventually removing the dessert plates. The pressure is off, but the enormous drudgery of collecting all the equipment and cleaning up is still ahead. It is very helpful to have one or two inexpensive cleanup staff who come in relatively late to relieve the tired serving and kitchen staff.

When all is finally complete, the client's kitchen looks better than it has for years, the truck is loaded up to its rim (for some unexplained reason there is always more to haul back than what you brought), and the exhausted staff can hardly drag themselves to do the loading.

Now it is time to present the invoice. You always hope that you will get a check for the balance of the invoice right away, but if not, cheerfully tell the clients that there is no problem with dropping it in the mail tomorrow.

It is up to you how you divide any gratuities that you might receive. You can do it in equal portions among the staff and yourself or in unequal portions as you see fit. Or keep it all to yourself if your staff did a lousy job.

Last, if your event was not a regular business meal, a thank-you note to the client is a thoughtful gesture. To make it sound personal, add a sentence mentioning something about the particular event.

5. AFTER THE EVENT

Once the event is over and the equipment and leftover food are transported back to the kitchen, the final step is cleaning up and putting everything back in its place, ready for the next time. Make sure that whoever is putting equipment away knows what goes where. You can't afford to waste time looking for items a half hour before departure time on the next event. If the cleanup person doesn't know what goes where, have him or her leave the clean equipment out for sorting instead of putting it away on the wrong shelf. Perfect order in your kitchen is another prerequisite for an efficient operation.

Carefully store any leftover food that can be used again and discard the rest. For instance, cheeses can be grated and frozen to be used in cooking. Vegetables may be used for stocks or soups or some can even be used in salads if they are in good condition. Pickled items are reusable, breads can be frozen, and leftover pasta is fine for salad. Only keep leftover and extra food if you feel it is absolutely safe and its quality on reuse fits your established standards.

To know what is absolutely safe and what is doubtful, you must be familiar with spoilage and deterioration rates of various foods. You must also know how each particular food was stored and handled since it left your kitchen. If something was sitting out on the kitchen counter or buffet table for several hours, be suspicious. If it is cheese, not much can go wrong with it except drying out. It will be perfectly fine for cooking, grating, and baking. Serve the leftover potato salad with mayonnaise dressing to your own staff only if you think it is really safe. Either you or a trusted staff person should sort the food and judge its usability as it is unloaded. Naturally you want to reduce waste to a minimum without risking your reputation. If you provide linen for an event, time must be scheduled for laundering as well.

The goal is to get your kitchen and storage room back to normal as soon as possible after an event. If you have other events planned soon after, then you want to clean and sort even faster so you can get on with preparing for the next event.

If you and your staff are especially busy with events during high-demand season, it may be a good idea to hire extra help just to keep the kitchen, work areas, and storage space clean and ready at all times.

PERFECT ORDER IN YOUR KITCHEN IS ANOTHER PREREQUISITE FOR AN EFFICIENT OPERATION.

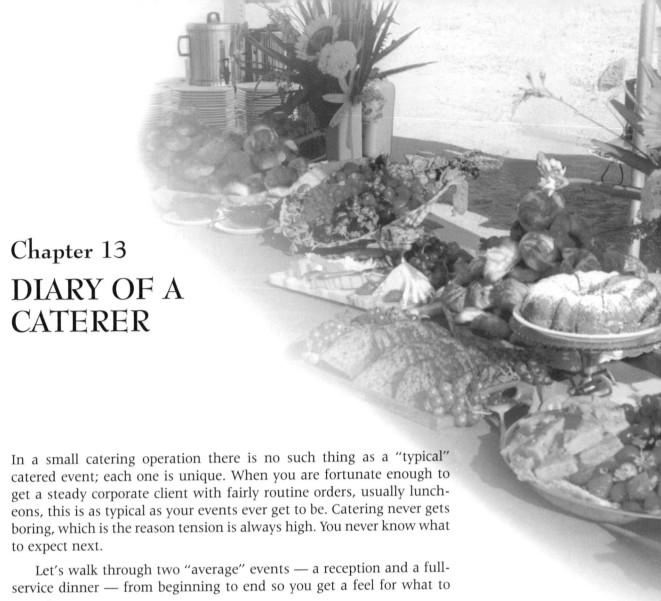

Chapter 13

DIARY OF A CATERER

In a small catering operation there is no such thing as a "typical" catered event; each one is unique. When you are fortunate enough to get a steady corporate client with fairly routine orders, usually luncheons, this is as typical as your events ever get to be. Catering never gets boring, which is the reason tension is always high. You never know what to expect next.

Let's walk through two "average" events — a reception and a full-service dinner — from beginning to end so you get a feel for what to expect.

1. EVENT 1: A RECEPTION

1.1 The beginning phase: Client-caterer contact

You receive a call from a Ms. Ginger Prosciutto from the Spiced Ham Distributing Company. She tells you that they are new in town, they are opening a branch office, and they are looking for a caterer for their grand opening reception six weeks from now on August 1. Your catering business was highly recommended to them by a client of yours in the building they just moved into. She wants to know prices, what is included, what you recommend for beverages, what types of food you serve, and so on.

You tell Ms. Prosciutto that you would be delighted and honored to cater the reception and you need to check your calendar to make sure August 1 is still open before further discussion. You put her on hold and look at your calendar. There is nothing scheduled for August 1. You tell Ms. Prosciutto that fortunately that date is not yet booked and the next step is to meet personally to talk about details, budgets, and menus. You also tell her that generally you recommend that new clients meet you in your office, so they can inspect your facilities and get an impression of how your operation works. She can even taste some fresh tidbits from your repertoire. Ms. Prosciutto agrees and you give a secret sigh of relief. It saves you a trip, and also it is an advantage to meet clients on your home ground.

Two days later Ms. Prosciutto shows up in your office on time, giving you a good impression of the kind of client you like to work with — professional, businesslike, and pleasant. She accepts and compliments you on a glass of your fresh peppermint iced tea. You give her your photo portfolio and menu to look at while you ready a tiny plateful of goodies that you carry in on a little silver tray. Now you are ready for business.

You may want to go through some of the photos in the portfolio and talk about the kind of event they represent, perhaps pointing out your professional-looking uniformed staff. Then you find out all about her reception — time of day, length, number of guests invited and expected, facilities available, type of food wanted, beverage service, and the budget allocated. This is what she tells you:

They are inviting about 130 guests and requesting an RSVP. They will invite the staff, some retailers, and other companies that are potential clients. They want to distribute their own spiced ham. They have scheduled an open house reception from 2:00 p.m. to 6:00 p.m. Their kitchen facilities are minimal — just a small lunchroom that doubles as the office storage room and is equipped with a tiny refrigerator and a microwave oven.

However, the office is in a prestigious, high-end, high-rent office building in a new development downtown. Ms. Prosciutto tells you that budget is no problem and they want a very classy affair. They want to impress their potential new clients as well as the old ones who are already distributing their ham. They want a full bar service. The only condition, she says, is that the food must feature their ginger-spiced prosciutto ham as one of the buffet items.

No problem, you say, since you know that their ham is excellent. So you discuss the menu in detail for the next 40 minutes. Ms. Prosciutto would like to have two of the items she has just sampled on the reception menu because she liked them so much. (This is one way to steer clients into choosing certain items.)

You tell her that a four-hour reception is hard on the host, staff, and the guests and could result in very thin attendance. You recommend no longer than two and a half hours. She agrees, provided her boss approves. The event is now tentatively scheduled from 3:00 p.m. to 5:30 p.m.

You also tell Ms. Prosciutto that to reserve the date, you will need about half of the expected total as a deposit as soon as possible, the balance being due at the time of the event. You offer to send a proposal letter with all the details and a copy of the contract the next day.

THE JOB IS NOT YOURS UNTIL YOU RECEIVE THE DEPOSIT.

The total consultation time takes one hour and fifteen minutes, and almost all the details for the reception are worked out. This is a fairly typical amount of time for a first consultation. You should generally expect to spend an hour to an hour and a half, including coffee and chitchat.

After Ginger Prosciutto leaves, you think about the meeting briefly, look at your notes and jot down anything you may have forgotten. The meeting went well. Ginger was impressed with you and your kitchen and she liked your food. You liked her, too. This will be a good client to work with. But the job is not yours until you receive the deposit.

The next day you send the client a letter of proposal (see Sample 8). This sets out the arrangements you have discussed and the cost.

Three days later Ms. Prosciutto calls to tell you that she received your letter, all looks fine, and she has requested a check for you from their head office. Mark your calendar in pencil for August 1. If you don't receive the deposit within the next week and someone else calls you about another function for August 1, consider whether you can do both. If not, call Ginger Prosciutto and explain the situation. If the check is already coming, tell her that you will refuse the other event but you cannot hold the date open for more than three days without the deposit.

The check and the signed contract arrive as promised. Now the event date is marked firmly in ink on your calendar and you can forget about it until July 22.

John Dough Catering Company
35 Batter Road
Crepeville, CA 94066

June 17, 20--

Ms. Ginger Prosciutto
Spiced Ham Distributing Co.
100 Clove Circle
Tarttown

Dear Ms. Prosciutto:

It was a pleasure to meet with you yesterday. We are honored to present you with this proposal for your grand opening reception on August 1. The menu we agreed to is as follows:

- Ginger-spiced prosciutto wrapped around honeydew melon wedges
- Poached whole Atlantic salmon
- Baked Brie en croûte with fresh-baked French bread and cracker squares
- Sour cherry and sweet potato tarts
- Italian pesto torta made with fresh basil
- Tortilla roulade with a spicy Tex-Mex flavor
- Cherry tomatoes with a southwestern corn salad filling
- Our own fresh-baked dessert display

This lavish meal will be presented elegantly and beautifully on buffet-style service with uniformed staff in attendance. We know that you, your staff, and your guests will be impressed with both our food and our service. The price will be $14.50 per person, assuming approximately 130 guests and including china and paper napkins.

One bartender should be able to provide full bar service with some help from our food staff at times of greatest demand. Should the number of guests go up, we may need two bartenders, though due to limited space, only one bar will be set up. Bartending service is $75 per bartender, including ice, fruit, and miscellaneous bar items. Glasses are $2 per person and I understand that you will supply all beverages, including mixes.

A 15% catering service charge and 7.75% tax will be added to the final bill. We would like to have a final guest count five days before the event.

We sincerely hope that you will choose John Dough Catering for this important function. We would be very pleased to serve you and will do everything we can to make this event memorable for you and your guests. We will reserve August 1 for your event as soon as we receive a deposit of $1,300 (about half of the expected total).

Sincerely,

John Dough

John Dough, Chef/Owner
John Dough Catering

So far this event has been very easy and has cost you only a couple of hours of work. This is not typical, though; for other clients it may take much more haggling, letter writing, and telephone follow-up. Business clients are more businesslike than social clients and they don't want to waste time any more than you do. Social catering clients, especially for weddings, are often much harder to pin down. Some take three, even four meetings, none shorter than an hour. These clients do not use caterers on a regular basis, they are uncertain and afraid of being "ripped off." Your first job is to convince them they can trust you.

1.2 The middle phase: Planning and organization

July 22 arrives — ten days before the event. It is time to reserve your staff. You haven't heard from Spiced Ham yet about the exact number of guests, but you don't expect that for a few more days. You assume there will be about 130 guests, and chances are that the number will go down as RSVPS slowly arrive. This is based on your experience with previous events.

The menu is not difficult. No food needs to be freshly prepared on site. The staff will replenish trays and cut up the full pans of food into portions. Excluding bartenders, you can handle it with one helper, but it will be tight. One bartender for that many guests is really cutting it close. As a compromise, reserve one bartender and two helpers, and one of your helpers can also assist the bartender from time to time. That way you have a total of four staff, including yourself.

Wait before reserving the second helper until you hear from the client about the final count, just in case the number goes down drastically. You know that it could easily drop 20 percent to 30 percent. Ginger appears to know what she is doing, but be ready for anything.

Look at your menu again with a critical eye. Any out-of-the-ordinary ingredients should be ordered ahead of time, as well as anything that needs special attention.

A week before the Spiced Ham event, on July 25, it is time to look at the menu and start planning. First, write down the staff schedule; don't leave it to memory. The bartender, Curry, should be on location an hour and fifteen minutes prior to the event, at 1:45 p.m. She is reliable and she should be able to set up well before 3:00 p.m. Your helper, Clove, will be in the kitchen at 8:00 a.m. on July 31. Put these notes in the Spiced Ham file.

Of the various menu items, you pick ones that can be done ahead of time to keep last-minute preparation to a minimum. Here are things you can do in advance: puff pastry wrap for Brie, pie pastry for sour cherry tarts, pesto, and possibly some desserts. You note that none of the items needs too much preparation. You can't begin any of them until the final guest count is given.

Fortunately the next day Ginger Prosciutto calls you and keeps the count at 125. Now you sit down and prepare a supply list and a detailed schedule. But first you should call the second helper and reserve his or her time. After calling several, you find that Pepper is available that day. He is reasonably reliable as a server but not very good in the kitchen. So you reserve him for August 1 to arrive in the kitchen at 1:00 p.m., dressed in your standard serving uniform.

Sample 9 is the menu showing reference page numbers in your recipe collection and the number of times the recipe should be scaled up. Sample 10 is the supply list and the detailed schedule (giving approximate preparation time in hours) for the event.

This schedule is a fairly complete list of jobs to be done for the event. The times given to accomplish each task are approximate, but with experience you can get rather close in your guess. It is best to schedule a generous time allowance.

RECEPTION MENU

Item	Recipe File	Scale of Original Recipe
Ham/melon	(no recipe) 250 skewers	
Salmon	p. 36	
Brie en croûte	p. 12	pastry 3X
Tart	p. 52	2.25X
Pesto	p. 54	3X
Roulade	p. 21	10X
Corn salad	p. 40	3X
Dessert:		
plum tartlets	p. 12	4X
lemon-walnut cookies	p. 43	4X
biscotti (already prepared)		

Here is a brief description of the preparation involved in some of the menu items:

- The prosciutto is thinly sliced and will be wrapped around bite-sized melon wedges, secured with a toothpick, and stuck into half a red cabbage. Once the red cabbage is full, the remainder is prepared and kept in a storage container for replenishment. This can be replenished very quickly so half a cabbage is enough.

- The salmon is garnished and ready to be put on the table. If you can get one large enough so only one is needed, then that goes on the table and is kept looking neat during the reception. If you have two pieces, the first one is replaced when most of it is gone. The Brie is also ready but there are four to six of them. Only two are garnished and ready to go and one is placed on the table; the other one is backup. The rest will be garnished and used as needed.

SUPPLY LIST AND DETAILED SCHEDULE

MEAT	DAIRY	PRODUCE	OTHER
12½ – 13 lb salmon	6 lb Brie	1 red cabbage	toothpicks
4 lb spiced prosciutto	7 lb butter	4 lge. honeydews	crackers
	10 lb cream cheese	12 lemons	7 baguettes
	24 eggs	8 limes	9 oz black olives
	3 c. milk	3 lb yams	hot chili oil
		3 bu. basil	stuffed olives
		2 lb corn	maras. cherries
		3 lb carrots	1 bt. wh. wine
		9 oz pimento	10 burritos
		120 cherry tomatoes	70 lb ice
		6 scallions	flowers
		2 bu. parsley	
		garnish: table	
		salmon	
		trays	
		greens for trays	

SCHEDULE

SAT		SUN		MON	
roulade mix	1.25	pesto torta	1.0	prep prosc/melon	1.5
puff pastry	1.5	poach salmon	1.5	cut up roulade	0.5
cookie dough	0.75	bake Brie	1.5	cherry tomatoes	1.5
tart pastry	0.5	corn salad	0.5	bake dessert	1.5
pesto	0.5	prep invoice	0.5	cut up tart	0.5
order bread		prep equip	1.5	tray dessert	0.5
		tray salmon	0.5	load	0.5
		wash truck	0.5	pick up bread	0.5
				contingencies	1.0
Totals	4.5 hrs		7.5 hrs		8.0 hrs

Depart 1:30 p.m.

Work to be done on site: Tray cherry tarts, tray and fill tomatoes

- The sour cherry tarts are cut up into small pieces, trayed, and garnished on the job site. There is always one plate prepared ahead ready to go on the table.

- The pesto torta is cut into several pieces, two are plated and garnished, one of which goes on the table. The rest is backup. The roulades are on two plates, ready to go. The remainder is cut up and can refill plates quickly. The dessert display is on two platters, the rest is on reserve. They are also quick to replenish.

The schedule shows that if you have the time on Saturday, you can do the work by yourself. You could also work on Sunday, if there is no other business and you want to save on labor costs. Monday, you and Clove have four hours each, so starting at no later than 8:00 a.m. is advisable, especially for you, as you may be interrupted by telephone calls and so on. But both of you should be able to finish and have a quick bite by noon. There should even be time for a fast cleanup. With Pepper's help you should be able to load the truck and be ready to roll by 1:30 p.m. The client's office is only 20 minutes away.

1.3 The final phase: Day of the event

Before you all leave, you go through the menu and your notes one more time, perhaps the third time, to make very sure everything is on the truck. Take your time to check off each item and think about every component that needs to be taken. Some of the food items are in more than one piece, like the cherry tomatoes. Remember the garnishes, flowers, ice, and fruit for the bartender. These should all be on your checklist. Then look into the refrigerators and freezer for a last-minute visual check in case a prepared plate is still hiding in there. The equipment was already carefully checked and loaded earlier. Your final check complete, the team is ready to take off.

A few minutes before two o'clock, you arrive in front of the office building. Curry, the bartender, is already there waiting.

Your two helpers, Pepper and Clove, can load up the rolling cart with Curry's help, while you go upstairs to check in with Ginger in Spiced Ham's office. Decide with Ginger where the bar table and food table are going to be. Your staging area will be very small but will have to do. The dining area you were told was small is really tiny, not much counter space, just a small table.

By 2:40 p.m., everything is upstairs and the empty truck is parked. One helper sets up the table, one takes care of the bar, and two of you prepare the trays that were left to be done on the job site. The loaded

IT WILL TAKE HALF
AN HOUR TO BREAK
EVERYTHING DOWN,
PACK ITEMS AWAY,
TAKE THEM DOWN
TO THE TRUCK,
AND RELOAD.

trays are checked for any necessary adjustment. By the time they are finished, the table is ready. A few minutes before three o'clock, both the bar and buffet table are ready. The food looks gorgeous. Ginger, her boss, and the office staff "ooh" and "ah" in front of the buffet. The guests start arriving shortly after.

You and your helpers can relax for a while. Only Curry will be busy at the bar. The guests attack the bar first and only a few will nibble.

By four o'clock the place is jammed and all your staff are busy. You can keep up without difficulty but Curry needs help. You assign Pepper to help Curry as needed. The food is going well but there is plenty of extra left by 5:15 p.m. The reception is obviously a success for the Spiced Ham Company as well as for you.

Although the reception was supposed to be over at 5:30 p.m., many guests are still hanging around both the bar and food tables at 5:45 p.m. There is no choice but to put a smile on your face and pretend you are thoroughly enjoying the extra half hour with these exciting people.

So that time is not completely wasted, you can all start collecting equipment without making it too obvious to the guests. Leave the buffet table and the bar alone. There are plenty of other things to clean up and pack into boxes or crates. Any extra food that you would rather not leave behind is now discreetly taken down to the truck to avoid discussion with the client later.

By 6:00 p.m., it is time for the bartender to go around with disposable wine glasses and ask everyone with a real glass for an exchange so you can pack up your glasses. Ask Ginger if you can break down the table. Ginger readily agrees, thinking that this may be a further hint to the last guests. It will take half an hour to break everything down, pack items away, take them down to the truck, and reload. In the meantime, all the guests have disappeared. Only Ginger, her boss, and a few office people remain, ready to lock up. You offer some food items that are safe for them to take home. From your catering box you take out a couple of paper plates, fill them up with food, wrap them tightly with plastic wrap, and give them to Ginger, along with the final invoice.

By 6:25 p.m., the truck is loaded, Curry is gone and you, Clove, and Pepper leave. The truck needs to be unloaded, which takes another 20 minutes. Things must be sorted and any perishables put away in the freezer or refrigerator. Let Pepper and Clove help themselves to whatever they want from the extra food. You take care of a few last-minute things in the office and by 7:30 p.m. you can lock up the kitchen.

Cleanup has to wait until tomorrow. You make a mental note to send a thank-you card to Ginger, mentioning what a pleasure it was to serve the Spiced Ham Distributing Company and adding something specific about the party.

YOU ARE HAPPIEST WHEN THE CLIENT TRUSTS YOU TO CHOOSE THE MENU.

2. EVENT 2: A FULL-SERVICE DINNER

For our second example, let's walk through an elegant full-service dinner party.

2.1 The beginning phase: Client-caterer contact

Mr. Chuck Roast is a partner in a law firm for whom you have catered everything from full receptions to holiday dinner parties. He calls to ask about catering for a surprise birthday dinner party for his wife, Tender Roast, in six weeks. You ask him for the exact date to make sure that your calendar is clear. It is scheduled for Friday, September 16. You inform Mr. Roast that the date is his. You set up an appointment in your office for Thursday.

He arrives at your office as scheduled, and since it is a warm day, you offer fresh iced tea, a piece of cranberry sweet potato tart, and some fresh lemon-walnut cookies. He accepts them with delight. Since he has attended several of your parties, he knows that he can trust your food and service. That eliminates a lot of sales talk, show-and-tell, and negotiating. You get down to business at once.

He is planning to invite 36 guests for his wife's 40th birthday celebration. It will be a surprise party. He wants a full-service, elegant dinner party and, though his budget is not unlimited, he will pay whatever it takes, within reason.

Here is what he wants: tables, chairs, and linen set up in his backyard, along with an ice sculpture, flaming torches all around the yard, flowers on the tables, and live musicians. He also wants a limousine service to take his wife on a hoax trip supposedly to meet him for dinner and keep her out of the way while things are being set up. Can you arrange it all? Of course, you assure Chuck, no problem at all.

As for the dinner, he wants your suggestion for an appropriate menu that is elegant, unique, and pleasing to every palate. He also needs a bartender for a full bar, along with china, glass, and silver. You say that your proposal will be in the mail within the next two days. Since you have no event scheduled for the rest of the day, you settle down to write it up. Easy, you think. You are happiest when the client trusts you to choose the menu. Menu items that are relatively easy on the caterer, hold well, and will be appreciated by the guests can be selected.

Occasionally a client comes to a caterer with a full, preconceived menu in mind. The menu is often completely inappropriate for several reasons. The food will not hold and must be served absolutely fresh, (e.g., sautéed fish), or it is a dish such as a stew that cannot be presented well, especially on a buffet table. The ingredients are too costly for the meager budget (the classic champagne taste on a beer budget), or the ingredients are out of season (asparagus in mid-summer). The items could be out of the caterer's style or range of food. Sometimes a client requests food that few guests would be willing to eat or appreciate, such as seviche or herring.

In mid-afternoon Mr. Roast calls to tell you that he also wants a birthday cake, something beautiful, not too sweet, and with a great flavor. In your files, you should have a cake cutting chart so you know how to cut the cake so there are enough pieces for each guest. (A cake cutting chart is included on the CD-ROM.) Also, he reminds you that all correspondence and telephone calls should be directed to his office, not his home.

It takes about an hour to prepare a proposal. You have all the subcontractors' prices in your files. Sample 11 is the proposal letter you type up for Mr. Roast.

You send this proposal the next day. Chuck Roast calls you two days later. He basically likes the menu and the proposal, but would like to change a few items. He doesn't care for The Squealing Pig Quartet. He would rather have a country western band, his wife's favorite. You agree that it is no problem to arrange this, but most country western bands are just too loud to accompany a dinner where guests would like to socialize. You promise to find one that is willing to turn the sound down (though you know this will cost you extra).

He is also uncertain about the iced sour cherry soup. You assure him that the sour cherry soup will be well received, though not everyone will be willing to taste it because it is so different in appearance and flavor. The older generation will love it. Younger guests will be suspicious. You remind him that it will be a very elegant beginning. Chuck finally agrees and says that you can make the reservation firm since he is putting a check in the mail today.

You mark your calendar from pencil to ink, complete your notes on the Roast affair and put the file away for four weeks. After you receive the deposit, call the musicians and the ice sculptor to reserve September 16. You will have to send a deposit to these subcontractors; others you will pay at the end of the event.

2.2 The middle phase: Planning and organization

On September 2, two weeks before the Roast party, you retrieve the file and take a look at the menu to refresh your memory. Is there anything you need to order ahead of time? No, there are no unusual or exotic ingredients that you cannot get from your usual sources. However, it is time to reserve the subcontractors. All of them are people you have worked with before; they all give you a 10 percent discount. The only exception is the country western band with whom you have already made arrangements after talking with Chuck Roast. This is a four-piece band, the Bellowing Bisons, with a female vocalist. They agreed very reluctantly to turn the volume way down. They will cost more than The Squealing Pig Quartet, so you need the client's approval.

NOW IT IS TIME TO RESERVE ALL THE SUBCONTRACTORS WHO WILL PROVIDE THE CAKE, THE FLOWERS, RENTAL EQUIPMENT, AND A LIMOUSINE.

Now it is time to reserve all the subcontractors who will provide the cake, the flowers, rental equipment, and a limousine, giving the sub-contractors an exact guest count (subject to change), the address, and any special instructions. The limousine will pick Mrs. Roast up at a friend's house. She thinks they will then pick up Chuck Roast and take both of them to an unspecified restaurant for dinner. The surprise is that she will be dropped off at her home with 34 guests and her loving husband waiting.

Reserve your staff. Curry will be your bartender again, and Cinnamon will be your chef. You'll help her plate the food in the kitchen, and Clove, Pepper, and a new helper, Chili, will be the servers. You reserve them tentatively, but since no firm schedule is set yet, you postpone telling them the exact hours of work until a few days later.

It is time to put the schedule on paper so the staff can plan their time. Sample 12 shows your planned schedule.

The numbers on the Friday schedule are estimated hours needed for each job. A total of 6.25 hours should finish the preparation. The Thursday hours are not specified since nothing is very time-consuming. Two and a half to three hours should complete the job; you will be doing this yourself. Departure time on Friday, considering rush-hour traffic and the fairly distant location, should be 4:20 p.m. Even if traffic is heavy, 30 minutes should be sufficient to get there and by 5:30 p.m. everything should be unloaded and organized in the kitchen.

John Dough Catering Company
35 Batter Rd
Crepeville, CA 94066

August 3, 20--

Mr. Chuck Roast
The Law Firm of Partridge, Squid, and Roast
1 Meat Avenue
Butcherville, CA 94067

Dear Mr. Roast:

It was my pleasure to meet with you yesterday regarding your plans for a surprise birthday party for your wife on September 16th. I can assure you that we will do our best to help you give Mrs. Roast and the invited guests a great meal with a beautiful presentation. Here is my tentative suggestion for the menu:

- Hors d'oeuvres: fresh-baked artichoke kisses, steamed marinated jumbo shrimp in snow peas and our own pesto torta with cracker squares (these will be passed around by the servers)
- Iced sour cherry soup served in melon halves
- Boneless fresh Atlantic salmon fillet with chopped eggs and dill in individual paper packets
- Pork tenderloin medallions with peppers in paprika sauce
- Seasonal vegetables
- Rosemary linguini
- Fresh-baked Italian bread, rolls, and butter
- Light chocolate cake with raspberry and Bavarian custard filling, decorated with fresh flowers (no inscription)
- Bite-sized fruit tartlets and lemon-walnut cookies
- Choice of fresh coffee and teas

The prices for 36 guests are as follows:

Food	@$31.50	$1,134.00
Dinner china, glass, silver	@$3.25	117.00
Ice sculpture		200.00
Flowers		180.00

5 tables @ $7.00, 36 chairs @ $1.00	71.00
Linens	53.00
Bartending service, including ice, fruit, bar glassware	121.00
Chocolate cake	120.00
Yard decoration and bar rental	285.00
Music, The Squealing Pig Quartet	320.00
Limousine	225.00
Subtotal	$2,826.00
15% catering service charge on food/beverage	170.10
7.75% tax on subtotal	219.02
Estimated total	$3,215.12

All setup will be completed before guests arrive at 6:00 p.m. We will start serving hors d'oeuvres by 6:30 p.m., giving early guests time to order drinks first. Champagne will be ready for toasting by 6:45 p.m., when Mrs. Roast is expected to arrive by limousine. Dinner will be served at about 7:30 p.m. We will have one bartender who will also help pour wine at the tables during dinner, a chef and a helper in the kitchen, and three servers. At the end of the meal, the kitchen will be cleaned up and refuse removed. Rental items will be stacked by the back door, ready to be picked up the next morning. The Squealing Pig Quartet will play from 7:00 p.m. to 10:00 p.m. with two short breaks. We will supply everything for the party except beverages, which will be supplied by you.

We have tentatively reserved September 16 for you. As soon as we receive half of the estimated total as a deposit, the reservation will be firm. We would like to know the final number of guests by September 11, though variations of up to three are acceptable until September 13. The price for the food is based on 36 guests. Since we have to reserve several subcontractors, we would appreciate hearing from you as soon as possible.

The weather should be pleasant on the date of the event, but if the forecast is for rain, we will arrange for tents to be brought in and set up.

Thank you for asking John Dough Catering to serve you. We will do everything possible to make Mrs. Roast's 40th birthday a memorable event.

Sincerely,

John Dough

John Dough, Chef/Owner
John Dough Catering

PREPARATION SCHEDULE FOR THE FULL-SERVICE DINNER

Prior	**Wednesday, 9/14**	
Prep marinade for shrimp	Defrost shrimp	
Order cake	Boil 4 eggs for salmon	
	Pastry for tartlets	
	Cookie dough	

Thursday, 9/15	**Friday, 9/16**	**Time (hours)**
Steam and marinate shrimp	Finish shrimp	0.5
Pesto torta	Artichoke kiss	1.0
Cherry soup	Tray pesto torta	0.25
Peel, chop eggs	Melon for soup	0.5
Bake tartlets	Prepare salmon	0.75
Invoice	Prepare, cook pork	1.0
Collect equipment	Pick up bread	0.5
	Bake cookies	0.5
	Tray dessert	0.25
	Load contingencies	1.0
	Fruit for bar	_____
	Total time	6.25

Ask Chili and Pepper to meet you at the Roast residence at 5:00 p.m. on the 16th. Chili, who has not worked for you before, needs to be reminded to wear a tuxedo shirt with black slacks. You tell him that you will bring the bow ties and aprons. Even though Chili appears to be reliable and was highly recommended to you, you have no experience with him, a slight cause for worry.

Clove, the third server, will take care of the torches and decorations, so she is instructed to arrive at 4:00 p.m. Rental equipment, including a portable bar and torches, will be delivered earlier the same day. (Mr. Roast has arranged for Tender to be away from the house for the full day).

You schedule Curry to be at the residence at 5:00 p.m. to set up the bar. It will take close to an hour to complete the job, including glassware. The fruits for drink garnishes will be prepared before you leave your kitchen. Cinnamon will be putting in about six hours in the kitchen doing the bulk of the dinner preparation. You will assist her as needed.

Flowers, the ice sculpture, and cake will be delivered by 5:00 p.m. Musicians will arrive at 5:45 p.m., and start playing at 6:30 p.m.

The next step is to prepare your supply list. Ordering on Monday, September 12, is adequate as this is a fairly easy, small dinner party. Sample 13 shows the order list.

This list does not include every ingredient you will need to prepare the menu. Spices and herbs are on the shelf. Before purchasing the supplies, you check the shelves for anything already available to eliminate duplication.

You'll need several shopping trips. Some supplies will be needed early in the week. The fresh produce and dairy products should be purchased on Thursday. Another buying trip is needed on Friday for the fresh bread, and the individually wrapped butter patties need to be taken out of the freezer. You always have a supply of those on hand.

2.3 The final phase: Day of the event

Your chef, Cinnamon, arrives at 10:00 a.m. on Friday. You give her a rundown of the menu and let her work at her own speed to have everything complete by 3:45 p.m. You take care of the bread pickup, loading the truck with equipment, and other basics, including the halved melons. She can do the rest comfortably.

The shrimp is marinated. One snow pea split in two will be wrapped around each, secured with a toothpick and stuck into half a red cabbage. Extras are transported in a covered pan. The artichoke kisses are prepared and half baked. The pesto torta is trayed, garnished, ready to be passed around, accompanied by crackers in a tiny basket.

The salmon fillet is cut into small serving pieces, allowing two ounces per person. Most guests will take a pork tenderloin as well, also in two-ounce pieces. If a guest doesn't eat pork, he or she can take two or more pieces of salmon. There are 40 servings of the salmon. Each piece is put on a square of parchment, sprinkled with chopped boiled egg and fresh dill, and closed to form a cute little packet. They will be baked just before serving. It only takes 12 to 14 minutes in a hot oven.

ORDER LIST

Item	Recipe file	Scale of Original Recipe
Artichoke kisses	p. 45	0.2X
Shrimp	p. 40	
Pesto torta	p. 50	0.5X
Crackers		
Cherry soup	p. 20	3.0X
Melon		
Salmon	p. 61	3.0X
Pork	p. 12	3.0X
Vegetables		
Linguini		
Bread/butter to pick up		
Cake ordered		
Fruit tartlet	p. 27	1.0X
Lemon cookies	p. 21	1.0X
Coffee, tea, cream		

Produce

2 lb onion
1 bu. scallion
50 large snow peas
1 bu. basil
1 bu. dill
1 bu. tarragon
1 red cabbage
4 lemons
2 limes
18 melons
1 lb red pepper
1 lb green pepper
7 lb mixed vegetable with entrée
Garnish for hors d'oeuvres

Meat

4 lb shrimp (21–25 count black tiger)
5 lb salmon fillet
5 lb pork tenderloin

Dairy

4 oz Parmesan
1 c. heavy cream
Cream for coffee
8 eggs
1 lb cream cheese
1 lb unsalted butter

Other

1 lb phyllo dough
25 oz marinated artichoke hearts
Crackers for pesto torta
3 lb canned sour cherries
1 bot. red wine for soup
24 oz tomato paste
4 lb linguini
50 lb ice

The pork is half finished. It will take about 20 minutes of cooking on site to finish it. Pasta can also be cooked in the host's kitchen. Freshly chopped rosemary is taken in a plastic wrap to be added to the pasta right after cooking. Vegetables are blanched and ready to be sautéed on site with garlic and fresh tarragon. They only take ten minutes to heat through and finish cooking.

The cherry soup is finished, resting calmly in the refrigerator. Heavy cream and the red wine need to be swirled into it as a final touch just before serving. Dessert will be trayed on-site and passed to guests. This is in addition to the cake, an extra touch, and most people will take one or the other. Some will take both. The cake will be cut in small portions.

You have scheduled enough helpers, so the bread can be sliced on-site, stacked in baskets for each table along with butter. The servers will replenish them as needed.

All is going according to plan. At the last minute it occurs to you that you neglected to provide some garnish for the soup. Is one needed? There is enough heavy cream, for example, to whip some up and add a tiny dab on top of each serving. Or a thin half slice of lemon could be hung on the edge of the scooped-out melon half in which the soup will be served. You confer with Cinnamon. She says no, it is overkill. The soup will be served in a fruit bowl and it is a dark-colored, unusual-looking soup. Anything extra will be too garish.

By 3:30 p.m. everything is just about complete. You and your crew have just enough time to give the kitchen a quick cleanup.

By 4:00 p.m. the truck is loaded except for a few things in the refrigerator and freezer, for which you have a separate checklist. You know that Clove is very reliable, and she will take care of everything at the Roast residence. Nevertheless, you are anxious to leave. You and Cinnamon go through the checklist of the menu one more time, then take the frozen and refrigerated items out and place them in the cooler on the truck. According to health regulations, any potentially spoilable food should maintain a temperature of less than 45°F (7°C) in transit. In this case, the shrimp and the salmon are the only potential hazards during a 30-minute transit. But you want to serve the pesto torta and the soup cold, too. They all fit in the cooler along with the 50 pounds of ice for Curry, the bartender.

You and Cinnamon have changed into your uniforms and are ready to leave shortly after 4:00 p.m. To your surprise, the Friday rush-hour

DESSERT WILL BE TRAYED ON-SITE AND PASSED TO GUESTS. THIS IS IN ADDITION TO THE CAKE, AN EXTRA TOUCH, AND MOST PEOPLE WILL TAKE ONE OR THE OTHER.

traffic is not too bad. Still, you drive at a respectably slow speed in consideration of your precious cargo. When you arrive at the party site at 4:40 p.m., the decorations are in place, the cake and ice sculpture have just arrived, and a few minutes later you see the rest of your staff driving up. Mr. Roast is not ready yet but comes out to greet the staff and tells you to do whatever you want, the house is now yours. He shows you where the trash is and the two refrigerators, one of which is half empty. The other is filled with champagne, wine, and a variety of other chilled drinks. Curry will soon take care of emptying that one, too.

By 5:15 p.m. the truck is unloaded, Cinnamon is busy in the kitchen, Curry is setting up the bar, and everyone else is working on the tables, chairs, linen, and silverware. The china remains in the kitchen. By 5:45 p.m. everything is done, including setting up the ice sculpture, flowers, and cake, and the place looks fabulous. The band is just setting up. They have brought their huge sound system. Will the lowest level still be too loud for a quiet conversation? It doesn't matter so much by the middle of the party when people have had enough to drink and the level of conversation is no longer quiet, but at least during the early part of the dinner the music should be kept at low volume.

A few minutes before 6:00 p.m. the bell rings; several guests have arrived already. You check progress in the kitchen and all seems fine. The shrimp and pesto torta are ready, the artichoke will not need to go into the oven until close to 6:30 p.m. Cinnamon does not need to do much with dinner until close to 7:00 p.m. Even though dinner is scheduled for 7:30 p.m., chances are it will not be served until later. These leisurely parties never stay on schedule.

By 6:30 p.m. the place is humming and so is the band. Surprisingly enough, the music is pleasant, relatively soft country ballads, very nice as background music. The female vocalist is excellent. The bar is busy, and you decide to wait with the food until more people arrive. You know that everything is ready in the kitchen. The oven was turned on 15 minutes ago, and the artichoke kisses will only take five minutes to bake.

Pepper reminds you that Tender should be arriving in ten minutes, and shouldn't we serve the hors d'oeuvres. You agree and the two servers appear with two trays, passing the food. All seems well so far. The hors d'oeuvres go fast, people seem to be hungry but there is a lot left in the kitchen. Only about half of the kisses have been baked. They are light, so they can be served even shortly before dinner without spoiling appetites.

The limousine arrives exactly on schedule at 6:45 p.m. Everyone is waiting at the front door and Curry has 36 champagne glasses ready inside on two trays. She will start with five bottles of champagne that are open and one bottle of nonalcoholic fizzy drink. That should be enough for the first round. The surprise for Tender is successful. Curry and the three servers pour and distribute the champagne for the toast. In just a few minutes everyone has a glass in hand. Curry returns to the bar and leaves several bottles of champagne with the servers for refills.

You check the kitchen. The water is ready to boil for the pasta, and the pork is being finished slowly. The melons are ready for the soup and the plates are stacked up, ready to be garnished once the soup is served. That will be your job. Everything else is last-minute preparation.

Check with Chuck Roast about dinner plans. He says he would prefer to postpone it a little since no one seems to be ready to break up the socializing. You and Chuck agree on 7:45 p.m. That means that the entrée won't be served until nearly 8:15 p.m., so you inform the chef of the new schedule. She agrees to put the salmon in the oven at 8:00 p.m., as well as the bread to warm up. The pasta can be cooked at 7:45 p.m., ready to be served by 8:00 p.m. (it holds well), and the vegetables can also be started at 7:45 p.m.

At 7:35 p.m. the soup is served in the melon half-shells and placed on the table at each place setting. Bread baskets and butter are put on each table, water glasses are filled with ice and water. Two servers distribute them; the third one is still passing the hors d'oeuvres, making sure that the host and Mrs. Roast are always served from a fresh plate.

The soup, like any unusual food, is a mixed success. Shortly after 8 o'clock the soup containers are collected and water glasses are refilled. Curry and one server are filling the wine glasses. Everyone else is in the kitchen helping to plate the entrée. The 36 plates are laid out on the counters and tables, and each one is garnished. The whole job takes four or five minutes. On every plate a packet of salmon, a portion of pork medallion, pasta, and vegetables are placed in a beautiful, colorful arrangement. As soon as half a dozen plates are finished (in less than a minute), they are taken out by the servers. Wine has been poured, so all three servers can work on the distribution of dinner. Another six plates are ready by the time the servers return for them.

Everyone has been instructed on what the food is. If a guest prefers no pork or no fish, then Cinnamon can make up a separate plate which is delivered with the next set. In less than ten minutes, the entire dinner

AS SOON AS HALF A DOZEN PLATES ARE FINISHED (IN LESS THAN A MINUTE), THEY ARE TAKEN OUT BY THE SERVERS.

is plated and served. It is time to replenish the water glasses, wine, bread, and butter. The pressure is off. The remainder of the meal should be slow and leisurely.

It is close to 9:00 p.m. by the time plates can be collected. A few of the guests ask for seconds. The amount of food left on the plates tells you a lot. If it is too much, you either served too large portions or they didn't like the food.

It is time again to refresh the wine glasses; there is no hurry with dessert. The coffee pots are ready, both regular and decaffeinated, and the electric kettle is plugged in to boil water for tea. In a few minutes the tables are rechecked to make sure nothing from dinner is left before the coffee is served.

By 9:15 p.m. the guests are ready for coffee. While Cinnamon is organizing the kitchen, you and the three servers distribute coffee with cream and sugar and tell guests that both black tea and a variety of herbal teas are available. Several prefer tea, so you bring out tea bags neatly arranged on a plate for choice. When someone makes a choice, you take the tea bag back to the kitchen, pour freshly boiling water over it in a cup, and bring it back to the guest.

You tell Mr. Roast that it is time to cut the cake. After a brief cere-mony and many good wishes, Tender cuts the first slice and Curry fin-ishes cutting 36 servings. They are distributed quickly and the fruit tartlets and cookies are passed by two servers. As predicted, almost everyone takes one or the other, or even both, in addition to the piece of cake in front of them.

By 10 p.m. no one wants to eat or drink anything more. The servers collect the plates and only leave the coffee cups on the tables. The kitchen is in good shape. All dinner china is rinsed and in bus tubs. With everyone helping, the rest of the china, silverware, and glasses can be put into crates fairly quickly.

By 11:00 p.m. most guests are gone. The band is packing up, the tables are cleared, and the truck is half loaded. Pay the balance due to the band, complimenting them on the very good job they did. By 11:15 p.m. only a few guests are left, probably close friends. Ask Mr. Roast if he would like to keep some extra food. He says yes, so Cinnamon wraps up a generous portion of leftovers and puts it in the refrigerator. The remainder of the cake is also wrapped and stored in the refrigerator. Other food is placed in the truck by the servers. In the meantime, you hand your invoice to Mr. Roast, who compliments you on a very successful event and superb food.

He returns in a few minutes with a check for the balance due. After verifying that the kitchen is scrupulously clean and neat, checking the refrigerator, the freezer, and for any of the catering utensils or equipment that may have been forgotten, you take one more look to make sure all the rental equipment is in crates and stacked neatly in one pile, ready to be picked up. You say farewell to Mrs. Roast and depart with the staff. The time is now 11:40 p.m. Back at the kitchen the truck is unloaded, extra food is quickly put in the refrigerator to be sorted out tomorrow, and dirty dishes are put in the sink to soak. It is well past midnight. The facilities are ready to be locked up.

There are two to three hours of work left to clean up equipment and the kitchen, put everything back in its proper place, and store or discard leftover food. There are also a few tasks in the office: mark the file, mentally check off the menu to see if any notations need to be added to the recipes regarding either portions or ingredients. Then add the gross earnings to your books, mark down staff time, pay the various subcontractor bills, and send a thank-you note to Mr. Roast.

You made a very good profit on this event. Adding to your own profit is 10 percent of each subcontractor's invoice. You planned it well, organized it down to the finest detail, and executed it perfectly with a good team. You deserve your profit.

BACK AT THE KITCHEN THE TRUCK IS UNLOADED, EXTRA FOOD IS QUICKLY PUT IN THE REFRIGERATOR TO BE SORTED OUT TOMORROW, AND DIRTY DISHES ARE PUT IN THE SINK TO SOAK.

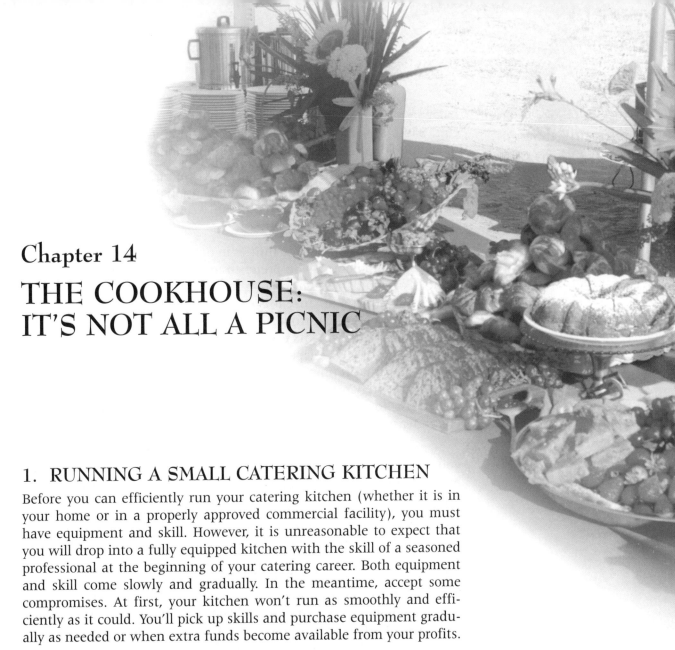

Chapter 14
THE COOKHOUSE: IT'S NOT ALL A PICNIC

1. RUNNING A SMALL CATERING KITCHEN

Before you can efficiently run your catering kitchen (whether it is in your home or in a properly approved commercial facility), you must have equipment and skill. However, it is unreasonable to expect that you will drop into a fully equipped kitchen with the skill of a seasoned professional at the beginning of your catering career. Both equipment and skill come slowly and gradually. In the meantime, accept some compromises. At first, your kitchen won't run as smoothly and efficiently as it could. You'll pick up skills and purchase equipment gradually as needed or when extra funds become available from your profits.

Let's assume that when you first start your business, you'll be in the process of acquiring many of the necessary physical skills for food preparation and cooking. Let's also assume that for quite some time now you have been busy testing recipes and accumulating a store of cooking and kitchen reference books. These activities are essential, no matter what sort of catering you have chosen.

2. RECIPES

Learn to write recipes in an abbreviated, professional way. You'll soon have enough cooking experience to need a minimum of explanation to

ONCE YOU BEGIN
COLLECTING RECIPES IN
EARNEST, YOU'LL SOON
REALIZE THAT YOU
NEED AN EXCELLENT
SYSTEM OF
ORGANIZING AND
RETRIEVING THEM.

follow a recipe. Often, the recipe becomes a mere checklist of ingredients. Sample 14 shows a simple recipe written for a novice. Compare it to Sample 15, a recipe written for the professional.

As you can see, the second recipe is written in shorthand style, giving you ingredients and pointers on preparation. You know the rest. The preparation is slightly altered for quantity commercial cooking, but the results will be the same.

What measure you list quantities in on your recipes depends on you and your equipment. If you prefer to use scales, use weight measurements. For liquids, use cups. For quantity cooking, weight is the most convenient method because it is easy to check and it is easy to scale a basic recipe up or down from the amounts indicated. Most commercial kitchens deal with weights even for liquid ingredients. Never write "to taste" on any of your recipes; it is hard to scale up or down. It will add to your preparation time when you have to think about how much salt to add to a french vanilla cream written for eight portions if salt is shown as "to taste." Change it to a definite quantity, perhaps one-eighth teaspoon; that way, 40 portions will be five-eighths teaspoon.

Once you begin collecting recipes in earnest, you'll soon realize that you need an excellent system of organizing and retrieving them. If you are a good organizer, develop your own system. Put recipes on a computer if you have easy access to one at all times, but you'll still need hard copies for kitchen use. Both professionals and nonprofessionals tend to organize recipes by class of food: meats, soups, desserts. That is how cookbooks are organized, too. However, there are other systems. The one that I use is especially suitable for commercial operations:

- Collect recipes in random order in any form you wish — loose leaf binder, index card, bound book, whatever you have. Number each page or card. Compile a master file in which each recipe is listed under the standard headings: soups, salads, chicken, fish, etc. You may want to divide each of these headings into subheadings. For desserts, for example, you can have subheadings for cookies, cakes, pies, miscellaneous pastries, and basic preparations.

- Only the name of the recipe and its page number appear in the master file. Of course, references can be made to cookbooks on your shelf, too. Just choose a brief name for each by title or author and the appropriate page number. To illustrate, say you are looking for a recipe for Bavarian Trifle. Open the master file

RECIPE FOR THE NOVICE COOK

HUNGARIAN CHICKEN PAPRIKA

1 cut-up chicken, about 3 pounds

1 chopped medium onion

3 Tbsp vegetable oil

4 tsp Hungarian paprika

1 tsp salt

1 chopped medium green pepper

1 chopped medium tomato or 1 Tbsp tomato paste

2 Tbsp sour cream

2 Tbsp flour

Brown onion and chicken pieces in the oil in a heavy pan over medium heat. Turn heat to low, sprinkle with paprika and salt, and stir until chicken is thoroughly covered with paprika. Cover pan and sauté on low heat with steam from chicken for 30 minutes.

Add tomato and green pepper, cover pan and continue cooking for another 30 minutes on low heat, stirring occasionally. Add a little water, if necessary, if there is not enough liquid in the pan.

Meanwhile, stir flour into sour cream in a small bowl with a wire whip or spoon, slowly adding some hot liquid from chicken until it forms a thin, smooth paste. Remove chicken pieces from pot, gently stir sour cream/flour paste into sauce, and heat slowly until almost boiling, stirring continually. Turn heat very low, continue stirring until sauce thickens. Return chicken pieces to pot, heat once more slowly. Serve over hot poppy seed noodles or spaetzle, accompanied by traditional Hungarian sweet-sour marinated cucumber.

Serves 4–5.

HUNGARIAN CHICKEN PAPRIKA

20 8-oz chicken breasts	1 lb chopped tomato or 1 c paste
24 oz chopped onion	½ c sour cream
5 T Hungarian paprika	¼ c flour
4 t salt	
24 oz chopped pepper	

Brown chicken breasts in oven. Sauté onion. Add paprika, salt, cook for few minutes, add tomato, pepper, cook 30". Blend sour cream, flour, little sauce, combine with rest of sauce. Pour over chicken, cook 30" in 300°F convect. oven or on range. Serves 20.

to Desserts. Trifles are found under the Miscellaneous subcategory since they don't fit into any other standard dessert preparation. It takes you 15 seconds to discover that Bavarian Trifle is on page 52 of your collection. Open the collection book (or card box) to page 52. In less than a minute, you have found the recipe. It is an excellent idea to have your own recipes on a computer as well as in two master files kept in separate locations.

The advantage of this system is that your collection can be completely random as long as either the pages or the recipes are numbered. It is foolproof, except when you cannot recall the name of the recipe or what category you put it under. This is when a computer comes in handy and wins over the manual system. Cross-indexing in your master file is advisable when something is ambiguous, for instance a lemon-herb salad dressing that can also be used as a dip should be listed under both salad dressings and dips.

When you are collecting new recipes, which should be a continual process, keep in mind the broad areas they should fall into. Think twice before keeping a new recipe if it cannot fit in any of your major food categories.

Your personal catering recipe collection, tested, revised, and modified over years, is an invaluable asset to your business. Losing your collection is something you cannot afford. It needs to be protected like any other valuable business asset. First of all, to protect the written recipe for everyday use, each page should be separate from the rest of the material so when you or your kitchen staff use a recipe in the kitchen, just that single page or index card leaves your office. If the page falls into the boiling minestrone soup, all you have to replace is that single page — no great tragedy. (The soup is fine, too.) But if the whole collection falls in, you have a much more serious issue.

Second, each page should be protected individually from spillage in the kitchen. Ideally, it should be sealed in a transparent, washable cover. While permanent sealing is the best protection, it also prevents you from adding remarks on timing, baking temperatures, serving sizes, and so on. Recipes in a good kitchen evolve continuously. No recipe is permanent; it should change with time, following food trends as well as changes in your own taste. Various transparent protection covers that the page or card can be slipped into are available in all sizes. They're a must since you can't avoid all spills no matter how careful you are.

Third, you should have a backup copy of your recipe collection at your home or at a location other than the main collection in case of fire, theft, flooding, or whatever. Treat your collection as one of your most important documents. Update it regularly with the notations you make when using the originals. The backup may be hard copies or on CD-ROM, and I keep mine in a safe. Losing an only copy is a tragedy for a caterer. I cannot emphasize strongly enough to keep one or more backup copies of all your recipes in a safe place.

Prepare a collection of menus from your recipes for different occasions; such lists make your job easy when discussing food items with a client. For example, have lists of breakfast dishes; lunch and brunch suggestions; lists of recipes for a specific ethnicity; a list for bar mitzvah and bat mitzvah; for picnics; for vegetarians, and so on. Examples of catering recipes are included on the CD-ROM enclosed with this book.

3. LABELING

Run your kitchen as if it were a laboratory as far as labeling is concerned. Every item in the freezer and refrigerator should be labeled and dated. This is also true for your regular shelf items; nothing can be left unlabeled.

Make sure that when food is prepared for an event, everything is also labeled as to which event it was prepared for. This may sound like an unnecessary step when you only have one event, but it looks better

I CANNOT EMPHASIZE STRONGLY ENOUGH TO KEEP ONE OR MORE BACKUP COPIES OF ALL YOUR RECIPES IN A SAFE PLACE.

when it is delivered to a client's home or office, suggesting a busy caterer's kitchen where several parties were prepared that day. That little unnecessary step may be a good client relation strategy.

This procedure is an absolute necessity when two or more events are being prepared during busy periods. It is important to read those labels with great care when loading the truck.

For one holiday party, someone was not careful enough and our wonderful freshly prepared cranberry sauce ended up on the wrong truck even though everything was meticulously labeled. It was meant to accompany a holiday turkey at a private, full-service dinner for about 30 guests. The meal was lavish, elegant, and beautiful. But there was no cranberry sauce anywhere. We didn't have much choice; someone quickly got in the truck (left on the street so no one could block it!) and ran off to the nearest supermarket for a few cans of mediocre cranberry sauce. The guests were grazing on their salad and the next course was due in a few minutes. No one could see our horrible crime of opening cans of cranberry sauce for the high-priced dinner. Since opening cans is an unusual occurrence, a can opener is something that we don't carry with us. However, we discovered an electric one sitting on the counter in front of us. We thought our troubles were over until we tried to operate it. It gave out a horrible screech and whine that could be heard by the whole neighborhood. Conversation stopped for a moment in the dining room until the host stood up and announced that it was just the can opener. He came in the kitchen to assist us. We were thoroughly embarrassed but he neither noticed what we were opening nor cared. The dinner was good enough that the third-rate cranberry sauce probably was not noticed very much. The nice homemade sauce was brought back from the other event and devoured by the staff. It was good!

4. CONTINUING YOUR EDUCATION

Continue collecting information from any source that suits you, whether it is magazines, new cookbooks, foreign cookbooks, your own old books, or the Internet (for web surfing, see suggestions and some websites on the accompanying CD-ROM). On your shelf alone there are thousands of untried recipes. Your changing recipe collection is a major marketing tool in the fierce competition among caterers.

Think about the staggering number of new cookbooks appearing every year, with hundreds of recipes in each, plus scores of food magazines with their own hundreds of recipes, not to mention the Internet food and cooking sites. But after you compare those many new recipes to the basics, you will quickly come to the conclusion that new recipes are not new at all.

Many recipes, especially desserts, are virtually the same in many cookbooks, with nothing more than a change of name and possibly a few minor changes in ingredients. Many of the new recipes are adaptations of older, standard recipes with trendier titles. "Spaghetti with tomato sauce and meatballs" becomes "angel hair pasta with ground eye of round smothered in Italian spring tomato sauce and herbs." Same thing, but the spaghetti was changed to a thinner cousin, angel hair pasta (previously known as vermicelli), with virtually no difference in flavor or appearance.

There are a few cookbooks with really new recipe collections, written by people who were able to successfully create their own new concoctions. Those are the books you're looking for, books that suit your taste and style. These will be the cornerstone of your research for new ideas. You can sometimes use the recipes as they are written, but more often you have to modify them to your taste and style. Don't blindly trust any cookbook. Your well-tested favorites are fine, but treat any new ones with caution. Some of them have obvious errors in them, which is bad news when you are testing recipes.

Even after you have tried out a recipe, the product may turn out quite differently than predicted. The more you know about food and cooking, the more likely you can predict the outcome of a new recipe and errors that you may make with a difficult preparation. Here is a simple example.

I was in charge of a church dinner once as a volunteer. The expected guests numbered 180. I planned the dessert to be fresh-baked lemon bars, a simple recipe with only a few ingredients producing very delicious, traditional lemon bars. Anyone with a minimum of baking skill can produce this recipe with minimal effort. I bought the ingredients for 180 servings, divided them into nine equal portions, and gave each portion to one of the nine volunteer bakers along with a photocopied recipe that gave instructions on how to prepare it in a standard 9" x 13" baking pan. Each person was to cut the dessert into 24 squares, plate them, dust them with icing sugar, then bring them to the dinner.

The results were totally astonishing. It was as if nine completely different recipes had been used. They looked vaguely similar, and with a few exceptions they all tasted good, although unexpectedly different.

DON'T BLINDLY TRUST ANY COOKBOOK. YOUR WELL-TESTED FAVORITES ARE FINE, BUT TREAT ANY NEW ONES WITH CAUTION.

MAKE SURE THAT ALL
YOUR KNIVES ARE
RAZOR SHARP ANY
TIME YOU USE THEM.

And the difference could have been due to only two factors: oven temperature and preparation. (Or did a few bakers keep the unsalted butter I bought and substitute margarine?)

Learning on the job is by far the best and most pleasant way to continue your education. But it is often by trial and error, a slow way of learning, as well as somewhat risky with your client's food. Learning through formal training is another way. Advanced cooking classes can be useful and from time to time classes are given specifically for caterers. Unfortunately, these are mostly geared for large caterers and hotel catering services. Nevertheless, useful information can be picked up at these workshops and seminars. Of course, they are costly.

5. SHARPENING

As mentioned in Chapter 5, sharp knives are the single most important tool for a chef or caterer. There is nothing you can do efficiently without them, unless your catering business is based on buying and reselling ready-made food products.

From your experience as a cook, you probably know the importance of having very sharp knives at all times. Sharp knives can be fully controlled; you know the result of each cut you make. Dull knives can slip and cut fingers.

You have probably attempted to use knives in other people's kitchens on occasion, and you may well wonder how they manage to cut butter with those knives. As a matter of fact, dull and poor-quality knives may be the single biggest reason why many people hate to work in the kitchen.

Make sure that all your knives are razor sharp any time you use them. If you have watched professional chefs and butchers work, you know they sharpen their knives often, every 15 minutes or half hour when working with them continuously. They can work faster and more safely with less effort, and they know it.

A good way to make certain your knife is sharp is to try dicing tomatoes. Tomato skin is tough; a not-quite-sharp knife has problems penetrating it. You have to exert pressure. A sharp knife cuts through a tomato as easily as through a ripe peach, with no effort and a minimum of pressure.

You can always send your knives out to have them sharpened, but it is much better to learn how to do it yourself. That way, your knives are always available when you need them. All you need is a sharpening stone and a sharpening steel (or ceramic). It is easy to resharpen knives provided they weren't misused or nicked, or left until they became very dull. For dull or nicked knives, power grinding is necessary to restore the original bevel (angle or slant) of the blade. You can achieve the same with a file and plenty of elbow grease.

THERE IS A DIFFERENCE BETWEEN SHARPENING AND HONING A KNIFE.

There is a difference between sharpening and honing a knife. A sharpening device, whether electric or manual, resharpens the steel of the knife by an abrasive action. A steel or ceramic honer does not sharpen but realigns the steel. After cutting with a knife for some time, the edge of the knife is no longer a straight line but becomes microscopically serrated — the knife feels dull. Pulling the edge a few times across the honing device as butchers do every few minutes realigns the edge and the knife is sharp again. Constant honing is the key to easy kitchen cutting, but sharpening is not necessary for several weeks or until honing no longer results in a razor-sharp knife.

Remember, too, that eventually sharpening steels lose their fine steel ridges and won't effectively hone your knives. Don't use a steel that seems to have too little resistance when a knife is drawn against it. It may be too old to do much good.

Three different cutting edges or bevels are used on common kitchen knives. The heavy French knife, your basic tool, has a V-shaped grind, the tip of the V coming to a sharp, very thin point in cross-sectional view of the blade. The edge that comes to a sharp point combined with a heavy blade will give you the sharpness and strength needed to do a lot of chopping. The carving knife has a thinner blade and the cross-sectional V-shape is narrower. This is called the hollow grind. Thanks to the thin blade, this knife is even sharper than the French knife, but it lacks the strength, so it is only used for carving reasonably soft food items. There is also a concave grind for even thinner bladed knives that are not used much in catering kitchens.

The first two knives mentioned above are the most useful for you. Don't worry about how to achieve a V-shape, hollow, or concave grind. Just sharpen the knife well and try to keep the original configuration of the blade.

The sharpening stone, or whetstone, can be used two ways: sharpen with a moist stone, dipping the stone into water often while sharpening, or keep an oil stone. If you use an oil stone, you don't need to add anything to it. To make the oil stone, soak a stone in light machine oil for several hours. Lift it out of the oil, wipe it clean, and you have an oil stone. Keep it in a plastic bag so dust won't settle on it, otherwise it may become clogged.

Most stones have a coarse and a fine surface. When your knife is quite dull, start sharpening on the coarse side, keeping the blade at the original angle against the stone. As soon as it appears sharper, switch over to the fine side and continue sharpening. For larger knives it is easier to hold the stone against the blade. For smaller knives, hold the knife against the stone. Keep up a good pressure on the blade, but gradually ease off the pressure until you just barely push the blade against the stone. For a sharp knife that only needs keening of the edge, the process takes 30 seconds. For a duller knife, it takes a minute or two.

A sharp edge becomes dull from contact with the cutting surface. Try not to cut on hard surfaces such as metal, pottery, or glass. Hard surfaces cause knives to dull fast. Wood is the gentlest surface for knives; plastic cutting boards are in between.

As the blade touches the cutting surface, the very fine cutting edge bends slightly on a microscopic scale and eventually loses its razor edge. To restore it while working with the knife, you don't need the whetstone. Just stroke the blade against the chef's steel for 15 seconds. Start with good pressure, then ease the pressure off gradually. Try this when cutting several pounds of tomatoes. Start with a sharpened knife and resharpen with a steel after dicing about two pounds of tomatoes. You can notice the difference immediately.

Whetstones are only used occasionally, when the edge of the knife is duller than a steel can remedy. You will be able to tell when it is time for the stone as you get used to working with well-sharpened knives.

A serrated knife rarely needs sharpening, but don't use it on anything other than fairly soft food material. It will keep its edge for a very long time. There is a special sharpening steel available for serrated knives, but it isn't commonly available. A well-equipped hardware store may have one if you feel the need for it. However, I find that a few pulls over a honing steel resharpen a serrated knife better than any other method.

The blade of a food processor also needs sharpening just like your knives. When it is used often, sharpen it often with a whetstone. Food processor blades have one beveled edge and one flat. When sharpening, keep these original angles. Sharpen the beveled edge only, and when it is sharp, pass the whetstone gently over the other flat side of the blade a few times to get rid of the rough surface that the whetstone produces while sharpening the beveled side. When cutting large quantities of certain acidic foods (such as parsley), manufacturers recommend resharpening the blade frequently.

One more item that should be sharp is the vegetable peeler. Replace it soon as it does not peel with the lightest touch.

If you don't yet know how to sharpen knives, learn how, either by yourself or have someone else show you the technique. Get into the habit of using these sharpening devices continually while working with knives. The habit will make your work much more efficient.

6. KITCHEN SUPPLIES: SHELF LIFE

Replenish all your supplies as soon as they get low. It is a sin, and a major dent in efficiency, to run out of a critical item in the middle of preparing a meal, when every minute counts. There is no choice but to run to the nearest store, wasting valuable time. Train your kitchen staff (and yourself) to write everything that needs replacing on a board or notepad and remember to add it to your shopping list.

For perishable items, use the refrigerator or freezer, but use good judgment and leave enough space for other food that needs to be kept cold.

When buying and storing your supplies, remember two things:

(a) You don't want to buy too small a quantity of items you use often, nor do you want to buy huge quantities that tie up your money and take up too much storage space. Find the balance that is correct for you. Consider cheaper unit prices when you buy in larger quantities. For example, capers are costly when bought in small jars. A small jar costs 80¢ per unit price. The price is much lower when you purchase a large jar for 52¢ per unit price. Since capers keep perfectly well in your refrigerator for a very long time, if you have the space and use them frequently, the larger jar makes better sense.

(b) Most items have a finite shelf life. There is no sense buying large quantities if the shelf life is much shorter than the time it would take you to use all of it. This is a common fault in household purchases. You see huge spice containers in many kitchens simply because it is cheaper in large containers. Four, five, or even ten years later the same containers are still sitting in that kitchen, and the cook is still using the same spices that lost their flavor three years ago. You might as well add talcum powder to that chicken dish instead of the five-year-old garlic powder; the taste will be the same, and talcum powder at least helps thicken the sauce!

You should learn the shelf life of items you stock in your commercial kitchen. There is no overall guideline for shelf life, unfortunately. You can study cookbooks, food manuals and reference books, home economics texts, and government publications. A wide range of values on the shelf life of various foodstuffs can be found. And when you see that some of them are obviously wrong, how can you trust the rest? One reference book mentions that salt and sugar have a shelf life of one year. But I know that they both keep indefinitely as long as they remain dry. Another says honey is no good after two years. Yet perfectly good honey was found in the Egyptian pyramids, proving that its shelf life is indefinite, at least for our purposes. I just haven't found a reliable guide to food shelf life.

Legumes, dry goods, and canned items will keep for years. The shelf life of items in your refrigerator and freezer will vary, and the taste will tell you when food has been kept too long. The guides you find in food reference books are much too conservative.

Once you read a great deal about food (and that is what I'm advising you to do), you can reason out shelf life for most things. For instance, storing food in the freezer can produce freezer burn if oxygen comes in contact with your food. Properly wrapped food suffers a minimum of freezer burn, but it is difficult to completely eliminate oxygen without a vacuum seal. In frozen fruits and vegetables, the enzyme action eventually breaks down flavor. If the produce is blanched before freezing, the enzyme action stops. Storage life will be much longer but not indefinite, as both the flavor and nutritional content will slowly decrease with time.

There should be very little deterioration in dry legumes. With years of storage they become even drier, requiring a slightly longer cooking time, but you can challenge anyone to tell the difference in flavor between a kidney bean stored for six months and one stored for six years.

Spices and herbs are another matter. They do lose their flavoring oils, called essential oils, with storage. These are the items you should purchase in very restricted quantities, certainly not more than a year's supply if the spice is ground. If it is whole, it will keep longer.

Discard spices and herbs when in doubt. Flavors are so important in your cooking that you can't afford to use old spices and herbs.

For your spice and dried-herb supplies, look for a source where you can buy in bulk (not commercially packaged) but in small amounts. Virtually any large, and many small, health food stores and food co-ops have a supply of bulk spices and herbs. Make sure the store has a good turnover of stock by smelling the spices and herbs. Buy them in unground form and grind spices and crush herbs fresh just shortly before you add them to a dish. They should have a fresh, pungent, spicy smell, not a dried, grasslike odor.

You may want to keep certain spices that you have to buy in ground form (curry and chili powder, paprika, ground chili, etc.) in the freezer to keep them fresh, if you have the space.

Find out what foods keep well in the freezer, which ones can be reused after defrosting, and which can only be used in cooking and baking. You will always have leftover food, much of which can be reused or recycled, including cheeses, dairy products, meats, fish, breads, and pastries.

7. WASTE REDUCTION

Wasted food is probably the single most serious plague of the food industry, a business already operating at marginal profit levels. Many restaurants and caterers go out of business because they cannot make enough profit to justify their existence.

There are two categories of wasted food in catering:

(a) Those beyond the caterer's control:

    (i)   The client overestimated the number of guests and ordered more food than needed.

    (ii) The guests consumed less food than expected.

    (iii) The event was canceled.

    (iv) Extra food was prepared to ensure sufficient amounts.

(b) Those within the caterer's control:

    (i)   Food that is wasted during preparation.

    (ii) The caterer overestimated the amount of ingredients needed.

    (iii) Food spoilage occurred.

    (iv) Food theft occurred.

WASTED FOOD IS PROBABLY THE SINGLE MOST SERIOUS PLAGUE OF THE FOOD INDUSTRY, A BUSINESS ALREADY OPERATING AT MARGINAL PROFIT LEVELS.

WASTE CAN BE
REDUCED
SIGNIFICANTLY
WITH GOOD
ORGANIZATIONAL
SKILL AND EFFICIENCY.

In the first category, food is actually wasted but is paid for by the client, so it doesn't cut into profits. Some of the extra food can be left with the client; it is not all wasted in the physical sense. How much extra food is prepared as insurance against running short of food is really within the caterer's control, but is necessary and included in the pricing. The number one complaint against caterers in general by the public is "they ran out of food." With experience, the amount of extra food prepared can be kept to a minimum to reduce waste. Ten percent is a good rule of thumb if you calculate your portions precisely. With lower budget catering it can be reduced even more, and for full-service preplated meals it is minimal. When preplating food, the chef or kitchen help carefully divides food on the prepared plates so there is just a little left in the pots when the last one is dished out.

The second category is the one you should worry about. In the first list, waste hurts for ethical reasons, simply because wasting food is a crime when much of the world's population is hungry. But at least you are not losing money on the food. In the second category, however, you waste not only the food but the money you paid for it.

Waste can be reduced significantly with good organizational skill and efficiency, but it can never be fully eliminated. Some waste is necessary to run your business efficiently. For example, you need to keep milk and coffee cream in your refrigerator for events and sometimes they become outdated or spoiled. That is a small expense compared to someone's unnecessary trip to the store just to get cream for the next morning's breakfast event because you ran out two days ago. Some of the extra food is there as an insurance policy against such contingencies and a small amount of waste is justified.

7.1 Supplies

Theft is a problem discussed in Chapter 3. This is usually well within your control, though eliminating it is not always easy. Losses due to theft could be significant. The larger your operation, the more likely you are to have a problem here.

Ordering supplies close to the right amount is an art that comes with experience. In some cases it is easy: if you need salmon steak for 34 guests, you order 34 pieces and a few extra for a possible increase in the number of guests. In the case of salads, you need to calculate the amount a person consumes plus 10 percent. But no matter what, you have to over-order somewhat to avoid unexpected problems — unacceptable pieces of fruit, errors in the kitchen, spillage, and sampling by staff all go into this category.

7.2 Staff

Another area of costly waste in catering is staff time. The more routine work your catering business does, the easier it is to plan staff time. If much of your business consists of corporate breakfasts and luncheons, they all have similar menus and you can predict preparation, delivery, setup, and cleanup times fairly closely. Your staff time waste is minimal.

But with a high-end reception where menu, setup, and everything else is completely different from one to another, you have to plan extra staff time for contingencies. You can't afford to schedule your staff so closely that as soon as they are finished in the kitchen, it is time to leave. Many things can go wrong. You have to allow extra staff hours for such eventualities, and at times everyone is finished an hour before the scheduled departure time. This is expensive but necessary.

The second most frequent complaint against caterers is that they arrive late. This is an easy problem to eliminate; usually all it takes is careful planning and organization.

7.3 Space

There are other kinds of waste to consider, too. If you are running a small business and you don't have many events scheduled to keep your kitchen busy, your rented space may be wasted if it sits idle too often. If you can find another entrepreneur in food preparation who can use your health-approved kitchen, sublet your space for some extra income. Make sure you don't interfere with each other's activities, and that the other person is properly insured, licensed, and trustworthy, and that you have permission to sublet from your landlord if you are renting the space yourself. Don't sublet to someone who may be or could be your competition. Keep your files and recipe collection under lock and key when you are not in your kitchen.

8. CLEANLINESS AND CLEANUP

It is vital to your business to be clean and hygienic at all times in the kitchen. One error and your business can be ruined. The following sections examine hygiene and food safety in more detail.

IF YOU CAN FIND ANOTHER ENTREPRENEUR IN FOOD PREPARATION WHO CAN USE YOUR HEALTH-APPROVED KITCHEN, SUBLET YOUR SPACE FOR SOME EXTRA INCOME.

8.1 Avoid contamination

Your food must be absolutely safe at all times. There should be no possibility, no matter how remote, of someone getting sick from your kitchen's product. Strictly observing all sensible rules and regulations of food preparation will virtually eliminate this possibility.

It is not enough to keep everything hospital clean. As a caterer and chef you need to learn and understand what causes food poisoning and how it can be eliminated.

In a nutshell, five microorganisms are the most common causes of food-borne illnesses:

(a) botulism, incubation period 12 to 36 hours, very serious

(b) salmonellosis, incubation period 12 to 24 hours, moderately serious

(c) trichinosis, incubation period two days, serious

(d) staphylococcus poisoning, incubation period three hours, not very serious

(e) clostridium perfringens poisoning, incubation period 10 to 12 hours, mild

All five are easy to prevent if you know just a little bit about them. Poisonings by salmonellosis and botulism have been increasing, while trichinosis has decreased over the years. The other two are rarely reported because they are rarely recognized as food-borne diseases and their symptoms are relatively mild. There are many books and websites available on the subject. Take a good reference book out of your library or download information from local, state, provincial, or federal government websites — there are dozens of them — and understand food-borne illnesses thoroughly.

In addition to knowing about these food-borne illnesses, you should stay up to date with reports in the food industry regarding their occurrences. For example, in the US, eggs were not reported as the cause of salmonella poisoning until the late 1980s when a large batch of salmonella-infected eggs from a New England farm found its way to consumers. Since then, raw or barely cooked eggs are no longer considered safe for you and your guests.

Many recipes use slightly cooked or raw eggs, including various sauces, poached eggs, eggs Benedict, and Caesar salad. Even though salmonella-infected eggs are very rare, many, if not most hotel and restaurant kitchens stopped preparing foods that call for raw or not-fully cooked eggs. You're the one who must decide whether you will also follow that safety precaution, or take a chance, tiny as it may be. It is just a question of time before perfectly safe eggs (perhaps irradiated to kill any possible infection) are available again. But it is your responsibility to seek out current information on food safety on a regular basis.

8.2 Staff

If you feel that your food preparation techniques are absolutely safe, your only worry is your staff's personal hygiene and food preparation practices. Observe how each staff member works in the kitchen. You can guess at their personal hygiene, too, after observing them.

It is mandatory in the food industry that staff wash hands with soap after using bathroom facilities so there is no chance of transferring any disease-prone organisms into the food. How do you check that? There is no easy way short of staying with them in the bathroom, and that isn't an acceptable option. Your next best alternative is to hire people who are clean in appearance and seem to take good care of themselves. Chances are their personal hygiene is good, too.

8.3 Utensils and equipment

Continuous cleanup is highly beneficial to kitchen efficiency. Pots, pans, utensils, and whatever is being used in the kitchen should be washed on a continual basis. As soon as one project is finished, utensils and containers should be washed. No matter how busy the kitchen is, mountains of unwashed dishes should never be present. It helps efficiency because whenever you need something, you know it is ready to use. It is psychologically beneficial, too. You don't have to contemplate an hour's washing up at the end of the cooking time. A few minutes here and there are far easier to swallow. Finally, it is much faster to wash almost anything right after it was used rather than hours later when food is congealed and caked on.

The continual cleanup mode requires that your kitchen equipment is washed well and thoroughly as you are working, but your floors, walls, sinks, and tables are only cleaned superficially during food preparation. After the food preparation is completed, usually after the event, a more thorough cleaning is needed so no remnants of spilled food are present. This eliminates bacterial growth as well as insect infestation.

BEWARE OF FOOD IN BOXES BROUGHT INTO YOUR KITCHEN, AS BOXES ARE POTENTIAL BUG CARRIERS.

Surfaces should be washed with disinfecting cleansers. Work tables and cutting boards are constantly in contact with food and are vulnerable to bacterial infections..Soap and water will do a good job, but occasionally the surfaces should be sprayed with chlorine for a thorough disinfection. Chlorine will also take food stains off cutting boards and work tables. If you are using any wooden surface, rub some vegetable oil into it from time to time to prevent drying out, thus preserving it for the long term.

Always keeping your kitchen spotless pays off in the long run. There is less chance of bacteria and insects, as well as a better working environment for you and your staff. A person working in a clean kitchen tends to clean up more as he or she goes along. A clean, spotless kitchen is also an excellent marketing tool when a new client visits your facilities. In fact, invite visiting clients to look at your kitchen.

8.4 Work space

A properly sealed kitchen should be virtually bug-free. Needless to say, all food must be in tightly sealed containers with nothing exposed even overnight. As long as there is nothing for bugs to eat, they will go to someone else's kitchen.

Spiders and flying insects are not so easy to keep out. The wonderful smells coming out of your kitchen will attract flies, and when you have to leave your door open for loading and unloading, they will sneak in. That keeps the spiders happy, too. So try to have the door open as little as possible. Obviously, no insect spray of any sort can be used in the kitchen. A fly swatter is one of the only weapons allowed. To kill ants, crawling insects, and spiders without using insecticides, you can use a spray bottle of laundry stain remover such as Spray 'n Wash. Even though it is not poisonous, make sure it is wiped off surfaces that will be in contact with food. When sprayed on insects, it kills them in seconds and is a perfect alternative to insecticides.

Beware of food in boxes brought into your kitchen, as boxes are potential bug carriers. Empty the boxes right away and remove them from your kitchen area.

Another kitchen problem to deal with is hair and fur. Few things will turn a guest off faster than a stray hair in a tantalizing dish. Hair in the food is a disaster. No animal of any sort should ever enter your kitchen. If you or one of your employees has a problem with flying hair, insist on a hair net for everyone. Never let anyone comb or brush their hair anywhere near the kitchen. Again, frequent cleaning of your facilities will reduce this problem.

Keeping your facility clean means you're always ready for an unexpected health department inspector's visit. You want the inspector as a friend; the fewer violations he or she finds, the less trouble you will have in the future. Once an inspector knows that your kitchen is always clean, he or she will not even look around much on visits and will just have you sign the papers. That "no violation at the time of inspection" notice gives you a wonderful feeling and can even be used as a marketing tool.

9. HEALTH DEPARTMENT CODE

Health department codes for your commercial facility are strict and vary depending on where you live. Generally, field inspectors visit all food facilities once or twice a year, in some cases three or four times a year.

Larger, more heavily populated areas have stricter codes. Enforcement is probably more strict in large metropolitan areas — with good reason, too, if you think of some of the sleazy-looking restaurants you may have passed in the seedier parts of town. Just looking at the restaurant's visible areas lets you imagine what the nonvisible kitchen and storage areas must look like.

In the United States, the federal model health code was introduced to have all states adopt a uniform code throughout the country, but due to the many regional variations and politics, it was never adopted, and probably won't be in the near future. Canadian and American regulations are quite similar, with variations ranging from province to province and state to state rather than across international borders. The differences are considerable within the same province or state between large municipalities and small communities. Investigate your local regulations. All health departments issue pamphlets or booklets that you should study thoroughly and follow meticulously. Do so and the health inspector will be your friend. Most state and provincial health departments also have websites with local health regulations, sometimes called the food compliance code. An online search should locate the relevant website in seconds.

To give you an idea of what the regulations are like, here is a summary from the California code, which is probably the strictest on the continent. Only the part of the code that may apply to small catering

GENERALLY, FIELD INSPECTORS VISIT ALL FOOD FACILITIES ONCE OR TWICE A YEAR, IN SOME CASES THREE OR FOUR TIMES A YEAR.

facilities is included here. These codes are strictly enforced, with inspectors visiting about once every six months. The visits are not announced so there is no chance to bring the kitchen up to par the day before. If your kitchen is well maintained and if it generally conforms to the code, you should have no problem with the inspections. In general, hygiene codes look at these problem areas:

(a) Doors and windows

   (i) Exterior door: rodent- and insect-proof with no opening greater than one-half inch and equipped with heavy-duty self-closer

   (ii) Screen door: equipped with heavy-duty self-closer

   (iii) Windows: equipped with screening

   (iv) Restroom doors: equipped with self-closers

   (v) Other openings entering buildings (pipes, etc.) sealed

(b) Interior material and finishes

   (i) Floor smooth and washable in all rooms where food is prepared or stored, and in toilets

   (ii) Base of continuous four-inch cove sealed between floor and walls

   (iii) Walls and ceiling smooth, washable, light colored, sealed

   (iv) Exceptions allowed where food is stored in unopened cans, bottles, cartons, sacks, or other original shipping containers

(c) Toilets

   (i) Hand-washing facilities within or adjacent to toilet room. Must provide soap dispenser, towel, paper dispenser, and hand wash sign

(d) Lighting

   (i) Minimum 20-foot candle intensity in food preparation area

   (ii) Minimum 10-foot candle in storage area, toilets, dressing room

   (iii) Protective cover over light bulbs or use of shatter-proof bulbs

(e) Ventilation

   (i) All areas must have sufficient ventilation to facilitate proper food storage and provide comfort for workers

    (ii) Toilet must have exhaust fan or openable screened window

(f) Kitchen

    (i) Canopy-type hood with six-inch overlap on ends and sides over stoves, grills, soup kettles, steam-jacketed kettles, and fryers. Duct, fan size, and air velocity must comply to specified code

    (ii) Thermometers in refrigerators and freezers, accurate within plus or minus 2°F (1°C)

    (iii) Tables, counters, shelves made of hardwood, formica, metal, or other approved easily cleanable material

    (iv) Food storage shelves six inches above floor

    (v) Utensil and equipment stored so as to be protected from contamination

(g) Washing facilities, four options:

    (i) Dishwashing machine with 180°F (82.2°C) rinse

    (ii) Dishwashing machine with 120° to 140°F (48.9° to 60°C) chemical rinse

    (iii) Undercounter dishwashing machine with 120° to 140°F (48.9° to 60°C) chemical rinse

    (iv) Three-compartment metal sink and hand washing according to code: dishwashers must have two metal drain boards or adjacent two-compartment sinks with two drain boards; sinks and drain boards must be stainless steel; vegetable sink with indirect waste connection to floor sink; dishwashing sink with direct waste connection; dishwashing machine with direct waste connection

(h) Refrigeration equipment

    (i) Indirect waste connection or self-contained evaporator unit

(i) Cleaning area, two options:

    (i) One-compartment nonporous janitorial sink, hot and cold water

    (ii) Concrete slab, curbed and sloped to drain, connected to sewer, hot and cold water with anti-siphon device

(j) Grease interceptor

    (i) If required, must be readily accessible for cleaning

(k) Water supply

- (i) Hot water heater minimum 120°F (48.9°C)

- (ii) Hot and cold water to all sinks

- (iii) Water of required minimum temperature to dishwashing machines

(l) Refuse

- (i) Adequate facilities to store and dispose of all waste material

(m) Other requirements regarding catering food facilities:

- (i) All potentially hazardous food must be held below 45°F (7.2°C) or above 140°F (60°C) at all times

- (ii) No food prepared or stored in a private home can be served for sale or given away in a food facility

- (iii) All food preparation employees must wear clean, washable outer garments or uniforms and keep their hands clean. They must wash hands and arms with cleanser and warm water before commencing work and after using toilet facilities. They must wear hairnets or caps. They must use tongs to serve food.

- (iv) No smoking in food preparation, storage, or cleaning areas

- (v) All poisonous substances, including cleaning materials and insecticides, must be labeled properly, kept in original container, and stored in separate closet away from any food material

- (vi) All waste is stored in leak- and rodent-proof containers and removed frequently. Food preparation facilities must be free of litter and rubbish

- (vii) Manual sanitization according to code specifications

- (viii) All living and sleeping quarters must be separated from the food preparation area by a wall. No door or other opening may connect the two directly

- (ix) Vehicle used in food transportation must have smooth, easily cleanable, easily accessible interior surfaces

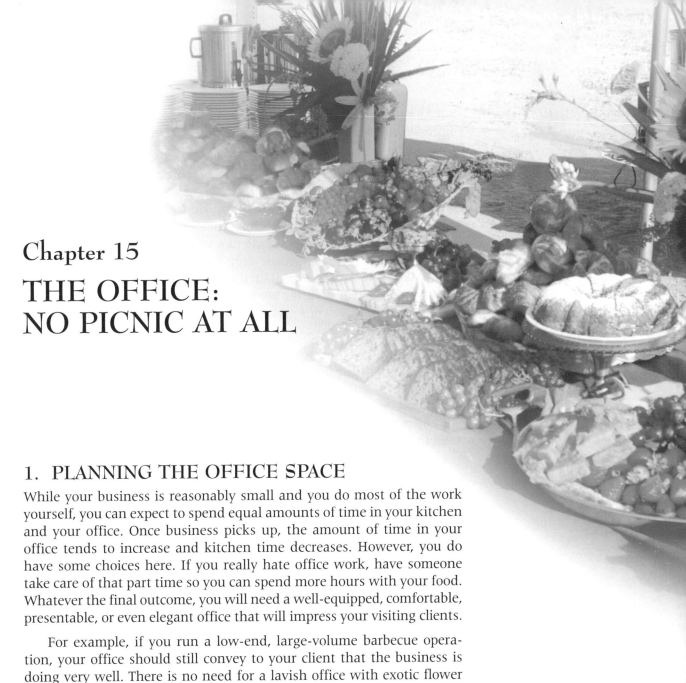

Chapter 15

THE OFFICE:
NO PICNIC AT ALL

1. PLANNING THE OFFICE SPACE

While your business is reasonably small and you do most of the work yourself, you can expect to spend equal amounts of time in your kitchen and your office. Once business picks up, the amount of time in your office tends to increase and kitchen time decreases. However, you do have some choices here. If you really hate office work, have someone take care of that part time so you can spend more hours with your food. Whatever the final outcome, you will need a well-equipped, comfortable, presentable, or even elegant office that will impress your visiting clients.

For example, if you run a low-end, large-volume barbecue operation, your office should still convey to your client that the business is doing very well. There is no need for a lavish office with exotic flower arrangements. The client may get the wrong impression, thinking that you are too pricey for a barbecue. A small bouquet, arranged by yourself, or even a few single stems are sufficient.

The higher the class of catering you run, the more presentable your office should be. Nevertheless, a personal touch in the office will help sell a client on you much faster than the cold, plastic look of an interior-designed bank manager's office. You need to give the client a favorable

MANY CLIENTS FIND
IT FUN TO VISIT A
CATERER AND SAMPLE
THE FOOD, SO EXTRA
PEOPLE MAY JOIN IN
AT THE LAST MINUTE.

first impression of you and of your establishment. Then you can impress him or her with your menu, pictures, and samples.

Your office should be comfortable for you and your clients, and it should definitely reflect the fact that a caterer occupies it. Many caterers, if they have the space, set up a little "tasting" table that will seat two to four guests. There your client can sip fresh iced coffee with little scones and plum jam, or taste tidbits that you pulled from your refrigerator. Whenever you expect a client's visit, plan to serve something fresh, even if it is just chocolate chip cookies. The aroma of anything freshly baked is welcome at that time. Your client will want to order whatever you serve for his or her event, so don't offer something out of season, or an item you don't like to prepare, or something obviously out of the client's budget.

If your office is too small to have a separate table for clients to sit around, have a little coffee table where you can set a beautiful tray of refreshments. Anticipate extra people showing up and prepare some extra food. Set four or five glasses in the freezer to serve chilled beverages on a summer day. Many clients find it fun to visit a caterer and sample the food, so extra people may join in at the last minute.

If your office is too small for that many visitors, set up a small reception area for guests elsewhere in your facility, if at all possible. Even if it is not very fancy, the clients will understand that this is primarily your working kitchen, not a reception room. Make serious attempts, though, to give your reception area a little zing.

2. BASIC EQUIPMENT FOR THE OFFICE

Your office needs a desk, filing cabinets, and bookshelves to store cookbooks and various items — your collection of antique tea kettles, for example. These items should preferably be food-related. A collection of antique rat poison containers may be frowned upon by your clients, as well as by the health inspector.

You will need a computer for billing and correspondence, storing your recipes, downloading photographs if you have a digital camera, and research. You will also need a good-quality printer, a fax machine, and perhaps a scanner.

There are many companies that sell software specifically for restaurateurs and caterers. Most of these are geared for large businesses, but a few are suitable for small-business caterers. I discussed this subject in Chapter 3.

Your standard office equipment should include a good calculator. (Put another small calculator in the kitchen, and one more in each of your catering boxes that are carried to all functions.) A telephone answering machine, voice mail, or answering service is a must for catering since someone cannot be near the telephone all the time and clients with last-minute changes in guest numbers or menu items should be able to leave messages for you.

A cellular phone is no longer optional. Most caterers equip their delivery vehicles with a cell phone for convenience. Not only are you easily accessible at any time, but you are not tied to your office quite so much. When heading to an event, a cell phone comes in very handy to keep in contact with your staff, your kitchen, and even the client (if you cannot find the address or you are slightly delayed). A cell phone is not very expensive, but if your budget is tight, it can wait until the business is bringing in a positive cash flow. A PDA (Personal Digital Assistant) can be very useful if you are into advanced electronic gadgets — and they are not expensive. It can do a lot more than storing your clients' phone numbers in its memory. As I discussed in Chapter 6, it can store data on prices and sources, making it an invaluable aid to shopping.

3. BOOKKEEPING AND OTHER RECORDS

There is constant office work of all sorts associated with any business that not only must be done, but is sometimes legally required. The secret to having all your books in order hinges on two basic tenets:

(a) Keep good written records of everything related to your business

(b) Keep your records and books fully up to date at all times

If those two principles are not observed, your office work will become a menacing black cloud over your head most of the time and a chore even if you generally don't mind keeping the books. On the other hand, if your records are good and orderly, the bookkeeping is not very difficult and spending a few minutes a day will take care of the majority of the necessary office chores. Once a month there will be extra office work to update monthly records, labor reports, payroll, and so on, and once a year your annual records, taxes, reporting of employee earnings, and similar tasks will keep you busy for hours, even if you have a bookkeeper.

You must keep records, no matter how busy you are, and you must keep your books up to date at all times. Even if you are working long hours and can barely keep up with catering events, keep up with the office work as best you can. Schedule a little office work into your general plans or just do it routinely. If you prefer to have someone else do this work, be sure the business records you hand over to the other person are orderly and up to date. He or she can only accomplish record keeping as good as the raw data you are supplying. If it is very poorly organized, it will cost you dearly to have your bookkeeper organize it for you.

As soon as you anticipate your first few business expenses, open a separate business checking account. Keep your business and personal checking accounts strictly separate — never mix the two. Choose the type of business checking account that fits your business needs best. Some small-business people use a simple system similar to a personal checking account, some prefer a more elaborate system, like "one-write" checks which produce a carbon copy of all checks, and a spreadsheet.

Accountants say that if you are processing more than 30 or 40 invoices a month, you should use a computer accounting system.

3.1 Records

Keep records of all your expenditures, supported by receipts or at least canceled checks. Even if your business is very small, it is wise to keep these records in a regular accountant's book with 10, 12, or 14 vertical columns for different expense categories. The vertical columns will automatically give you the breakdown of expenses that is required for tax purposes once a year.

You can break the expenses down into categories any way you like, but it is preferable to have them in groups that will eventually help calculate your taxes. If you have a tax accountant, he or she will give you the categories. Here is an example:

(a) Food and related supplies

(b) Office expenses

(c) Insurance

(d) Advertising

(e) Rent

(f) Utilities

(g) Repair

(h) Equipment purchase

(i) Vehicles

(j) Rental, flowers, subcontractors, miscellaneous

(k) Salaries

(l) Total

Have a separate set of records for each month. Each entry should include the date of purchase, where the purchase was made and, if it is out of the ordinary, what the item was. To keep up such a record is easy and best done by you even if you have a part-time bookkeeper. Even if you have to undergo a tax audit, a missing receipt would probably be acceptable, provided a receipt is difficult to obtain, the item is not expensive, and it is infrequent in occurrence. For example, if you purchased produce at a local farmer's market, you can record it on a piece of paper with the date and approximate total purchase price, and sign it. Include it in the collection of receipts.

3.2 Records of employee hours worked

You can keep records of employee hours in a separate book on regular employee time cards. At pay time, multiply the hours by your employees' hourly wages and mark the amount paid on the card.

3.3 Events and appointments

Never leave these to memory. If you forget to mark down an item you purchased or your chef's hours for a day, you may end up with slightly misleading records or a dispute with your chef. If an event didn't get on your calendar, you have a disaster on your hands. Make sure that all events you are asked to cater are written on the calendar at once! Also mark any deposit you have received from a client. An unmarked deposit can lead to unpleasant consequences, too.

3.4 Client and event records

As soon as you are contacted by a client, open a file for him or her. The system you use is immaterial as long as you are consistent and the records are easy to retrieve. You can use a separate file folder or just a sheet of paper for each client where you record the date of first contact, name, address, telephone number (preferably both home and business), and two pieces of clearly visible information: the date of the prospective event and the number of guests expected. Add any details about the event that you have been told, including price or price range quoted. All subsequent contacts with this client should be recorded on

MAKE SURE THAT ALL EVENTS YOU ARE ASKED TO CATER ARE WRITTEN ON THE CALENDAR AT ONCE!

the same paper or in the same file folder, including everything that is new in connection with the party.

Every item can be useful in planning the party, so your notes should be detailed. File the information so that you can retrieve it readily. Reserved events can be filed together by month. If you don't have too many, each event can be randomly placed within the folder for each month. If you have many events, you may want to separate them by weeks or alphabetically. However, keep in mind that since you cannot remember each client's name, alphabetical listing is only helpful if you have cross-referenced the name, maybe to your event calendar. For example, if you remember that the event is in May, you can scan your calendar until the client's name in May comes up, and find your event notes in the May folder. Whatever way you choose, make sure it works for you.

This is an area where a computer is very useful. Input the information and separate events into folders any way you wish. Should you be looking for a specific event that happened years ago, your search function can find it for you faster than you can open your filing cabinet drawer.

3.5 Invoicing events

The easiest, most straightforward way of invoicing is to take an invoice with you to present to your client at the end of the event. This is a common way of billing in social catering. Hand your client the invoice, and thank him or her for choosing your catering company for the event. Often you will get a check for the balance right away. This saves time and you have a check in hand ready to be deposited in your bank.

For corporate catering, a check must often be requisitioned, which will take a few weeks, but carrying the final invoice with you will save some time in mailing. Chances are you will get your check a few days earlier. Some corporate clients carry a blank check with them, so having a ready invoice with you can pay off.

In some cases, however, you cannot make up an invoice until after the event. For such clients, you must send the invoice by mail, e-mail, or fax. The sooner you send it, the sooner you get paid. For more frequent clients, you may choose to bill monthly. This bill should be made up as soon as you know all the event totals for that month. It is best to schedule invoicing time as part of your event planning time.

3.6 Accounts of events

As soon as an event is over, you should record it or input it into the computer with a brief summary of the event on a single line or two, the name of the client, date of the event, type of event, number of guests, gross receipts, and the amount of sales tax included in the gross. Include a column to check off and record the date once you receive payment. To double-check the receipt of payment, it is a good idea to mark outstanding invoices in the client's file as well. Since many clients are potential repeat customers, mark down anything that may be useful for you to know for a future event for the same client — names of relatives or close friends, food likes and dislikes, and so on.

3.7 Notes on past events

Once you become a seasoned, well-established caterer, you will rarely need notes on an event you catered, but even then you might want to mark down anything new that happened from the caterer's point of view. When you are still learning (this goes on for a long time), it is important to learn from mistakes you made. Write down anything unexpected and significant, especially with regard to food. Was the quantity enough or too much? Did you run out of an item too soon? Did everything arrive in top condition? Did the guests especially like or dislike a menu item? Make notes on staff, too. Did you plan for just the right number or were idle staff talking in the corners? All these observations should be filed in the appropriate pigeon holes — notes about the staff in one file, and food quantities in the recipe file. Again, if your notes are on the computer, file information in specific folders.

3.8 Inquiries and requests

Many of the calls coming in are from potential clients who are not ready to make reservations. Respond to these appropriately: sending the information requested, making notes with enough detail for the next call from the potential client, and filing this information separately from the reserved events. Again, the best method is to set up monthly files, either hard copies or on the computer. Some inquiries are general, with no specific event in the client's mind. These cannot be filed by event date, so keep them in a separate folder called "General Inquiries." Check this folder from time to time and contact the potential clients again.

WHEN YOU ARE STILL LEARNING, IT IS IMPORTANT TO LEARN FROM MISTAKES YOU MADE.

YOU WANT TO KNOW
IF YOUR CASH FLOW IS
A TRICKLE, OR IF IT IS
FLOWING OUT
INSTEAD OF IN. YOU
NEED TO REMEDY
THAT SITUATION FAST.

3.9 Paying your bills

Prompt payment of your bills is essential, particularly when starting up a new business, to establish your credit and to gain the confidence of your suppliers. That will eliminate future problems and headaches. Of course, during the beginning period, virtually all suppliers demand to be paid on pickup or delivery of your order. No one trusts a brand new business until it has been financially established and proven itself to be viable.

Your orders will be rather small and suppliers don't always appreciate small orders, so establishing the image of a trustworthy business is a good idea. There are times when you need their help with a sudden, last-minute emergency order, or when they have to drop off an order by your back door when no one is in your kitchen and trust you to send a check by mail. You adore the client who carries a blank check with him or her to an event to pay you with. This kind of prompt payment will be just as appreciated by your suppliers. While you are small, you depend on them more than they depend on you.

Utility bills, rent, and other invoices should be paid promptly, too. To anyone supplying you with anything, their only proof of your reliability is your payment.

4. MONTHLY SUMMARY

It is a good habit to add up your books once a month and feel the pulse of your business. No doubt, you have some idea how you are doing, but sometimes those numbers come back with a different answer than you expected. Sometimes it's a pleasant surprise, other times it is not so pleasant. You want to know if your cash flow is a trickle, or if it is flowing out instead of in. You need to remedy that situation fast. The books or the computer printouts will give you an answer and if you don't add them up at least once a month, you won't know what's going on. Also, if the business is doing better than you suspected, you can afford to adjust your pricing a little for new requests, and you can refuse marginally profitable events that you don't want to waste time on. This is important!

At the end of each month, add up your total expenses by categories, check if there are some unjustified expense leaks, and add up your receipts as well. After subtracting the sales tax and any other expenses that were either collected on someone else's behalf or not related to your business, compare the total receipts to your total expenses to get the approximate bottom line figure of how your business did that month. This figure will not be quite accurate as it does not take into account any change in inventory, but in a small catering business that is not a significant figure. Provided you kept your records up to date at all times, adding up your books monthly should take minimal effort, especially if you have accounting software.

5. PAYROLL

Organizing your payroll can be done in several different ways. People working for you on an occasional basis generally want to be paid frequently, often right after each event. For a really occasional worker, there is no problem with that. For someone working more frequently, weekly, bi-weekly, or monthly payment is preferable. You want to keep your staff happy and working for you in the future.

Even if you are not a pleasant boss to work for, the bottom line for them is your prompt payment. Your helper will swallow a lot if he or she knows that the expected checks are forthcoming regularly and promptly. Make sure that they are not disappointed. Establish your credibility with them as carefully as you do with your suppliers. When they know that they can count on punctual payment, they will be more likely to work for you in an emergency situation.

In addition to your regular record keeping and payroll chores, there are also periodic legal requirements that you must observe. (These are discussed in full in Chapter 16.) They include filing business records, renewal of licenses, and completing tax returns. Again, do these things promptly. If there is payment involved, the forms are often sent to you months in advance, in which case prompt payment is not a good idea. Put the deadline date on your calendar, especially if a missed deadline will result in a fine. Establish a system to help you remember deadlines if you have a habit of ignoring the calendar.

6. ANNUAL SUMMARY

Once a year, add up the total of each of your monthly summaries to feel the average annual pulse of your business. Again, if you did your homework every month, this is not a big job and it will tell you a great deal about the progress of your business. The procedure is no different than your monthly summaries, but you will have to deal with 12 sets of figures, one for each month. This chore is a snap with a suitable software program.

7. INCOME TAXES

Your annual tax returns are more complicated when you own a business. Most small business owners find it best to have a professional accountant familiar with small business taxes do their taxes. Business tax laws change from year to year, and you may have difficulty keeping up with the changes on your own. In addition, a good tax accountant will be able to advise you with the right combination of various allowable deductions and options on equipment depreciation so you pay the minimum of income taxes. Unless you know a lot about business income taxes, your accountant's fee is well justified. In order to save on accountant's fees, provide him or her with good records in good order. Remember that with incomplete records on your expenses you will have lower business deductions and will be paying higher taxes. And if you miss recording some of your events, you may have problems if you are ever audited.

Next best thing to a CPA is an income tax software program — but you still have to input the data manually.

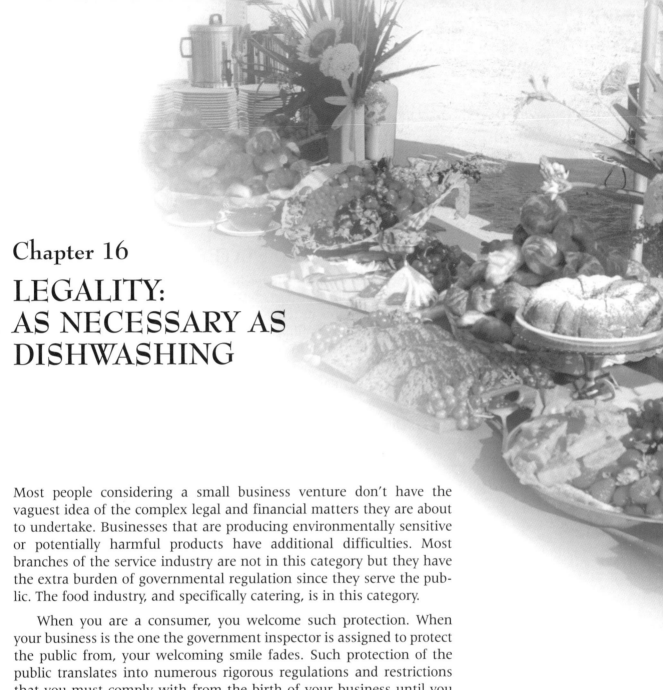

Chapter 16
LEGALITY: AS NECESSARY AS DISHWASHING

Most people considering a small business venture don't have the vaguest idea of the complex legal and financial matters they are about to undertake. Businesses that are producing environmentally sensitive or potentially harmful products have additional difficulties. Most branches of the service industry are not in this category but they have the extra burden of governmental regulation since they serve the public. The food industry, and specifically catering, is in this category.

When you are a consumer, you welcome such protection. When your business is the one the government inspector is assigned to protect the public from, your welcoming smile fades. Such protection of the public translates into numerous rigorous regulations and restrictions that you must comply with from the birth of your business until you close the doors.

I suspect that if a potential entrepreneur were confronted with all the regulations he or she must conform to early on, the entrepreneurial enthusiasm would all but vanish. It really is a formidable list if you live in an area that takes regulation seriously. As difficult as conforming may be, it can be done if you accept the rules, go about acquiring permits and licenses step by step, swallow your frustration, and attempt to enjoy the time you have to spend standing in line at the health department, or waiting weeks for a necessary certificate or license to arrive. The problem comes when you already have catering events to execute and a money-making business to run. The time needed to get your official and legal documents, generally during regular business hours only, is often long and can cut seriously into the time you need to plan and execute your events.

1. IN THE UNITED STATES

Sometimes it is more fortunate to still be waiting for paying clients while getting the legal aspects settled. Let's review what a small catering business requires in terms of permits. The following example outlines the situation in California, one of the most restrictive places in the United States in which to conduct business. If you live elsewhere, you may get off a little easier. Also, smaller municipalities generally have less restrictive regulations than larger ones, but the guidelines are often similar:

(a) Once you've made your decision about operating as a sole proprietor or incorporating your business, you act accordingly regarding legal matters. There is generally no additional legal requirement if you are a sole proprietor. If you incorporate, papers have to be filed, forms filled out, fees paid, and incorporation recorded, so it is best to use your lawyer to be certain that the procedure is legally correct and no step is left out. Partnerships are also legally complex; legal advice or assistance is advisable.

(b) Business name. Decide what name you want to use for your business, visit the county recorder's office, and search the files to determine if anyone else may have reserved the name. Both active and inactive files must be searched. If a name has not been actively used for a certain number of years, it is no longer reserved and you are free to use it. After finding that your chosen name is not being used by anyone else (by the way, never print up business cards or brochures until you know the name you've chosen is available), fill out forms, pay a fee to record it, and then run a fictitious business name statement in a local, legally qualified newspaper for a certain length of time (generally four times in a weekly paper). If no one protests, the name is officially yours. At the county recorder's office, find out how long you can use the name without refiling. A fictitious name is not yours for eternity, even if you are actively using it. It must be re-recorded before the expiration date, which is usually several years after the initial filing.

(c) Get a federal tax number for your business (also called the employer identification number). For a small business operating as a sole proprietorship and with only occasional employees, your social security number may be sufficient, but check with the federal tax department.

(d) A resale license proves to your suppliers that you are in a legitimate business and have the right to purchase from a wholesaler. And since you are reselling, you will not be charged sales tax on products that are resold in your business. For example, you will be taxed on cleaning supplies but not on disposable plates. If foods, beverages, and services are taxable where you live, this resale number will authorize you to collect sales tax from your clients on behalf of the state. You pay the collected taxes to the state at regular intervals, either monthly or quarterly. You may have to leave a security deposit if you are a new business owner without previous history of collecting sales tax. The amount of the deposit is based on the expected annual gross, so make sure you expect a small figure for this to keep the deposit low. After a given period of time, if you pay your sales taxes faithfully, the state will return your deposit, but you may have to request it.

(e) Business tax is either a city or county tax, and you pay it annually based on your gross receipts. Call your local administration offices to get information on what this entails.

(f) While city tax is paid simply because you are in business, the county assesses you for equipment, supplies, and property that you own. You file county property tax annually, listing all your equipment or supplies, and any changes from the previous year. The amount of tax is determined by the total value you declare.

(g) A health department permit is usually a county requirement. As explained previously, once your commercial kitchen has passed an inspection based on health department regulations, you can operate from the kitchen as a legitimate business provided all other permits and licenses are in order. However, a health inspector is likely to visit your facilities regularly without notice. If you are near the business district with many restaurants

ONCE YOUR COMMERCIAL KITCHEN HAS PASSED AN INSPECTION BASED ON HEALTH DEPARTMENT REGULATIONS, YOU CAN OPERATE FROM THE KITCHEN AS A LEGITIMATE BUSINESS PROVIDED ALL OTHER PERMITS AND LICENSES ARE IN ORDER.

IT IS VERY RISKY TO
DO ANY BUSINESS,
ESPECIALLY CATERING,
WITHOUT PROPER
BUSINESS INSURANCE
COVERAGE.

around, you can expect more frequent visits. If you are located away from the main part of town, you will probably be visited less frequently, or not at all. You will be sent an annual bill to cover the cost of the health inspector. The fee may seem unreasonably high, but you have no choice but to pay it.

(h) If you start from new kitchen facilities, you will also need the building inspector's approval before the health inspector can approve them.

(i) If you have employees (even sporadic employment counts in California), you are required to enroll in the state program for workers' compensation insurance in case of job-related injury, illness, or disability. The premium is based on your annual payroll and you pay it once or twice a year. If you don't have a regular payroll, you will be charged a predetermined minimum premium.

(j) If you have employees, you must withhold the required percentage from each of your employees' paychecks for Social Security Insurance (FICA), and you must contribute your share as well. This is a federal law.

(k) Unemployment insurance is a state deduction, and it is paid entirely by the employer.

(l) In some states you are required to have disability insurance. Inquire about the status of this in your location.

(m) Many caterers don't bother with any business insurance coverage when they are just starting out, partly because they cannot afford the additional and very substantial cost, but mainly because no insurance company will insure an unlicensed caterer. It is very risky to do any business, especially catering, without proper business insurance coverage. You risk losing everything you own in these lawsuit-prone times. If just one guest bites into a missed olive pit, he or she can take you to court and demand replacement of a bridge and plastic surgery on chin and cheeks, plus a million dollars to compensate for pain and suffering. And he or she might even get it, or at least part of it.

If you are uninsured or work out of an unapproved kitchen, you are automatically in the wrong no matter how absurd the demand is. Each situation is different, but with an insurance agent and your expected income you can come up with a minimum insurance coverage necessary to operate safely.

Insurance will likely be your second highest overhead item after rent. The premium for business insurance is based on your estimated gross revenues and revised once you know the exact gross. If the gross is less than expected, you will get a refund that is applied to your next premium. If it is more, you will be charged the additional amounts of premium that you underpaid. Generally, the cost for adequate insurance for a year is about 1 percent to 2 percent of your annual total sales.

(n) Whether you're renting or purchasing, make sure that the local zoning laws allow your type of operation on that location. You have to be absolutely certain or you will have big problems. Don't rely on what the landlord thinks might be true. If there are restaurants in the neighborhood, chances are that zoning regulations permit off-premise catering.

(o) If you are planning to serve and sell liquor, you need a liquor license. If you are planning to serve and sell occasionally, you can get a license for one day only in most states. If you are planning to serve your clients' liquor but there is no exchange of money for it, you may not need a liquor license, but you still need liquor liability insurance. Find out all the local and state regulations for future reference and keep the information in your files.

IF YOU ARE PLANNING TO SERVE AND SELL LIQUOR, YOU NEED A LIQUOR LICENSE.

No doubt, many municipalities will not require all the permits listed above, and some may require more. However, of one thing you can be certain: for each one there is a charge, often an annual charge, and you will be required to pay several sets of taxes every year in addition to your income tax.

Many of these required taxes you may pay electronically through the Internet once you set up an account.

2. IN CANADA

In Canada, each province has its own laws, codes, and regulations. Your business must comply with applicable federal, provincial, and municipal laws. Generally, each municipality has special health requirements and licenses for food service businesses.

SINCE LICENSING
AND OPERATING
REQUIREMENTS MAY
DIFFER FROM REGION
TO REGION, CONTACT
YOUR LOCAL LICENSING
AUTHORITIES FOR
SPECIFICS.

(a) A business may operate as a sole proprietorship, a partnership, or a corporation. If your company name is an important part of your business, you might want to consider registering it as an official trademark.

(b) Businesses must apply to Canada Revenue Agency (CRA) for a provincial or federal tax number, also called a business number, which exempts payment of tax on merchandise purchased for resale. A business number is used on your account when paying your provincial and federal taxes. All businesses pay federal income tax.

If you own your business property, you also pay property tax. If you rent, the tax is included in your rental payment.

(c) Businesses with gross revenue of over CDN$30,000 must charge 6 percent (promised to be reduced to 5 percent eventually) goods and services tax (GST) on the goods and services they provide. They must also pay GST on anything they buy. Registration is mandatory with CRA. It allows you to recover any GST that you spend on business purchases. Small businesses that the Canada Revenue Agency defines as "Small Suppliers" — with under CDN$30,000 gross revenue — do not have to charge GST. Even if you are a Small Supplier, it is wise to register for the GST in order to reclaim any GST you paid on business purchases.

(d) Employers must also pay unemployment insurance premiums and make Canada Pension Plan (CPP) contributions for each employee. Long-term disability insurance and business insurance are optional and are handled through private companies.

(e) In some provinces, businesses of a certain size must contribute to a provincial health plan for their employees. In other provinces, employees must make their own contributions.

You may pay your taxes electronically through the Internet once you set up an account.

These are just a few of the regulations that businesses in Canada must follow. Since licensing and operating requirements may differ from region to region, contact your local licensing authorities for specifics. For further discussion about the legal aspects of setting up a business in Canada, see also *Starting a Successful Business in Canada*, another title in the Self-Counsel Business Series.

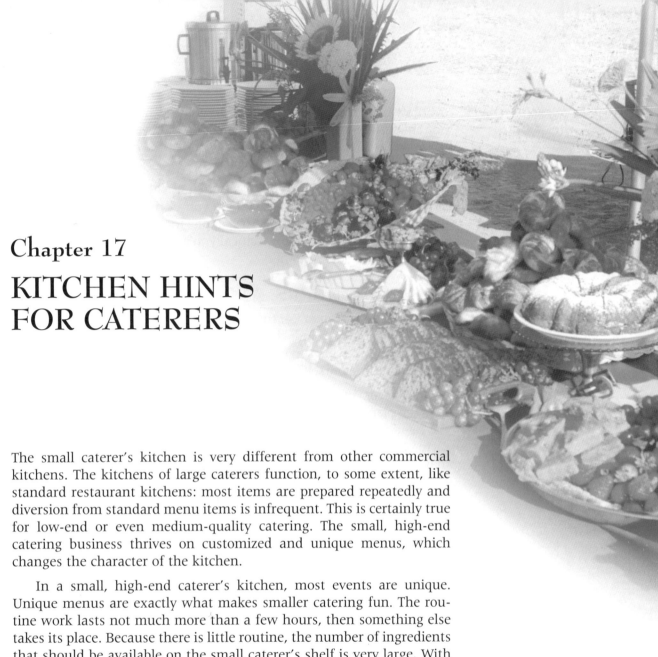

Chapter 17
KITCHEN HINTS FOR CATERERS

The small caterer's kitchen is very different from other commercial kitchens. The kitchens of large caterers function, to some extent, like standard restaurant kitchens: most items are prepared repeatedly and diversion from standard menu items is infrequent. This is certainly true for low-end or even medium-quality catering. The small, high-end catering business thrives on customized and unique menus, which changes the character of the kitchen.

In a small, high-end caterer's kitchen, most events are unique. Unique menus are exactly what makes smaller catering fun. The routine work lasts not much more than a few hours, then something else takes its place. Because there is little routine, the number of ingredients that should be available on the small caterer's shelf is very large. With a fixed menu, you can get away with only ingredients that the standard menu items require. With customized menus, you'll need items for a dozen different types of foreign cuisines, regional dishes, local ethnic specialties, and food preferences of groups demanding out-of-the-ordinary cooking — vegetarian, heart-healthy, California lite, or kosher, to mention just a few.

The other difference is your kitchen's erratic use. For two days all the machines are purring, refrigerators and freezers are jammed to overflowing, the large collection of bowls, pots, and pans is seemingly not enough to keep up with the demand, and everyone is fighting for space on the prep tables. Then all of a sudden the event is over, and the kitchen is quiet for days, even weeks.

Managing such a kitchen and running it with top efficiency is challenging. The following hints will help you in running your own catering kitchen efficiently. Some tips apply to any kitchen, some to a caterer's kitchen, and some specifically to a small caterer's kitchen. Use what applies to your situation.

1. SPICES, HERBS, AND FLAVORINGS

As discussed in Chapter 14, the shelf life of spices and herbs is not very long. The finer the grind, the quicker the essential oils escape. Whole seeds, by the way, preserve their flavor for a long time, perhaps years. Experiment for yourself.

The flavors of spices and herbs usually come from the essential oils that the plant materials contain. Essential oil may be in the seed and the cavities between the cells in leaves and stems, such as those in the carrot family (caraway, coriander, cumin, dill, fennel, parsley). Or it may be in specialized hairlike oil glands covering leaves and stems, such as in the mint family (basil, marjoram, oregano, mint, rosemary, sage, thyme). Drying organic material reduces the chance of its spoiling. By breaking down the cell structure in the course of drying, it is easier to extract the essential oils when the spices are added to foods. It may surprise you that dried herbs can be much more potent than fresh ones — more oil can be extracted during the cooking process.

In citrus fruit the volatile oils are in specialized oil glands in the skin. They volatilize (vaporize) fairly fast, and in fresh form they should be used immediately after grating. Most essential oils are slightly volatile and leave their host plant material slowly. That's why you should buy herbs and spices in small quantities and not store them for too long.

You'll want a complete collection of spices and herbs you may use in your kitchen. If your repertoire inclines toward relatively simple food and your menu is basic, then stock your spice and herb collection with only basic ones. But if you need some sophisticated items for clients who want ethnic, regional, trendy, or unusual flavors, have a larger variety on hand. Anything you use frequently that keeps well frozen can be kept in the freezer. Examples are chopped parsley, dill, grated orange and lemon peel (you can chop them in the food processor with sugar), chopped garlic and ginger, and fresh lemon juice. There are certain herbs that don't freeze well because they lose their volatile oil after chopping. These include cilantro, oregano, and basil.

Garlic is best kept in two or even three different forms — chopped and stored in the freezer, chopped and stored in oil in the refrigerator, and kept fresh in whole cloves. The commercially available fresh-chopped garlic in oil, sold in jars, is not as flavorful and powerful as the garlic you chop fresh yourself.

You should stock the usual extracts such as vanilla, lemon, orange, and almond. Extracts are alcohol-based and have a very long shelf life, so you are safe to buy them in large containers.

Finally, there is a little known form of many spices and herbs — the highly concentrated essential oils that you can buy in natural food stores. They come in tiny quantities (generally half-ounce bottles) and are very powerful — don't use too much. Their dispensers are like eye droppers. In place of one teaspoonful of lemon extract, for example, you would use one to two drops of the essential oil of lemon. Essential oils give a wonderful flavor and are available for many spices and herbs. There is no general guide for them that I have found, so experiment with them yourself.

Try peppermint oil to start with. Prepare a gallon of good iced tea from real tea leaves or tea bags and add two drops of the essential oil of peppermint. You will have a prize-winning peppermint iced tea.

2. ONIONS

You will find an endless amount of advice on how to chop onions without tears. There are two foolproof ways I've found to chop onions without the powerful irritation to my eyes. One is to wear a pair of tight-fitting swimming goggles. Your staff will stop giggling after they've tried this method, too. Or, to drive the fumes away, have a small electric fan blow the air past the onion so the fumes will not reach your eyes.

If you have a small mountain of onions to chop, a food processor is fast but doesn't give the uniform results of hand chopping. Cut the onions into eights or smaller chunks, process with the machine pulsing on and off just for seconds, and scrape the sides down frequently. This method is quick and painless. But avoid the danger of overprocessing: if the onion starts letting liquid out, you can no longer brown it. Reserve it in the freezer for soups and start over again.

ESSENTIAL OILS GIVE A WONDERFUL FLAVOR AND ARE AVAILABLE FOR MANY SPICES AND HERBS.

3. BREADS

People love good bread almost more than anything else. You need a good source of bread for your events. You could bake it yourself, but it is time consuming and you may not be equipped to bake breads and rolls for large groups. That's a bakery's job. However, there is no reason why you can't bake for a small gathering if you find time for it.

You should always take plenty of fresh bread to any event. For luncheons, count on two to three average slices per person. For dinner, provide one and a half to two slices, or about one and a half rolls per person. You will probably end up with extra bread — in fact, you should. You can use the leftovers in many recipes. If bread is getting stale, dry it and use it for bread crumbs. Unsliced loaves go right into the freezer. Even if bread has been sitting out for several hours, freeze it. When you need it again, remove it from the freezer several hours before an event, sprinkle it with water, and pop it into a hot oven for five minutes. It will taste like fresh bread straight out of the oven. If it was frozen when already stale, instead of sprinkling it with water, give it a very quick shower under the running tap.

Never keep bread in the refrigerator. The staling of bread is a chemical reaction. This reaction is unusual in that it proceeds at a moderate pace at room temperature, very slowly below freezing, and very quickly at around 40°F (5°C) — the temperature inside your refrigerator. Some commercial bread-baking companies have considered putting a message on their bread wrappers to warn people not to store it in the refrigerator, but I haven't seen such a label yet.

4. LEGUMES

Dry legumes are a useful ingredient in the catering business. They are inexpensive, and when cooked fresh (instead of opening a can), they give a nice flavor and texture to all kinds of foods. They are wonderful in salads, they give bulk at a low cost, especially in the winter when fresh vegetables are expensive, and they are very easy to prepare.

All my cookbooks say legumes need to be soaked overnight and cooked for hours. This is a myth. It is a good idea to soak legumes overnight to shorten the cooking time by about 50 percent but this is not essential. Very few legumes take more than one hour to cook, even if they are really old. Just take the beans, wash them well, boil water (about four times the volume of beans), and add one tablespoon of salt per gallon of water. When the water is boiling, add the legumes, turn the burner down to simmer, and set your timer. Most beans are cooked tender in 45 to 50 minutes. Lentils and split peas only take 20 to 25 minutes. Store a variety of legumes on your shelf, especially black beans, red beans, and kidney beans. Depending on what color you need in your salad, select the beans, and add approximately 0.5 dry ounces (15 grams) per person.

One more hint about legumes: they cook only in neutral or slightly alkaline liquids. If you will be adding sauce to the beans, make sure they are fully cooked before the sauce is added. Most sauces, especially with tomato in them, are acidic. As soon as you add it to the beans, they stop cooking. Veteran chili makers know this. Once the beans are added to the chili sauce, they can cook it for hours and the beans will never be overcooked.

5. STOCKS

Restaurant kitchens use stocks far more than catering kitchens. That's because soups are a daily menu item in restaurants while caterers don't often provide soups because they are awkward to transport and serve.

Nevertheless, stocks are used in catering kitchens, and it is nice to have either ready-made stock or ingredients for it in your freezer. You can get a full-flavored, wonderful stock from food parts you would otherwise discard. For vegetable stock, use the peelings and other vegetable parts that are discarded but have flavor. (Make sure you wash the vegetable thoroughly before peeling.) Any vegetable peels, leaves (such as celery), pea pods, roots (such as celery bottoms), unusable but still flavorful and healthy parts of scallion, the center and outer layers of onions, mushroom trimmings, tomato pieces, and parsley stems can be used. Don't include parts that have no flavor (taste it if you have doubts): papery outer peels of onions and garlic, and inner pith, seeds, and membranes of peppers. Anything you save for stock should be perfectly healthy, so when preparing vegetables, the blemished and spoiled parts should go in the waste pile, not the stock pile. Keep all the good vegetable material in a plastic bag in the freezer, labeled "for stock." When you have more peelings and trimmings, add them to the bag.

Find a good stock recipe and collect material in approximate proportion to what the recipe calls for. You need a lot of carrot, celery, and onion — the basic ingredients of stock — and much smaller portions of any other vegetables. The stronger the flavor of the vegetable trimming, the less of it you want to add, so the flavor won't overpower the stock.

FOR VEGETABLE STOCK, USE THE PEELINGS AND OTHER VEGETABLE PARTS THAT ARE DISCARDED BUT HAVE FLAVOR.

Some vegetables are so strong flavored that you should avoid them altogether, including cabbage and Brussels sprouts. Others will give too much color, like beets.

Don't collect any more than you need, as trimmings take up space in your freezer. When you need a vegetable stock, pull the collection, dump it into a pot, cover with water, and add salt, peppercorns, or other spices and herbs. Bring the mixture to a boil, simmer for a couple of hours, and you have fresh vegetable broth. Vegetable stock needs only a short time to simmer because the vegetable cells break down fast and flavors are quickly extracted. Cool, strain, and store the broth. If you didn't use too much water, you get a rich stock or even a concentrate that you can dilute.

For chicken and meat stocks, the procedure is the same. Save the trimmings and bones of chickens and meat. You cannot make a good stock from meat trimmings alone, but you can make stock from chicken trimmings, including the skins. When you're ready to make a chicken stock, add both vegetable and chicken trimmings to the pot. Go through the same procedure as for vegetable stock, but simmer it a little longer — three hours with just chicken trimmings, four hours with bones. Once you have strained and cooled the stock, put it in the refrigerator. The fat will collect on top and congeal, and then you can remove it all for a fat-free stock, or leave just a little for flavor and appearance. Using chicken trimmings with no bones will give you virtually every bit as good and full-bodied a stock as if you used a whole stewing hen. Try making chicken stock both ways if you don't believe me.

For meat stock you need to use the bones, and that takes longer simmering, about six hours.

One more item about stocks: when you finish making your stock, cookbooks recommended chilling it quickly to avoid bacterial contamination while cooling. However, if there is fat in the stock, the fat layer on top seals the stock from bacteria in the air. Nothing penetrates the layer of fat. You can let the stock sit on top of the stove until cool and it should be perfectly safe. To add an extra measure of safety, don't remove the lid after you turn off the stove. Stocks are almost always boiled again before using them in cooking, which is another safeguard.

Any stock or concentrate can be frozen or refrigerated. Don't freeze it in large volumes unless you expect to use a lot at a time. It is better to package it in smaller units, like one- or two-quart containers, so you can defrost smaller volumes at a time. Ziplock bags are great for freezing stocks. They take minimal space in the freezer and there's nothing to wash after defrosting. When you need to add stock to a dish, you can even cut the plastic off the frozen chunk and dump it into the pot without defrosting.

6. VEGETARIAN COOKING

If your catering business specializes in vegetarian menus, you can skip this section. But most caterers are stumped when the client asks for a totally vegetarian event. Cooking for vegetarians and presentation of vegetarian dishes is challenging. A breast of chicken, a center-cut pork loin, or a steak is easy to present, whether buffet style or preplated. Vegetarian meals are often not in individual serving portions but in stewlike or baked lasagna-shaped dishes that test your creativity for presentation.

If you don't cook many vegetarian dishes, learn at least a dozen good ones that have great flavor, are different than the standard spinach lasagna, and have potential for fine presentation even at a classy wedding. Vegetarian meals need to be high in protein to be nutritious. The proteins that meat, poultry, and seafood provide are replaced with ones found in nuts, seeds, legumes, and grains. Fortunately for cooks, these are all richly flavored and have good texture, but they all need seasoning with generous use of spices and herbs. These are the ingredients you should concentrate on for your own recipe collection and for presenting to your clients who request vegetarian catering.

When using nuts and seeds, and to a lesser extent grains, toasting them in the oven or on the stove top increases flavor tremendously. Toasting is an extra cooking step that I consider essential even if a recipe doesn't mention it.

All legumes must be freshly cooked, never out of a can, except perhaps for use in low-budget catering. Soybean and its derivatives — tofu, tempeh, miso, and seitan — are particularly emphasized in vegetarian cooking because of their extra-high protein content. Tofu is flavorless but absorbs flavors like a sponge in soups, salads, and any dish in which it is incorporated. But tempeh, miso, and seitan are highly flavored, so learn to use at least one of them in your vegetarian menus.

Vegetarian cooking is not hard or costly, but it is labor intensive. If your client asks you to cater a vegan affair, think twice before accepting. Vegan meals are hard to make tasty, and they are challenging to present well.

7. USING YOUR FREEZER

No matter how large a freezer you have, it's never big enough. Be judicious about what you fill the shelves with. A small quantity of often-used ingredients is nice to have at all times. My freezer usually holds chopped herbs (especially parsley), fresh lemon juice, yeast (in the freezer it will remain alive but dormant for a very long time), tomato paste (any part of the can you have not used) wrapped in plastic wrap so it is easy to cut part off while still frozen, lemon and orange zest, leftover egg white and egg yolk, bread and rolls, and pastry dough.

Leftover egg white freezes well and is worth saving in a jar. Whenever you need only the yolk, add the white to the jar in your freezer. Compile a collection of recipes that use a lot of egg whites. The whites of seven large eggs fill one cup.

Occasionally you have extra egg yolks. Yolks freeze well, too, but they need to be stabilized either by gently stirring a little salt or sugar into them in a proportion of a dash of salt or one tablespoon sugar (or honey) to three egg yolks. Gentle stirring eliminates trapped air that would oxidize the yolk in the freezer. Freeze egg yolk in small batches; you won't need too much at a time. Plastic egg carton cups are good receptacles to freeze them in. After the yolks are solid, you can repack them in a plastic bag. About 13 egg yolks make one cup. For short-term storage, mix the yolk with a little water so it won't dry out; then keep it in the refrigerator.

Storing some vegetables in the freezer is a good idea, too. Not many are suitable — the best are green peas and corn.

Unless you have a great memory, keep a written inventory of the contents of your freezer. List items by shelves, remembering to cross out items you remove and adding items to your list when putting them in your freezer. It is much easier to study a list than to search through masses of frozen items. And needless to say, everything in your freezer should be labeled, dated, and well wrapped.

It is questionable whether it is better to have a large freezer or the equivalent volume in two smaller ones. It depends on your business and your personal preference. Two smaller freezers take more space than one larger one. But often you only need to run one for your daily use, so you can turn on the second one only during peak periods — the wedding months and holiday season. A smaller freezer is more energy efficient to run than a large one. Another consideration is that if your freezer fails, you need to have a backup plan to protect the contents, which represent a fairly substantial investment. You can use the second freezer as a backup, transferring everything into the working one. If you have only one large freezer, you've got a real problem if it fails.

8. BLANCHING

Blanching is a great idea in better-class catering. It will produce a different vegetable than the guests usually expect. Blanching is also necessary before you marinate vegetables. It definitely takes extra time and involves extra steps, but that's when you are justified in charging a little extra. It also stops enzyme action that otherwise continues to ripen and eventually overripen the vegetables, so blanched vegetables keep longer. Blanching has two major benefits for a caterer: it produces more intense colors — deep orange in carrots, deep green in broccoli and snow peas — and it takes the raw taste away but still retains the crispness. Vegetables to be blanched should be cut to size first.

To blanch vegetables, you need a large pot of boiling salted water and a basket with a long handle in which you immerse the vegetables into the water. The more water, the faster it comes to a boil again, so don't blanch too many vegetables at a time. For carrots, it takes about two minutes (depending on the size they were cut); for broccoli, half a minute; for green beans, four to six minutes; and for zucchini, half a minute. Snow peas only take about 20 seconds.

Cookbooks say that after taking them out of the boiling water, the blanched vegetables should be quickly immersed in iced water. That is unnecessary. A large bowl of cold water is just fine.

Another possibility is to steam vegetables. For that you need a large steamer with several stacking compartments, such as a Chinese three-story steamer that allows you to do three batches of vegetables at the same time. The disadvantage is that they take longer to steam than to blanch and you have to remove different vegetables at different times as they are done. Once you calculate the correct steaming times for different vegetables, write them down on a chart and use several timers to remind you to stop steaming the various batches. In my experience, steaming never gives you the same crisp, intensely bright, appetizing-looking vegetables that blanching does.

9. BROWNING MEAT AND CHICKEN

Browning meat and chicken is often a problem for a caterer. Your limited budget allows limited space. You may not have large ranges either.

IN MY EXPERIENCE, STEAMING NEVER GIVES YOU THE SAME CRISP, INTENSELY BRIGHT, APPETIZING-LOOKING VEGETABLES THAT BLANCHING DOES.

To get around the problem, brown in the oven, especially when you need a hundred or even several hundred pieces of meat or chicken breasts. The results will not be identical but are perfectly acceptable. The difference in flavor of browning in hot fat or in the oven will not be significant. The advantage is twofold. Browning in the oven is much faster and adds much less oil to your dish.

To oven brown, place the meat or chicken on oiled pans and brush the top with oil. Place the meat in a very hot oven (500°F or 260°C conventional and 450°F or 235°C convection oven) until it's brown on top. If you wish, turn to brown the other side.

This is an equally good method for browning large amounts of vegetables when frying is one of the steps (e.g., eggplant slices for moussaka). You will have not even a quarter of the amount of oil soaked up by the eggplant compared to frying it.

10. EXTRA FOOD

You will be returning from most events with a substantial amount of leftover food. Eventually you will learn what can be used now or reused later. Fresh produce of any sort is often a loss. You and your staff can use it, perhaps, but it has no further value to your business. Some salads hold well for several days, but they are not for reuse in your business. Whole fruits are fine, but cut-up fruits are not unless you are making a fruit salad the next day. Leftover salads can be chopped up fine in the food processor, mixed with mayonnaise or sour cream, and served as dips.

Milk, cream, and half-and-half all freeze well. They can be used for cooking and baking after being defrosted, though defrosted milk is perfectly wholesome for drinking or coffee. Cheese can best be grated and frozen for future use. Many recipes call for cheese so it is rarely wasted. Most pastries, cookies, pies, and cakes freeze very well, and you can barely tell the difference between fresh and defrosted products. This includes savory pastries, too, such as quiche. Heat them just before serving and they will be perfectly good.

Bread and rolls, whether yeast or baking-powder types, freeze well too, but you should freeze them before they get stale. Rolls can be baked without defrosting, directly from the freezer. If yeast products were not very fresh when frozen, or if they have been in the freezer too long, sprinkle them with water before putting them into the hot oven so they regain their lost moisture.

11. BRAND-NAME OR STORE-BRAND PRODUCTS

A few decades ago, generic foods, wrapped in black-and-white labels, were on the least desirable bottom shelves in stores. Only thrifty shoppers bothered with them — their quality was not very good. They represented a mere 1 to 2 percent of food purchases. Today, they are not even called generic foods anymore but store-brand or "private label" products, and they represent 17 percent of food purchases and more than one-third of foods sold at supermarkets. Are shoppers more thrifty? No, store-brand foods became equal in quality to national labels. A US national survey found that many private label products were designed to be of higher quality than national brands even though their prices are lower. To keep your costs low and still maintain high quality, test some of these private label brands in your kitchen. If you like them, stick with them.

Kitchen tests are easy to do, and they may save you money while retaining top quality. Such experiments will certainly teach you a lot about food.

12. FLAVORING FOODS

Some cookbooks tell you that when preparing in large quantity, you don't increase herbs and spices in proportion to the increased quantities of other ingredients or the food will be overwhelmed by that flavor. Disregard this advice. Scale the recipe up in direct proportion, including all spices and herbs, and it will be just right. Test it for yourself, of course.

The trend is for more spices and herbs, and stronger flavors in all foods. However, caterers are advised to increase spices and herbs even slightly more. Not to a degree that the food is overpowered by the flavorings, but enough so that the guests notice it. The idea is to give their tastebuds a sudden kick. That's how they notice your food, and that's how they will remember that they ate something different at your event. The common tossed green salad will gain flavor when you add some chopped fresh herbs. Guests will notice that salad. Or give a simple Boeuf Bourguignonne some extra garlic and thyme, and your guests will definitely notice if they have the slightest interest in what they are eating.

13. DEFROSTING

Defrosting requires planning ahead or quality will suffer, in some cases drastically so. Do you remember the rubber chicken breasts often served at hotel banquets? Do you know why they are so dry, chewy, and rubbery? When hotels have large functions, they often get their supplies on the day of the event. (They don't have space to store three or four hundred chicken breasts.) The supplier delivers them in the morning, the food prep people open up the packages, put the breasts under running water for half an hour, and the breasts are instantly defrosted. This method of defrosting is the worst, and quality suffers severely. Natural juices are lost from the cells, resulting in rubbery chicken breasts.

The way to defrost meat in order to preserve the most meat juices and the highest quality, is slowly in the refrigerator. Defrosting 50 chicken breasts in the refrigerator will take several days, so you must plan ahead when to pull them from the freezer. If you do it right, your chicken will be like fresh.

Some items can be defrosted fast without deterioration — milk, juices, breads, anything baked, and anything that does not release juices from the cells. It is still a good idea to plan ahead and place such items in the refrigerator well ahead of time instead of letting them defrost on the counter.

14. SAFE EGGS

As I discussed in Chapter 14, since the late 1980s, raw eggs are no longer safe to use in any preparation, including many French sauces, eggs Benedict, Caesar salad, and a number of desserts calling for raw egg yolks. Raw egg whites are perfectly safe — harmful microorganisms cannot grow in them — but egg yolks are not. Even though the occurrence of salmonella in egg yolks is very rare, in a commercial food business you cannot risk making someone ill. Here is the remedy to make raw yolks safe.

Stir egg yolk and part of the liquid of the recipe (at least 2 tablespoons liquid for every yolk), and slowly heat it in a heavy saucepan. Cook very slowly, stirring constantly, until the mixture begins to coat a metal spoon with a thin film. At this point the mixture is above 150°F (66°C) and it's perfectly safe. If you have an accurate kitchen thermometer, use it to help you bring the mixture to this temperature. Remove the saucepan from heat, scoop egg mixture into a metal bowl and let the bowl sit over cold water to chill, then proceed with your recipe.

Heating eggs in the microwave does not make them safe because these ovens heat very unevenly, leaving cold and "unsafe" spots. Heating for longer to make them safe makes them unfit to either eat or use in recipes.

What about omelets, scrambled eggs, fried eggs, and eggs sunny-side-up? This is a little tricky. Egg white solidifies (coagulates) at a lower temperature than egg yolk, between 144° and 149°F (62° and 65°C). By the time the egg white is solid, the egg yolk is perfectly safe to eat even if it is a little runny because the critical temperature to kill microorganisms has been reached.

When you scramble whites and yolks, the coagulation temperature is higher, 156°F (69°C). When this cooked mixture becomes solid (and dry), you've gone well beyond the safety factor. You can take omelets and scrambled eggs off the heat when the mixture is just barely set. They will be perfectly safe to eat.

15. WINE IN COOKING

Some time ago, I visited a chef I know in a chic vegetarian restaurant's kitchen. What I remember most from this visit is a remark she made as she tasted one of her dishes: "If the flavor of the dish is not quite up to my standard, I stir in a good-sized dab of butter or a generous splash of wine."

Indeed, wine is a powerful and unique flavoring ingredient, and it is suitable in most any dish, especially in sauces, soups, and stews. Bottles of wine sit next to the Worcestershire sauce, soy sauce, and balsamic vinegar on a chef's shelves, but never, ever bottles labeled "cooking wine." Wine used for cooking must be of moderately good quality, but it need not be an expensive dinner wine. Cooking wine is heavily salted and low quality; it is not suitable for professional cooking.

Wise cooks don't use wine indiscriminately in their dishes or their foods will taste too uniform. Also, not all foods benefit from the flavor of wine. Pungently hot and highly spiced, salty, acidic, or very sweet foods are, in general, not enhanced by wine.

Choose a wine for cooking as you would choose one to serve with dinner. Poultry and most fish and seafood favor light-bodied white wine, while other meat dishes, stews, game, and even some oily fish favor full-bodied red wine. If your dish is acidic, use a wine that tends to be acidic. In less acidic foods, fruity wines bring out flavors without overpowering them.

WISE COOKS DON'T USE WINE INDISCRIMINATELY IN THEIR DISHES OR THEIR FOODS WILL TASTE TOO UNIFORM.

According to common belief, alcohol evaporates from a dish within about ten minutes of cooking. Unfortunately, this is a myth.

Your guests should be aware if you used more wine than just a splash in your cooking, since people who abstain from alcohol will want to avoid those dishes. According to common belief, alcohol evaporates from a dish within about ten minutes of cooking. Unfortunately, this is a myth. Food scientists' tests show that cooking a dish with alcohol for an hour and a half still retains 5 percent of the original alcohol content. Chicken cooked in a wine-rich sauce for 10 minutes preserves 40 percent of the alcohol, while flambéed cherries jubilee retains a full 75 percent of the alcohol when served.

16. EXOTIC AND RARE INGREDIENTS

Today's cooking must be distinctive in order to appeal to catering clients, as many of them are also sophisticated restaurant patrons. One way to impress them is to use exotic or rare ingredients that are spelled out distinctly in the name of the dish, for example, "sautéed fava beans with crushed garlic and thyme flowers." There are not many ways to get fresh thyme flowers. They have to be special ordered or picked from a garden. Will they give a distinctively different flavor to your fava beans? Absolutely not. Or do you think the shiitake mushrooms added to the soup will make it taste any different than adding ordinary garden-variety commercial ones? Not really, but the dish sounds better and you have to charge more for it because shiitake costs four times as much as the common mushroom.

Another way to make your dish exotic is to use readily available ingredients, but be extravagant about the sheer number you use, for example, "six-pepper fillet of pork with blue cheese." The flavor will be guaranteed to be indistinguishable, whether you use two or six peppers. But such little gimmicks make your catering menu distinctive from an ordinary restaurant or neighborhood bistro.

To be sure, exotic and rare ingredients are essential in truly ethnic cooking. However, an authentic ethnic dish, such as a genuine Ceylon curry, would be quite difficult to swallow (literally) by most people with an average Western palate. The dish would be much too hot and much too spicy. Most ethnic restaurants, unless their clientele is almost exclusively from that ethnic background, alter and tone down their authentic food drastically to suit the local palate. If you have the opportunity, try Italian food in Italy, Greek food in Greece, or Thai food in Thailand. They are not for the average North American.

However, take a look at the produce selection of a large, well-stocked supermarket. Chances are they will have some unusual fruits and vegetables most people wouldn't be able to even name. Supermarkets will stock them not just for selling but as a relatively inexpensive way of making their display look lavish, elegant, and unusual. It attracts customers and makes the supermarket stand out for its wonderful selection.

A problem you will run into with exotic and rare ingredients is lack of freshness. Because they are expensive and there is a low demand for them, they may have passed their peak by the time you need them.

The following samples, reference materials, recipes, and web links are included on the enclosed CD-ROM for use on a Windows-based PC. The forms and recipes are all in PDF format. Full color photos are also incuded.

Sample Forms

- Client questionnaire
- Cover letter for client questionnaire
- Contract and order forms
- Cover letters
- Event checklist
- Letter of agreement
- Pricing a recipe
- Proposal letter: Full-service dinner
- Proposal letter: Reception
- Sample brochure
- Sample entrée menu
- Sample party menu

Reference Materials

- Cake cutting diagrams
- Quantities and yields
- Temperature guide

Recipes for Success

- Hors d'oeuvres
- Salads
- Entrées
- Vegetarian
- Desserts

Useful Websites for Caterers

Photo Gallery

OTHER TITLES IN THE
SELF-COUNSEL BUSINESS SERIES

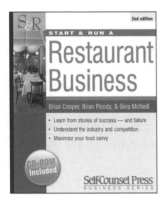

Start & Run a Restaurant Business

Brian Cooper, Brian Floody, and Gina McNeill
ISBN 10: 1-55180-632-0
ISBN 13: 978-1-55180-632-7
US $17.95 / Can $22.95

Every year tens of thousands of resturants open with great expectations, and every year almost as many close down. The successful restaurateur is a combination of entrepreneur, entertainer, and magician. *Start & Run a Restaurant Business* is a practical guide in "how to" and "how not to" proceed in this volatile business, covering the following topics:

- Formulating a business plan
- Budgeting and financing
- Choosing a location
- Designing a menu
- Hiring and managing
- Creating atmosphere through décor
- Attracting customers

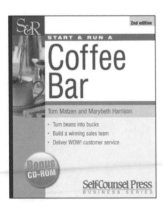

Start & Run a Coffee Bar

Tom Matzen and Marybeth Harrison
ISBN 10: 1-55180-354-2
ISBN 13: 978-1-55180-354-8
US $17.95 / Can $22.95

A comprehensive guide on what to expect when owning and operating a coffee bar/tea shop. This step-by-step book includes everything from choosing a unique identity to roasting, making, and serving coffee, espresso, and tea.

The two authors share their inside perspective on running a coffee bar, answering questions such as:

- How do I prepare a business plan?
- How do I market my coffee bar?
- What special equipment will I need?
- What will it cost to get started?

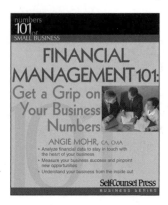

Financial Management 101:
Get a Grip on Your Business Numbers

Angie Mohr
ISBN 10: 1-55180-448-4
ISBN 13: 978-1-55180-448-4
US $14.95 / Can $19.95

This book covers business planning, from understanding financial statements to budgeting for advertising. Angie Mohr's easy-to-understand approach to small-business planning and management ensures that the money coming in is always greater than the money going out!

Financial Management 101 is an in-depth guide on business planning. It's a kick-start course for new entrepreneurs and a wake-up call for small-business owners.

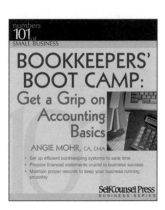

Bookkeepers' Boot Camp:
Get a Grip on Accounting Basics

Angie Mohr
ISBN 10: 1-55180-449-2
ISBN 13: 978-1-55180-449-1
US $14.95 / Can $19.95

Bookkeepers' Boot Camp teaches you how to sort through the masses of information and paperwork, how to record what is important for your business, and how to grow your business for success!

This book will show you the essentials of record keeping for a small business and why it's necessary to track information. It will give you a deeper knowledge of your business and how it works, covering topics such as:

- Managing paper flow
- Understanding the balance sheet
- Learning the basics of income statements and cash flow statements
- Recording the sales cycle
- Accounting for inventory
- Monitoring your budget and cash flow
- Understanding transactions between the company and its owners